Systemic Choices

Systemic Choices

Nonlinear Dynamics and Practical Management

Gregory A. Daneke

Ann Arbor

THE UNIVERSITY OF MICHIGAN PRESS

To the memory of
Erich Jantsch (1929–80)

(H   Copyright © by the University of Michigan 1999
All rights reserved
Published in the United States of America by
The University of Michigan Press
Manufactured in the United States of America
♾ Printed on acid-free paper

2002   2001   2000   1999   4   3   2   1

A CIP catalog record for this book is available
from the British Library.

Library of Congress Cataloging-in-Publication
data applied for
ISBN 0-472-11049-7 (hardcover)

Contents

Preface

This book was begun fifteen years ago, while I was a visiting professor in engineering at Stanford. However, my interest in the curious dynamics of complex systems goes back at least an additional decade. The Spanish-born philosopher and poet George Santayana (1863–1953) is credited with saying everyone is born either a Platonist or an Aristotelian, and they cannot change. I have often thought this must be true for systems theorists as well. And, if this is true, then those of us who aspire to not only see the forest for the trees but the process of forestation must have been preordained to this pursuit. Why else would we persist in an era where such pursuits were in such ill favor? Given disciplinary pressures, particularly present at tenure time, who would choose to be a hiking boot in a world of tuxedos? We are not heroic or merely foolhardy; we simply cannot help ourselves.

Given this preexisting condition, I tended to unconsciously resist, rather than emulate, the various fine scholars who earnestly tried to train me in more accepted ways of thinking. Actually, early on, a few biology and physics professors reinforced my innate tendencies as well as gave me a view of the scientific enterprise that seemed increasingly incongruous as I gradually shifted into the social sciences. Nonetheless, a handful of scholars of society had a profound effect on my perspectives, even if they could not divert me from my philosophical proclivities. These include University of California–Santa Barbara professors Dean Mann (a political scientist), Walter Mead (an economist), and Garrett Hardin (a biologist who spoke like an economist).

Having escaped my graduate work relatively unscathed, I immediately gravitated toward those who shared my systems affliction. At one point, I dreamed of postdoctoral study at Berkeley with Erich Jantsch (a physicist turned management scholar), one of my personal heroes. But I quickly learned, and was much puzzled by the fact, that he had somewhat less than postdoctoral status there himself. Jantsch grew ill and died a few years later, and he remains to this day one of the tragically unheralded figures of modern social inquiry.

Meanwhile, I began a teaching career in earnest, within the systems group at Virginia Tech and found a mentor in Alan Steiss. Al, who has been a research administrator at the University of Michigan since the mid–1980s, was back then a hard-core systems scholar with a practical tools orientation. It was his methodological encouragements, combined with my technology-policy interests, that inspired me to try my hand at actual policy analysis. However, after a brief stint in Washington, DC, during the Carter administration, I learned that policy and analysis were very far removed from one another. As the old saying goes, "There are two things one should never see made, sausage and policy." Despite the Department of Energy's able "systems-dynamics" modelers (like Denis Meadow's student Roger Naill), analysis was most often used to provide "backfill" and to justify decisions already made by political actors. Tens of hundreds of structural equations can hide mountains of political pressures and patronage. Moreover, arguments for markets, amid highly cartelized systems, provided an additional smoke screen for special interests. This later function of economic rhetoric became even more pronounced during another brief stint with the White House during the Reagan years. Then models were perverted to prove the piety of social privilege. Overall my experiences with strategizing, both in government and in industry, convinced me that our models were not only being abused, but their picture of social reality was largely inaccurate. Their lack of contextual understanding was dire. Moreover, their failure to represent the interaction of individuals and institutions as well as physical processes was appalling. Unfortunately, more contextually rich and dynamically accurate models were extremely difficult to validate; and if valid, they were equally—if not more—subject to political manipulation.

This later issue is probably endemic; however the former issue could be addressed in the same way that physics became the flagship of the hard sciences, by clarifying the dynamic processes. Back at the University of Michigan, where I taught in the School of Natural Resources (SNR) from 1978 to 1980, a small handful of scholars was beginning to explore this very path. Michigan was a literal hotbed of intellectual vitality, and it has always been a source of great disappointment that the impending demise of the School of Natural Resources forced me to leave there after such a short stay. For example, in the economics department (in a house next door to SNR until it burned down), young Turks like Hal Varian were redefining the boundaries of microeconomic theory. But by far the most interesting work was being done by colleagues over in the Institute for Public Policy Studies, Bob Axelrod and Mike Cohen (both political scientists). These two were members of the now-famous BACH (an informal study group), which included Art Burks (and his colleague John Holland) from computer science and William Hamilton (an evolutionary biologist). Most of these individuals have now become legendary figures in the study of "complexity." At the time, what struck me so profoundly about this nascent movement was that this blending of the biological and computer sciences with the studies of economics and politics would ultimately vindicate the railings of earlier systems theorists. What was unique about emerging complexity studies, however, was that they provided remedies to earlier systems' shortcomings. Paramount among these contributions is the ability to cut through the daunting density of social systems. Complexity, it turns out, might be more accurately called *simplicity*. These studies have not merely rediscovered the critical dynamics that engender both order and chaos, they are developing tools and perspectives that will eventually make these insights much more accessible, especially to social scientists.

The mounting success and respectability of these former Michigan colleagues and their students have added credence to my belief that a more generalized ecological approach to social inquiry is indeed very near at hand. However, my own ecological vision has been shaped and influenced more directly by a variety of other scholars. For example, animal ecologist Buzz (C. S.) Holling and other past and present colleagues at the International Institute for Applied Systems Analysis in Austria stand out as constant sources of inspiration. My colleagues at the University of British Columbia (in the Business Strategy Group) were gracious while holding my feet to the fire of neoclassical economics. The late Don Campbell was also extremely generous with both praise and criticism, and his sage comments are sorely missed. Likewise I miss my fellow at arms, Sam Overman, who was far too young to have joined Don, a few months after his mentor. Finally, I have acquired valuable insights from my "three amigos" in chaos: Kevin Dooley, Steve Guastello, and Doug Kiel.

I have also always admired, albeit from afar, the small remaining remnants of the sociotechnical systems tradition. In Europe, these folks are more or less represented by the Travistock Institute. In the United States, while greatly modified, elements of this movement are still manifest through the work of Harold Linstone and his colleagues in the systems-doctoral program at Portland State University and Ian Mitroff at the University of Southern California.

While not necessarily convinced of the merit of my perspectives, a special group of friends and colleagues has provided general moral and professional support over the years. Hence, they are partially responsible for this work being completed. In alphabetical order, they are Paul Adler, Heather Campbell, Ed Epstein, Jim March, Paula McClain, Elmer Staats, Fred Thompson, Susan Tolchin, Aidan Vining, and the late great Aaron Wildavsky.

Numerous graduate students, too numerous to mention, have been exposed to these ideas in various forms in the past decade. All of them added to this articulation. A much smaller group of students assisted in my research and/or provided particular inputs to my thinking. These include Jim Bly, Allen Brown, Dion Dennis, Brian Gregory, Steve Light, Nick Lopez, Bev Owens, B. J. Moore, Steve Sorenson, Jim Walsh, and Avery Wright.

Most of this writing was accomplished during summers in Oregon. Thus, my extremely kind and gracious hosts there in the Atkinson Graduate School of Management at Willamette University deserve much of the credit for this work finally emerging. There are a number of individuals who helped in the actual production. Janet Soper, Mary Fran Draisker and Roisan Rubio of the College of Public Programs' Publication Assistance Center at Arizona State University performed magic in the manuscript preparation. It is very fitting, given my attachments to Michigan mentioned earlier, that the University of Michigan Press is publishing this work. I especially appreciate the able assistance of Ellen McCarthy, my editor, and Alja Kooistra, the copyediting coordinator. Finally, I would like to thank John Miller and Richard Priesmeyer for their contribution to many of the ideas and a few of the figures found within.

Greg Daneke
Salem, Oregon

CHAPTER 1

The Long-Awaited Revolution: An Introduction and Overview

As Yale historian Paul Kennedy (1993) maintains, the twenty-first century will be one of monumental challenges for humankind. Overpopulation, environmental degradation, regional strife, and pandemic plagues loom on the horizon. Beyond the obvious challenges to the geophysical and medical sciences, the next millennia will place inordinate demands upon the social sciences, especially those that underpin the administration of human affairs. Particularly challenging will be the design and maintenance of much more adaptive institutions. Such challenges have already begun to accelerate the emergence of new metaphors and methods at the very basic levels of social inquiry. *Primary among these are tools for exploring the fundamentally nonlinear and thus systemic nature of institutional choice and change.* While these tools have profited from recent advances in the physical and computational sciences, their philosophical underpinnings harken back to a bygone era in social inquiry, namely the systems theory movement of the 1950s and 1960s. Hence in true dialectical fashion, the current era is both a merger and a reemergence of a previous intellectual epoch. Nonlinearity was a key feature of earlier systems theoretics (see von Bertalanffy 1950), but at the time, the computational tools and concepts did not exist to operationalize it fully. Now these tools are the tail that wags the systems theory dog. To reverse this juxtaposition is a central theme of this book. However, in the process, the centrality of nonlinearity will also be explored at length. For in an era of increasing turbulence and surprises, nonlinearity—which is *the science of surprise*—should be a vital element of any social inquiry, particularly those which purport to improve practical policy and management.

The notion of having a nonlinear social science, let alone a science of surprise, may seem a bit curious. It is especially odd, given the preoccupation with linear methods of description, prediction, and prescription in the social sciences. Yet initially, nonlinearity can be defined as any ongoing process combining elements in a fashion more complex and convoluted than possible through simple addition. One often ends up with more than one started with. To be precise, nonlinearity can produce "emergent properties." It is an essential feature of all living systems. Thus, it should be found in abundance in the social as well as the natural world. This is not to say that human systems are identical to biological or physical systems, merely that nonlinear processes are actively at work in both.

In the past twenty-five years, the significance of nonlinear dynamics has become increasingly appreciated in the physical sciences, and in the next twenty-five it will become perhaps even more vital to social inquiry—that is, if social scientists seek to aid in the process of institutional adaptation and change. The lessons derived from the science of nonlinear dynamic systems are themselves intricate and convoluted; however, for the purposes of this introduction and overview they might be summarized as follows.

- Even simple social systems exhibit "complexity" (behaviors with convoluted and indeterminate causal paths) despite being deterministic;
- Complex social systems exhibit "self-organization" (spontaneous reordering) and "chaos" (e.g., nearly random behavior);
- Complex social systems are driven by "feedback" (both positive and negative), and small changes often engender disproportional effects;
- Individual choices emerge from complex social systems; and
- Complex social systems are, at root, the result of simple rules and institutions interacting with turbulent external environments.

Almost since its inception, when the enterprise moved from philosophical speculation to quasi-scientific exploration, the notion of a *social science* has had a rather precarious status. A continuing concern has been whether the vast complexity, as well as various mercurial behavioral elements, of social phenomena made its study a difference of "kind" rather than merely a difference of "degree" from the physical sciences (see Winch 1958). Apparently this grand debate, to the extent that it has ever been resolved, was settled on the side of "degree." However, this fragile consensus was just gathering momentum in the social sciences at the very time that the paradigms of the physical sciences were experiencing significant upheaval. Since the quantum revolution at the dawn of the twentieth century, the physical sciences have sought to shed their more mechanistic models in favor of regaining their earlier organic representations. Meanwhile, social scientists have struggled to apply a nineteenth-century idea of science and thus extricate themselves from the various natural elements that had once animated their inquiries. In recent years, however, a handful of scholars has sought to refashion social inquiry along lines similar to advances in late-twentieth-century science. Among other things, this enterprise would include a number of unique features derived from the study of ecological interactions. Of particular interest are those interactions governed by the curious dynamics of nonlinear systems.

Over the years, awareness has grown among physicists, chemists, and biologists regarding the inherently nonlinear character of the natural world. These insights have, in recent years, become associated with the so-called new sciences of chaos and complexity (good nontechnical reviews are provided by Gleick 1987; Waldrop 1992; Johnson 1996; for technical treatments, see Cohen and Stewart 1994; Coveney and Highfield 1995). These various explorations of *nonlinear dynamic systems* not only provide a different model of the scientific enterprise, they establish a number of tools and concepts directly useful to social inquiry. While most of these applications remain merely metaphorical, a handful of intrepid social scientists have begun developing more technical investigations (Schieve and Allen 1982; Anderson et al. 1988; Richards 1990; Kiel and Elliott 1996; Epstein and Axtell 1996; Carley 1998; Richards and Hays 1998). While insightful in their own right, these investigators of nonlinear social phenomena often fail to discuss the underlying theoretical issues. Hence they largely ignore some of the conceptual problems associated with integrating these insights with conventional modes of inquiry.

It is one of the essential purposes of this book to raise and resolve some of these conceptual issues. Reasons for this emphasis are manifold but include at least the following three concerns. One, like a splice of foreign tissue, the current grafting of new methods onto old foundations may or may not adhere. Two, the actual intellectual heritage of the new methods may be misrepresented. Three, as a result, the full force of revolutionary scientific implications may be misunderstood. Stated simply, the study of nonlinearity in the social sciences has roots in systems theory. In order to facilitate a true intellectual firestorm, the fuel of nonlinear science must be reunited with the smoldering embers of this earlier epoch. This reunification requires a number of profound conceptual reconciliations. Foremost among these is the resolution of the long-standing conflict between "methodological individualism" (the autonomous agent as the unit of analysis) and more "holistic" (systemically determined) perspectives. These conceptual lacunae will be elaborated at length subsequently. For now, suffice it to say that these types of minor misnomers have been amplified though disciplinary reductionism and hidden ideological agendas into major stumbling blocks. Meanwhile, naive intellectual exuberance has generated numerous unkept promises, further inflaming an already jaded generation of scholars. Despite all these mishaps, a new level of reconciliation, if not actual reenchantment, is near at hand.

In order to initiate reconciliation, a number of disparate intellectual traditions must be refurbished as well as reintegrated under the rubric of *general systems theory* (GST). Among others, these include

- behavioral and institutional economics;

- information theory and cybernetics; and
- evolutionary biology and ecology.

From this vantage point a set of specific explorations into the dynamical workings of human artifacts and institutions can be forged, ones that highlight the ecological nature of many social choices. Hence, for lack of a better term, the decision processes that drive, as well as are driven by, this complex *institutional ecology* are labeled *systemic choices,* so as to distinguish them from conventional notions of "rational" (i.e., individualized) choice. As will be shown, these are not merely semantic distinctions; rather they represent a fundamental transformation in social inquiry (see table 1).

Revolutionary Rumblings

The epistemology (theory of knowledge) most often associated with the traditional model of science is positivism (or logical empiricism). This philosophical position, which holds that conventional scientific methods apply equally well to social knowledge (see Ayer 1946), has dominated social inquiry for the better part of the twentieth century. However, this rather narrow view has also been attacked from various fronts, ranging from phenomenology and "critical theory" (e.g., Habermas 1979) to feminist epistemology (see Henderson 1991) and "postmodernism" (Bauman 1988). Of late, these critical voices have reached a crescendo, ushering in the era of *postpositivism* with its concern for the "social

TABLE 1. Shifting Paradigms

Traditional Model	New Science Model
Largely static, linear, Newtonian, mechanical world view	Ever-fluid, nonlinear, complex, "living systems"
At or seeking equilibrium	Occasionally orderly but generally turbulent
Statistics used to separate predictable from random and intractable; with *processes* as probabilities	*Chaos and complexity* mathematics used to locate the deterministic amid the unpredictable; with *products* as probabilities
Focus on quantities and the pricing mechanisms	Focus on processes, patterns, potentialities and diverse values
Reductionist	Transdisciplinary
Individual as unit of analysis; with "rational choice" parameters	Synergistic, co-evolving individuals and institutions, with *systemic choice* parameters
Economics as architectonic social science	Ecology (social/institutional as well as biological) as the architectonic science

construction of reality" and its ethnographic-like (e.g., cultural anthropology) approaches. Unfortunately, postpositivism often promotes an unmanageable level of methodological relativism, ultimately leading to a sort of epistemological nihilism—that is, a state in which there is no final arbiter of the relative viability of a given contextual interpretation.

In the midst of this epistemological battle, the paradigmatic alternative of a previous era provides a new rallying point. Systems theory, while recognizing diverse contextual elements, is not so relativistic. Systems approaches might be thought of as the *pre-postpositivism,* both chronologically and methodologically. Systems theory not only foreshadowed the importance of social constructions, it anticipated the current emergence of nonlinear methods. Furthermore, systems theory provides a viable alternative to the reigning paradigm of applied social inquiry, largely derived from *neoclassical economic theory.* As Austrian economist Joseph Schumpeter once observed, when it comes to social science, one cannot merely displace a theory with facts: "it takes a theory to kill a theory."

By the mid-twentieth century, the tools and concepts derived from the most successful theoretical elements of Western economics (known as neoclassical economic theory) had become fairly ubiquitous, especially in schools of business and public policy. Moreover, the basic approach to social organization known as *rational choice* had become the central theme in political science and sociology. The rise of economics to the status of *architectonic science* might be exceedingly odd to the Greeks since they coined the term to refer to the mundane "affairs of the household." For them, politics was the ultimate realm of inquiry, as the state was the window to the soul and the cosmos. In Plato's *Republic,* the tripartite state was emblematic of the tripartite soul (see Jowett 1972). Yet, economics' preeminent position is not at all surprising. Its mathematical sophistication, unified body of theory, and aspirations to "social physics" make it the hardest of the so-called soft sciences. It is the only social science for which a Nobel prize is given.

Armed with their infamous "ceteris paribus" (all other things being equal) assumption, economists have developed powerful explanations of human behavior. Of course, bands of internal dissenters have questioned this assumption and developed more contextually rich explanations under the banners of *behavioral* and *neoinstitutional economics* (see Eggertsson 1990). Moreover, active countercultures have joined the more traditional "noble opposition" of *institutional* or *evolutionary* economists (Gruchy 1987). For example the *Society for the Advancement of Socioeconomics* (note Etzioni and Lawrence 1991) and the *International Society for Ecological Economics* (see Costanza 1991) call to question the hegemony of monetized values. However, from the standpoint of a methodological imperative, neoclassical theory, while much modified, has also become more reified over the years.

The most formidable challenge to the ahistorical/path dependent models of modern economics is the exploration of various nonlinear dynamic relationships. Under the rubric of *chaos* or *complexity* studies, a handful of scholars (including economists) raise questions regarding the core assumptions of the neoclassical approach (e.g., Anderson et al. 1988). Meanwhile, nonlinearity is also being introduced as a powerful new managerial metaphor (see Stacey 1992; Wheatley 1992; Lissack 1997; Polley 1997; Kelly and Allison 1999) and as a guide to new managerial technique (Kiel 1994; Priesmeyer 1992; also note Carley 1998). Yet, these do not necessarily a paradigmatic revolution make. What is lacking from these efforts, thus far, is an integrated body of theory. Moreover, by getting the methodological cart out in front of the epistemological horse, some of these studies have made such integration more difficult. Some social scientists appear to believe that nonlinear findings can merely be blended with conventional approaches. A certain level of conceptual blending is to be expected and is not necessarily dysfunctional. But as will hopefully be demonstrated subsequently, the application of nonlinear methods is much more congruent with a new socioecological paradigm. Moreover, as several physical scientists have already come to appreciate, nonlinear dynamic systems constitute a vital new approach to science, generally.

From Glacial to Gathering Pace

The origins of nonlinear science date back over a century. Consider, for example, the work of the brilliant French mathematician Henri Poincaré (1890). His analysis of the "three-body problem" (as in astrophysics) was a harbinger of current work in *chaos theory*. Yet, it remained relatively unappreciated for nearly eighty years. More widely influential was the development of *quantum theory;* however, it took nearly fifty years for it to take hold in physics. It was not until the late 1960s that biology widely adopted the formal and the statistical techniques of modern physics, but when it did, pathbreaking work proceeded pell-mell (note Mayr 1982). During the ensuing years, physicists and chemists working on persistent yet heretofore intractable problems in fluid and thermodynamics (Nicholis and Prigogine 1971, 1977) began to rediscover the curious organizing processes that literally generate "order out of chaos." At another extreme, the stepchildren of cybernetics, information theory, and physiological psychology were forming a new discipline labeled *cognitive science* and developing systems of "artificial intelligence" (AI). Facilitated by developments in supercomputing, this new discipline has begun to isolate the critical dynamics of complex human thought processes. At the same time, discoveries in diverse realms from weather forecasting (Lorenz 1963) to ecosystems management (Holling 1976) continued to demonstrate the ubiquitous character of these nonlinear dynamic phenomena. As a result of the mathematical advances, a new range of techniques was developed and applied to an increasingly broad range of phenomena, including human systems (see Schieve and Allen 1982).

It would seem, given various compelling features, that this revolution would swiftly overtake the social sciences, namely, economics, sociology, and political science, as well as the applied realms of business and public administration. However, this transformation has been gradual, to say the least. A measure of this laggardness is precipitated by the lack of a unified theoretical foundation. Yet one might expect that with or without such a foundation, forces of change will continue to gather momentum. As with advances in the physical sciences, the solution of persistent practical problems may spur theoretical development. The burgeoning management literature (e.g., Kelly and Allison 1999), while primarily metaphorical, alludes to a number of specific problems that might yield to nonlinear science. Of course, one can always invoke management gurus such as William Edwards Deming (1993) who couch their calls for radical reforms in the context of the mounting "competitive crisis." Such crises have certainly been instrumental in development of new public management techniques, as political mobilization is always a crucial ingredient. For example problems ranging from traffic congestion to "global environmental change," have led to the use of alternative methodologies. Paul Diesing (1982) argues that given the lack of replications and other standard methods of validation, social science paradigms yield more readily to unresolved policy crises than to conventional scientific arguments. The ongoing global transition to more sustainable resource use in general, and energy use in particular, presents an ideal case of the type of "policy crises" in which the current mix of institutions, decision rules, and tools of design merely forestalls the necessary adaptations. If the emerging paradigm of institutional ecology can help break down the barriers to a meaningful resource transition, then it would certainly be deemed a success. However, the basic integrity of the tools and concepts presented subsequently is not necessarily contingent upon such a momentous test. Furthermore, understanding social dynamics does not commit one to a particular policy agenda. This is not the dreaded "social engineering," which many feared but few experienced in previous versions of social ecology. The very nature of the understandings generated (e.g., the lack of predictability in otherwise deterministic systems) goes a long way toward reducing any hubris that might remain from earlier epochs. Moreover, the importance of open and widespread participation as a precondition to institutional evolution greatly reduces the role of elite judgment.

Reorganizing for Deep Dynamics

Despite the gradual character of this transition, the impact will be profound. The largely static, linear mechanical worldview will be displaced by a "living systems" or ecological worldview. Such systems have a set of deep dynamics, generating "perpetual novelty" (see Holland 1992). They are often orderly in appearance and yet governed by processes that only occasionally resemble equilibrium. These dynamics were originally discovered by studying various "far-from-equilibrium" phenomena (such as anabolic/catabolic reacting in chemistry); hence the term *disequilibrium* is often used to describe them. Since complex reordering is driven by these nonlinear dynamics, the phrases "order out of chaos" (Prigogine and Stengers 1984) and/or "order at the edge of chaos" (see Waldrop 1992) are also used to represent this fluid state of being, or rather *state of becoming.*

Social science, predicated upon static linear relationships, has problems with these *emergent* phenomena. Nonlinear dynamics are at once deterministic and unpredictable; thus they wreak havoc on standard statistical interpretations. Generally speaking, statistics play a substantially different role in chaos mathematics and have a very discrete meaning in the subfield known as "statistical mechanics." Like in quantum physics, it is the processes that are known and the products that are probabilistic. As one might expect, currently popular social methods, such as linear regression, would become less widely utilized in a world that focuses on nonlinear dynamics. However, once social scientists abandon their linear causal approaches, they are faced with overwhelming contextual complexity. This is where the deep reordering dynamics of a nonlinear systems perspective become so handy. In essence, ecological principles begin to replace the misperceived explanatory power of simple empiricism. As C. S. Holling (1987) points out, ecology is the primary path to "simplifying the complex." More importantly, Holling describes how it reduces the level of "surprise" (or disappointment) in human affairs. He explains that

> complexity is relative to a frame of reference that gives order to under-standing, expectation and action. Ecology, as with other sciences, has evolved a sequence of such frames of reference, each developed to give comprehension to some set of paradoxes, to some mismatch between theory and perceived reality. . . . Ecological systems have those features that now seem to frustrate both understanding and action in so many areas of man's interest. . . . The variables are connected in a web of interrelations that are fundamentally nonlinear. Thresholds and limits, lags and discontinuities are all inherent to ecological reality. (139–40)

Given disciplinary blinders and associated turf factors, the most suitable place to invigorate the ecological study of institutions is within professional schools and/or highly applied programs (business, public policy, and public administration). They already have an extensive multidisciplinary orientation. Through a new ecology perspective, the vast web of previously intractable individual and institutional interactions could be made both more intelligible and manageable. In this way, perhaps, these pursuits might obtain a more thoroughgoing blend of theory and action (designated by the ancients with the term *praxis*). In modern times, the "practice" of medicine is the only enterprise that is nearly so integrated. While the "arts" of policy and management only approximate a similar level of scientific integration, the impacts might be dramatic. The study of management, whether public or private is by definition an attempt to lend order to a turbulent world. Purposeful interventions under any conditions, but especially amid such turbulence, entail an appreciation of the fact that the world has a strange order of its own. That is, it has a set of evolutionary processes seeking the type of temporary stability that humans misconstrue as equilibrium. An ecological perspective, which appreciates the dynamics of order amid disequilibrium, could be used to design institutions that work with, as opposed to against, these inherent processes and resulting patterns. The result would be greater "resilience" or fluid order in the face of accelerating turbulence, and this would be the true embodiment of praxis.

Toward Praxis

Having identified this path to increased prominence, it is well to acknowledge that the gulf between theory and practice in the actual management of human affairs is not only often wide, it is also littered with significant stumbling blocks. First and foremost among these is that management theory has multiple meanings. For many practitioners, a theory is merely the most popularized and/or simple repackaging of the parochial wisdom. This does not necessarily imply that relevancy is merely a matter of marketing. Occasionally, a popular managerial axiom is one that strikes a cogent chord or unlocks a particularly intricate insight. Usually, popularity is merely based in fear, greed, or both (see Mickelthwait and Wooldridge 1996). If one suspects that competitors are "reengineering" in any form, then certainly one should at least look into it. The actual empirical content or even practical payoff of some of these popular theories is often quite suspect. As a result, theory among managerial academics (i.e., research oriented business or public administration professors) is generally an entirely different matter. While some scholars attempt to confirm or deny a given popular concept, especially when it becomes well embedded in practice, most remain aloof from these pedestrian protocols. This "ivory tower" mentality, when coupled with narrow notions of scientific activity, creates an almost atheoretical empiricism. Theory building becomes mostly concerned with low level and/or short-term causal explanations that rarely facilitate generalizations very far beyond the scope of the immediate data. "Grand theories," which reflect upon larger societal or epistemological implications, hardly ever enter into this type of simple linear theorizing. Many of these exercises in short-term factual analysis either ignore underlying conceptual issues and/or assume they could be resolved by resorting to reigning economic or sociological constructs. Plus, remaining epistemic questions are rendered moot through the hidden maintenance of logical positivism. Since these connections are loosely made, if at all, the gap between theory and practice grows even wider.

Given the antiepistemic preoccupation of many management scholars, it is not surprising that nonlinear policy and management have emerged initially as a few disembodied tools. These are methods in advance of meaning. Conversely, given the lucrative motivation inherent in being a management fad as alluded to earlier, nonlinearity has also arisen as vaguely defined concepts, without much in the way of methodological sophistication. Moreover, the arrival of a carefully integrated set of tools and concepts is greatly complicated by the inherent pragmatic propensity of technique to often outpace science. Technological advances occasionally precede scientific understanding by several years. Case in point, the steam engine moved into widespread usage long before its thermodynamics were given a full accounting. In this regard, some pop-management texts may produce applications well in advance of complete explanation. Just as Peter Senge's (1990) pronouncements and parochial wisdom are being adopted by many executives who will never fully understand the underlying "systems dynamics," *chaos* and *complexity* may become "buzzwords" well in advance of the conceptual clarification.

There are, of course, obvious dangers in becoming a management fad. Even in management circles where practicality is prized, there is always the possibility of an intellectual backlash if conceptual development doesn't quickly catch up. Furthermore, without conceptual undergirding, certain applications can be misapplied to antiquated paradigms. Worse yet, if certain premature applications prove faulty, there are numerous skeptics eager to "cast out the baby with the bathwater." The inevitable pressures for popularity create a fertile environment of partially baked ideas and incomplete understandings. Recall the initial excitement and extreme disillusionment associated with the *cold fusion* fiasco. Novel ideas will usually have many an opportunistic supporter, but truly viable paths should survive multiple missteps. Therefore, a new ecological approach will probably survive and perhaps even thrive amid a number of ill-conceived applications of nonlinear methods. As applied social science, ecologically enhanced understandings should impact specific managerial advances.

In turn, these practical examples of nonlinear methods should amplify the historical and conceptual explorations. By way of preview, very elemental techniques for mapping the types of changes a firm is experiencing in any number of its basic measures (e.g., market share, profit margin, inventory, productivity, return on assets) can be utilized to completely reinterpret its performance picture. These pictures, when combined with various strategic adaptations of "critical trajectories," exhibit multiple paths to significant improvements. As will be demonstrated, various nonlinear dynamics, especially those associated with chaos concepts, describe a system that is so sensitive to minor structural changes that myriad leverage points present themselves.

At the more macro level, gaping "black holes" in economic theory, regarding the status of *technological development* and *entrepreneurial behavior,* can be filled in using similar analyses of nonlinear trajectories. The fate of entire industrial sectors might be retrieved from the grip of inexorable forces. More importantly, technological choices can be informed by various regional and global environmental concerns. Systemic consequences can be understood in the context of industrial policies (both private and public). The global future need not be more predictable to be much more manageable.

Beyond the Clockworks

Achieving praxis in applied social inquiry requires movement away from the basic "clockworks"metaphor of science. Not only is the linear mechanical model of science out of step with the advances of the twentieth century and the promise of the twenty-first, its methods and metaphors do not really allow for human choice, either individual or systemic. Beginning with quantum physics, early in the twentieth century, a vastly different model of science has been taking shape. This new model emphasizes process dynamics and the complex interconnectedness of the natural world. According to Fritjof Capra (1975 1982), ecological thinking is needed to understand these "webs" of interrelationship. In returning to the rhythms and cycles of the prescientific perspective, the physical sciences had become more contextually rich as well as open to the prospects of "self-organization" and surprise. Capra (1982) invokes the ancient Taoist symbol (the yin and the yang) to represent this reunification. According to Taoism, the universal order required a balance of the light (active, warm, dry, procreative, masculine) and the dark (passive, cool, wet, fertile, feminine) modes of energy. When scientific thought took over in the late Middle Ages, it left behind the organic and relational processes of living systems for more mechanical metaphors. Not until the development of quantum theory did a bit of the balance return, and Capra maintained that the full-scale reintegration required for authentic science demanded further development in the direction of "ecological" approaches and a "systems view" (see 1982, 36–42). Gradually, as the quantum view took hold, old categories such as matter, energy, and position gave way to more fluid notions of "complementarity" and "potentia" (à la Bohr 1958). In a similar fashion, a new set of interactive concepts provides the basis for a new social science. Moreover, when combined with methods and metaphors emerging from the study of the human brain, the concepts provide powerful new tools for enhancing the human condition.

The Quantum Revolution

In the year 1900, Max Planck presented his paper on the problem of *blackbody radiation,* in which he implied that classical physics was incomplete and that certain phenomena are inherently discontinuous. He invented the term *quanta* to describe "packets of energy" and *quantized* to represent these unusual oscillations. Classical physics had been so successful in unifying fields ranging from acoustics to astronomy that Planck's work was initially viewed as heresy. At the time it was widely assumed that energy simply radiated in a uniform flow as it dissipated. By contrast, Planck's *quantized oscillators* moved in fits and starts until the oscillation itself subsided.

It would take another twenty-five years for *quantum mechanics* to be fully elaborated, for in the intervening years much of the spotlight was being stolen by a brilliant young physicist by the name of Albert Einstein. Starting in 1905 he published several papers that both built upon and distracted from the quantum message. In his paper on the *photoelectric effect,* he extended Planck's analysis and demonstrated the quantized nature of energy itself. Yet Einstein remained disturbed by the odd blend of chance and necessity found in quantum mechanics, prompting his famous quote, "God does not play dice."

The quantum juggernaut gained increased momentum as the result of Neils Bohr's (1934, 1958) conceptualizations. For example, his notion of *complementarity* held that light comprised a mix of wave and particle behaviors. Bohr, of course, was also the father of the "Copenhagen interpretation," which held that God could indeed play dice with the universe. This interpretation was amplified by Werner Heisenberg's famed *uncertainty principle.* Essentially, this principle banished Newton's notions of position and momentum from the subatomic realm by demonstrating that the establishment of one makes the other inherently uncertain (see Heisenberg 1958).

This unreality or what some have interpreted as the subjective reality of the quantum world was provided with a mascot by Erwin Schrödinger in 1935. His famed *cat in the box problem* provided amusement for many a physicist and philosopher of science for generations (see Gribbin 1984). Schrödinger had contributed to development of quantum mechanics by working out the equations for the *wave function* and linking it to *matrix mechanics* (note 1943, 1951). Yet he is best known for his little thought experiment in which a poor cat is placed in a theoretical box with an equally likely chance of receiving poison or food. The problem is to demonstrate that one does not know the state of a phenomenon (an analogy to the wave vs. particle state) until it is observed. It is one's curiosity that kills (or feeds) the cat. In short, observation establishes the state of affairs. By the time the helpless cat arrived on the scene, the quantum dance was in full swing.

Confrontations and refutations would continue, of course, and new elements would be added. Elaborate thought as well as empirical experiments clarified and/or modified quantum concepts while successful applications continued to mount. The great debates were varied, but beyond the nature of reality (alluded to earlier), the possibility of *nonlocal causality* generated, perhaps, the most controversy. Stated simply, quantum theory implies that events clearly separated in space can still somehow affect one another. In the year of "the cat," Albert Einstein, Boris Podolsky, and Nathan Rosen (1935) questioned the completeness of the quantum-mechanical description of reality and posited their *EPR experiment.* The *EPR* raises the issue of how particles communicate. In essence, if one were to change the position and/or momentum of one particle, one would also create a similar effect on its distant and yet unknown counterpart. Moreover, the effect is *superluminal* (faster than the speed of light). In sum, the *EPR* is set up to suggest that either common experience of causality (i.e., locality) is wrong or the quantum reality is incomplete. While expressly designed to contest quantum logic, the *EPR* opened the door to an even stranger world of "quantum entanglement." In this world, distinct probabilities could blend into what Richard Feynman (1948) labeled "probability amplitudes." In one of his many notable lectures, Feynman referred to this emerging quantum reality in the following terms: "Nature uses only the longest threads to weave her patterns, so each small piece of her fabric reveals the organization of the entire tapestry" (Glick 1992, 13). As Fritjof Capra (1982) points out, "in quantum theory you never end up with things; you always deal with interconnectedness" (80).

Order, Chaos, and Complexity

As the enterprise of science began to focus on the interconnectedness of systems, and again listen for the unique rhythms of nature, a number of potentially more revolutionary observations emerged. As James Gleick (1987) explains, until recently (last twenty years), most scientists adhered to a set of axiomatic beliefs regarding the behavior of complex systems: (1) "simple systems behave in simple ways"; (2) "complex behavior implies complex systems;" (3) "different systems behave differently." He proceeds to observe:

> Now all that has changed. In the intervening twenty years, physicists, mathematicians, biologists, and astronomers have created an alternative set of ideas. Simple systems give rise to complex behavior. Complex systems give rise to simple behavior. And most important, the laws of complexity hold universally. (304)

Stated simply, order, chaos, and complexity are not separate processes but temporary states within the same process. All arise within the dynamics of complex evolutionary systems. To isolate *chaos* without talking about its counterparts (e.g., self-organization) is a tale halftold. In times past, it was *order,* homeostasis, or equilibrium that was isolated from the dynamic processes. *Complexity,* meanwhile, in the words of Heinz Pagels (1988), is a midway point between "simple order and complete chaos" (54–55). In this netherland, complex systems exhibit "indeterminate causal pathways." Hence, they are best understood through focusing on their nonlinear organizing dynamics. Ilya Prigogine and Isabel Stengers (1984) identify the crux of this interposition in the title of their book *Order out of Chaos.* In short, order and chaos are different sides of the same coin, and the evolution of natural and social systems is driven by the tossing.

Perhaps the best way to picture these stages in the dance between chaos and order is an old-fashioned step chart. With all apologies to Arthur Murray, the chart for this dance makes the cha-cha look simple, but, in fact, these steps are actually amazing in their simplicity (see fig. 1). With thermal equilibrium as a starting point, all living systems would, of course, be dead. Thus, the dance really gets started when structures begin *self-organizing* themselves. More often than not these structures evolve into the next stage of the dance where mild buffetings produce the semiorderly patterns of *standard attractors.* In the next stage, sensitivity to small changes creates the erratic steps associated with *chaotic* systems. If turbulence continues to intensify, coherent structures can dissolve into *high-dimensional chaos* and eventually arrive at complete *randomness.* However, at most stages of the dance, it is also possible for the system to return to the previous stage. Dancing backward is especially possible for *cybernetic* and/or human systems. In short, the dance of chaos is also the dance of order, and hence these fundamental dynamics are a sort of "deep ecology" of social enterprise, in its broadest terms.

Decades before Gleick labeled chaos theory the *new science,* the study of nonlinear dynamics was well under way under the rubric of *self-organizing systems* and the *mathematics of discontinuities.* Discontinuity mathematics

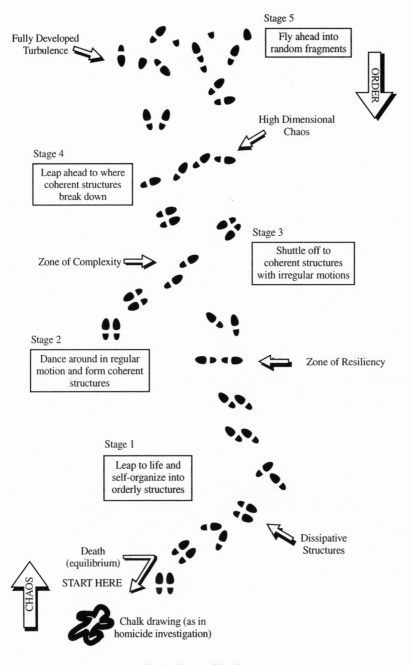

Stage 5
Fly ahead into
random fragments

Fully Developed
Turbulence

ORDER

High Dimensional
Chaos

Stage 4
Leap ahead to where
coherent structures
break down

Stage 3
Shuttle off to
coherent structures
with irregular motions

Zone of Complexity

Stage 2
Dance around in regular
motion and form coherent
structures

Zone of Resiliency

Stage 1
Leap to life and
self-organize into
orderly structures

Death
(equilibrium)

START HERE

Dissipative
Structures

CHAOS

Chalk drawing (as in
homicide investigation)

Fig. 1. Chaos: The Dance

actually finds its origins in the brilliance of Henri Poincaré (1890). Poincaré destroyed the simplified Laplacean worldview through his formulation of the *qualitative theory of differential equations* and demonstrated its application to the famed "*n*-body problem" (i.e., the interaction of three or more planets in a gravitational system). Such systems, Poincaré speculated, might exhibit asymptotic stability while being structurally unstable. Thus they may be in need of further specification to account for qualitative changes generated by periodic *bifurcations*. Building upon this work, René Thom (1972) developed *catastrophe theory* to look at large scale discontinuities in which certain types of sudden and dramatic changes tend to correspond to specific geometric shapes or *topologies* (i.e., the cusp). Moreover, by modeling discontinuities in major state variables, it was noted that various control variables reach critical *bifurcation* values at the point of discontinuity.

In contrast what is now being called chaos theory grew out of specific applications of bifurcation and oscillation mathematics to problems of turbulence. For example, Lewis Fry Richardson's (1926) study of turbulence in fluid dynamics identified the scalar self-similarities that would later be clarified in terms of Feigenbaum's (1978, 1980) cascade model and Mandelbrot's (1983) fractal geometry. Similarly, bifurcation studies, especially those undertaken by David Ruelle and Floris Takens (1971), engendered a characterization of chaos transitions in terms of strange attractors. These basic approaches have been applied to a range of diverse phenomena from healthy heart irregularities and stock-market bubbles to electoral behavior and the evolution of entire cultures.

Studies of nonlinearity are, of course, rarer in the social realm. Moreover, these studies have in recent years been eclipsed by the banner complexity, which generally refers to problems of labyrinthine causality. This term, popularized primarily by the Santa Fe Institute via its biographers (e.g., Waldrop 1992), was initially applied to a rather narrow set of perspectives. However, it has come to represent the full range of inquiries into nonlinear dynamics. Essentially the study of complexity relates to how simple things arise from complex systems, while chaos is about how complex things arise from simple systems (see Cohen and Stewart 1994, 2). At this generic level, it is easy to see how the concepts become muddled. In social applications, complexity theory equates to the study of how individuals and simple rules evolve through nonlinear processes into complex behaviors and/or institutional settings. In other words, complexity is the study of emergence, or the processes by which small patterns of interaction create large "structures" with novel "properties." As such, it is merely a subset of larger systems theoretics and their inherent nonlinear dynamics (Capra 1996).

The Merger of Metaphors

While various nonlinear systems dynamics provide the primary departure point for this excursion, it is the reformulation of a basic systems framework that is the ultimate destination. As the coming chapters will demonstrate the music of the new sciences is one of multiple metaphors (see table 2), and systems theory is the orchestration. The task of orchestration is complicated by the fact that elements from various metaphors and methodologies continue to have appropriate applications within the particular branches of science. For example, Newtonian physics and Euclidian geometry still have a number of important applications despite their overall incompleteness. Nonetheless, among the range of possible metaphors, there are obviously those that demonstrate greater

TABLE 2. Multiple Metaphors of Science

The Metaphor	The Clock	The Solar System	The Laser	The Brain
The meaning	Mechanical linear	Gravitational simple nonlinearity	Synergetic nonlinearity and chaos	Cybernetic nonlinearity and complexity
The focus	Two bodies internalizing	A few bodies interacting	Many atoms colliding	Synapses, cells, nerve impulses and coevolutionary ecosystems
The process	General equilibrium	Instabilities, asymmetries and catastrophes	"Order out of chaos," self-organization	Perception, cognition, learning, memory, connectivity, synaptic strength
The products	Static model of "the firm" and "the market," prequantum physics	Masses, distances, astrophysics	Thermo and fluid dynamics, physical chemistry, particle physics	Artificial life, adaptive agents, neural networks, parallel processing
Social science applications	Engineering and management problems (e.g., inventory and stock control) where human factors are minimal	Trade, warfare, and certain "game theoretic" problems	Opinion formation, revolution and/or "resilient" systems	Strategic management and creatively adaptive institutions

methodological potential with regard to social inquiry, especially the subarea of managerial studies. Some metaphors are primarily associated with a particular era or epoch. In some cases, metaphors peacefully coexist within the same era. Hence, the boundaries between applications are not nearly as neatly maintained as this characterization might suggest.

Different facets of this multifaceted enterprise are exposed through different avenues of research—some social, but mostly within the physical and now the cognitive sciences. Furthermore, even among those social scientists who contributed to a particular domain, the contribution was often very indirect and unintended. In some cases, a particular metaphor has been directly invoked in a context that clearly confuses its larger scientific meaning. Nowhere perhaps is the potential for misplacing metaphors greater than in the social realm. For example, *synergetics* has a number of useful analogues in social inquiry, but they are few and far between. Likewise, maintaining the possibility of *chaos* enriches one's understandings of institutional dynamics. Yet while the methods derived from "chaos theory" (e.g., phase planes) have a number of interesting managerial applications (as later chapters will show), the actual event of *chaotic attractors* may remain a rare social phenomenon. Meanwhile, other more arcane concepts such as *self-organization* and *dissipative structures* may be quite common occurrences. *Complexity* on the other hand, while even more ubiquitous, is, by its very nature (i.e., the deep organizing principles of systems), more difficult to capture from a methodological standpoint. Yet, given its metaphorical proximity to the processes of the human intellect (and its machine counterparts), these *creatively adaptive systems* are perhaps the most compelling. For instance, the "brain" is probably a more apt metaphorical tool in affairs of statecraft (trade, warfare, etc.) than the "solar system." Applying these more powerful, or merely promising, metaphors is relatively easy. Understanding the underlying theory that energizes them and gives them their explanatory punch is much more difficult. Nonetheless, this is the task that lies ahead.

Chapter Summaries

This book is designed to pull threads from a vast array of heretofore disparate literatures and weave them into a new conceptual tapestry. Thus, it may be useful to provide a brief overview of its constituent elements, chapter by chapter. At this point, the purposes of this particular chapter (chap. 1) should be relatively transparent. The theme of this chapter is the theme of the entire book. Stated directly, it is that nonlinear methods and metaphors as applied to social phenomena represent a restoration of the ideals of systems theory. Those ideals, in turn, include an ecological vision and a sensitivity to critical processes and their underlying dynamics. These ideals will be magnified through all the chapters that follow. The fact that these ideals have yet to be fully manifest in a successful paradigm of social inquiry relates to the more generic theme of chapter 1, in essence, that of impending paradigmatic revolution. While not identical, parallels can be drawn to similar revolutionary shifts in the physical sciences, in particular the rise of quantum theory.

Chapter 2 reviews the formal mathematical and empirical breakthroughs that have contributed to the new science of nonlinearity. Again, the theme of a gradually unfolding revolution is used to develop an appreciation for the potential impacts of these emerging mathematical methods. While some of these methods have been around for nearly a century, the gradualism, if not recalcitrance, of social scientific progress forestalled widespread appreciation. Massive advances in computational power have now made the methods commonplace, yet widespread adoption may still await the development of a comprehensive framework, such as systems theory.

Chapter 3 extends the review of mathematical insights through a tour of increasingly prominent tools and concepts. A key point is that while the social sciences will benefit from applications of chaos and complexity theory, not all the work being done will be of equal value. Of interest are tools and concepts that have a shared heritage stemming from cybernetics and general systems theoretics. Three particular domains are only tangent to social inquiry at present. These include cellular automata, neural nets, and fuzzy set theory. "Cellular automata" can facilitate the graphic display of evolutionary dynamics and can, in social science settings, illustrate the nonlinear evolution of strategic choice. "Fuzzy sets," with their existence being represented by probabilities, can be used to build learning models. These models, in turn, can be used to design more adaptive institutional processes.

Game theory provides a useful device for representing strategic interactions and how the decisions of one entity affect the decisions of another. The nonlinear ebb and flow of cooperative dynamics greatly extend the conceptual utility of game approaches. For example, "genetic algorithms" can be viewed as stimulating nonlinear evolution through the creation of binary-based organisms that evaluate, select, and recombine based on predispositions as well as on environmental factors. These recombinations, in turn, will have "implications" for the design of learning systems. Fields—such as economics—that already use game theory can apply nonlinear games to create an environment in which different institutional designs could be grown and tested for robustness.

Chapter 4 contains a historical review of systems theory and pulls out elements for revival and reconceptualization. In the 1950s, von Bertalanffy's general systems theory (GST) anticipated many of the current conceptual requirements. However, GST lost its status as a basic research *paradigm* by the late 1960s, and with it went the important distinction between living and mechanical systems. The success of certain narrow mechanical, engineering, and management applications has distorted systems theory's more generic utility.

A number of forgotten theorists sought to maintain a more general systems orientation during this hiatus period. For example, Stephen Pepper, Walter Buckley, and Edgar Dunn provide a foundation for the reformulation of the basic GST paradigm. Buckley, a sociologist, wanted to free his discipline from its association with simple structural/functionalism. Pepper, a philosopher, rejected the static equilibrium approach that formed the basis for "closed-systems" applications and developed a new contextual orientation. Dunn, an economist, described economic development in systemic and adaptive-learning terms. Similar contributions can be gleaned from "cybernetics," the subfield of systems thinking concerned with interaction of human and machine learning. One of its main contributors was W. Ross Ashby, who explored how systems regulate disturbances through variety. These insights formed the basis of "information process theory."

This chapter concludes with a discussion of unresolved issues. In particular, the hallmark of systems thinking, "holism," is also a major stumbling block to its increased utilization. Unless this position can be reconciled with "methodological individualism," systems' ascendancy might be forestalled indefinitely. A few formulations, such as the famed "garbage-can model," point toward such reconciliation, and these concepts might be further strengthened through the nonlinear dynamic characterization of "systemic choices."

Ecological thinking and its antecedent elements from "institutional" and "behavioral" economics are the primary themes of chapter 5. Principal among these antecedent formulations were the works of Veblen, Mitchell, and Commons. Veblen was a pioneer in the application of cultural anthropology to contemporary economic issues. Mitchell worked on understanding the interplay of social conventions and external forces on the results of government actions. Commons worked in the interplay of law, economics, and social dynamics. These writers are icons in the somewhat dormant institutionalist perspective. These institutionalists' insights can be combined with various elements from behavior economics and remnants of earlier social-ecology approaches to form a rejuvenated framework of *institutional ecology*.

Chapter 6 identifies perspectives similar to this ecological framework in the writings of business strategy and in the characterizations of Japanese management practices. Collectively, these perspectives describe nonlinear processes of organizational and societal learning and adaptation. In particular, the learning dynamics are manifest in successful applications of "total quality management" (TQM) and associated managerial innovations

Chapter 7 further extends this ecology of commerce perspective through the direct application of nonlinear tools to a number of specific management assessment activities. Via the illustration of "phase plane diagrams," a nonlinear accounting device is applied to managerial tasks ranging from inventory control to budgeting and financial accounting. Essentially these diagrams overlie measures of change and produce a picture of interaction between critical internal forces. These pictures expand the diagnosis of corporate health by capturing the overall metabolism of a given firm. When combined with strategic simulations using the nonlinear game approaches discussed earlier, corporate decision making could be sensitized to a fuller spectrum of evolving industrial ecosystems.

Chapter 8 expands this microecological perspective to the macroeconomic level. This chapter explores how nonlinearities exhibited in such common phenomena as the "business cycle" may, over time, accumulate into longer waves of economic boom and bust. Furthermore, since nonlinear dynamics are very prominent in the evolution of technological trajectories, and technological change may represent the critical initial condition (or "butterfly") within a given long-wave cycle, then nonlinearity may be the most central feature of any given macroeconomic theory. This feature is especially critical to understanding the current transformation from a manufacturing-based to an information-based industrial structure.

Chapter 9, the final chapter, prescribes the application of institutional ecology and associated nonlinear lessons to the resolution of various long-standing social dilemmas, such as environmental degradation. Examples of the micro- and macrodynamics of "sustainable development" are key cases in point. Here again, the systemic and institutional character of strategic choices is highlighted. It is argued that traditional mechanisms ranging along a continuum of markets to governmental regulation should be reevaluated from the vantage point of institutional ecology. Institutional redesign, it is argued, is the central challenge for social inquiry in the twenty-first century.

Conclusions

As an ill-prepared society rushes headlong into the new millennium, the problem of brittle (nonadaptive) institutions is compounded by ill-conceived models of human choice. An unfortunate by-product of the "millennial madness" manifest by certain cults and fringe groups is the more widespread belief that various inexorable forces are at work and that humankind is simply at their mercy. Even respected scholars and pundits portray waves of societal change breaking over a hapless populace (see Thurow 1996). This sense of fatalism—at the level of Greek tragedy—is not, interestingly enough, diminished by currently popular notions of "rational choice" derived from neoclassical economic theory. This impotence stems from a concept of choice that is too sweeping on the one hand and not really supportive of "free will" on the other. The concept of systemic choice, by contrast, is both more modest in scope and yet more authentic in its characterization of human agency. It goes much further toward clarifying the role of individual activity within complex webs and networks than the false idols of autonomy perpetuated in popular economic and political models. The design of more adaptive institutions is hardly aided by the existing models of decision making that inaccurately depict the processes of strategic choice. While the choice dynamics, derived from a revival of systems thinking, do not necessarily engender overwhelming optimism, neither do they enhance the prevailing pessimism. By unlocking the intricacies of various invisible dynamics, belief in, as well as maintenance of, "market" and associated signaling mechanisms, need not be matters of blind faith. Greater understanding promotes confidence, and confidence fuels competence. If institutional redesign is to be the hallmark of the twenty-first century, then such competence should be vigorously sought after.

CHAPTER 2

The Crux of Chaos and Complex Systems

The basic mathematics of nonlinear systems were investigated initially in the nineteenth century but remained relatively obscure for over a hundred years. Specific technical problems might have yielded to these curious mathematics at least fifty years ago. Many scientists and engineers preferred, however, to think of these problems as intractable and/or seemed satisfied with only partial solutions. As Nobel prize winner Ilya Prigogine and his colleague Isabelle Stengers (1984) observed, "oscillating chemical reactions could have been discovered many years ago, but the study of these nonequilibrium problems was repressed in the cultural and ideological context of those times" (19–20). Even as inquiries into discontinuity began to gather momentum in physics and chemistry, standard models tended to merely explain away the dynamics that result in chaos and complexity. Until very recently, nonlinear studies were dominated by models of *conservative* systems (also called hamiltonian) in which no energy loss occurs. As Stephen Kellert (1993) suggests, "physics concentrated on these cases, treating all others as exceptions to be approximated by a simple solution or else ignored" (143).

Occasionally over the years, a few scholars have sought to better understand these various exceptions to the rules of linear continuous phenomena. Gradually from studies of "discontinuities," they began to realize that some of these exceptions may be much more ubiquitous and in many cases may prove the rule. Ultimately, these and related explorations have yielded a much clearer picture of causality. For example, nonlinear methods can detect the potential for exponential expansion around a relatively weak causal pattern (one with little direct correlation and no statistical significance via traditional tests). In other instances of convoluted causality, one can now more nearly locate the proverbial "needle in the haystack." More importantly, the processes of unforeseen change and/or "hidden order" can be exposed. In other words, the crux of chaos and complexity studies is that they not only isolate the straw, but also explain the camel's broken back.

From Catastrophe to Chaos

The study of *discontinuities* in otherwise linear systems actually dates back well into the nineteenth century. During this particular era, Laplace argued from the extension of Newton's mechanical worldview to provide a completely deterministic system of linear equations for much of science. A mere handful remained unconvinced. The most significant challenge to Laplace's dream of a completely predictable system came from Henri Poincaré. Poincaré reintroduced a more organic notion of mathematics through his development of topological analysis. Moreover, he directly confronted the reigning theories of celestial mechanics by introducing a novel solution to the *n-body problem*—that is, an approach that accounts for the interaction of three or more bodies, as in the solar system. Poincaré's system also attempted to account for mechanisms of qualitative change and anticipated many of the current developments in chaos theory. Being so far ahead of its time, most of this work was ill appreciated for decades, yet it did inspire a small number of scholars to focus upon the mapping of discontinuities via topological characterizations. Topology is the branch of mathematics that maps properties of geometric forms with invariant transformational characteristics, and this particular focus on bifurcations dynamics was given the provocative label *catastrophic theory.*

Catastrophe theory was the brainchild of another French mathematician, and Fields Medalist, René Thom (1972). Essentially, it describes instances in which continuous causes (i.e., changes in evolutionary landscapes) produce discontinuous impacts. For Thom (1983), the study of catastrophes was a crucial addendum to "general systems theory," since it captured the internal dynamics of "morphogenesis" one of the more vital characteristics of living systems. Thom's breakthrough was the isolation of seven simple geometric shapes that he believed described most discontinuities (see table 3). Thom's (1972) famed *classification theorem* was the culmination of nearly twenty years of work on the transformation qualities of bifurcation mathematics. By formally exploring the effects of perturbations on curious states, known as *singularities,* Thom arrived at his *transversality concept* to describe the symmetry in what are now called symmetry-breaking events. For Thom, bifurcation points became the *catastrophe manifold.*

Catastrophe theory is not mere abstraction. Thom was originally influenced by specific issues of qualitative change in biological populations. In this regard, catastrophe theory also draws from the pathbreaking work of d'Arey Thompson (1917) on the geometric structure of a particular species or organism. Thompson's characterization of *homeomorphism* described how *continuous coordinate changes* occur between organisms located in roughly the same topological space (e.g., similar genomes). In other words, phenotypes undergo constant transformations in which similar organisms are "deformed into each other," such as the chimpanzee and the baboon (see Casti 1989, 12–13). This work also influenced the famed bioecologist Conrad H. Waddington, who saw it as a prelude theory to self-organizing systems (note Jantsch and Waddington 1976).

The greatest elaboration of catastrophes came through the efforts of Sir Christopher Zeeman (1977), who identified specific "behavioral patterns" for particular structures. For example, the cusp exhibits "bimodality, inaccessibility, hysteresis, and divergence." Zeeman is also credited for the most ambitious claims for topological analysis. Like Thom, Zeeman envisioned multiple applications for this theory of structural change. Their perspective has produced applications in embryology and morphology, as well as in numerous other physical science and engineering fields. Yet Zeeman's prognostications regarding economics, political science, and so on, have yet to be completely fulfilled. Examples, such as a cusp model of monopoly formation (Woodcock and Davis 1978), are fairly rare. Thom attributes this glaring lack of interest to the persistence of "neopositive epistemology." Moreover, he maintains that science itself has a dramatic bifurcation point between understanding and acting effectively. Understanding involves qualitative classification and geometry, while acting requires quantified models that are locally specific (Thom 1983, chap. 1).

TABLE 3. The Magnificent Seven (Catastrophes)

Name	No. of State Variables	No. of Control Variables	Germ	Perturbation	Meaning
Fold	1	1	x^3	cx	The *boundary* where processes begin or end.
Cusp	1	2	x^4	$c_1x + c^2x^2$	The *fault line* where processes snap or unite.
Swallowtail	1	1	x^3	$x^5c_1x + c_2x^2 + c_3x^3$	The *corner* where processes cleave or stitch.
Butterfly	1	4	x^6	$c_1x + c_2x^2 + c_3x^3 + c_4x^4$	The *pocket* where processes peel off or exfoliate.
Hyperbolic umbilic	2	3	$x_1^3 + x_2^3$	$c_1x_1 + c_2x^2 + c_3x_1x_2$	The *crest* of a wave where processes collapse or recover.
Elliptic umbilic	2	3	$x_1^3x_1x^2$	$c_1x_1 + c_2x_2 + x_3(x_1^2 + x_2^2)$	The *pike* where processes pierce or fill a sharp wound.
Parabolic umbilic	2	4	$x_1^2x_2 + x_2^4$	$c_1x_1 + c_2x_2 + c_3x_1^2 + c_4x_2^2$	The *jet* where processes throw off or bind.

As Stephen Guastello (1988, 1995) demonstrates, catastrophe theory has a number of possible practical applications in domains ranging from "personnel selection" and psychotherapy to "policy and evaluation." Guastello (1995) also illustrates throughout his book that catastrophes' plots provide a powerful graphic display. Moreover, he is quick to point out that catastrophe calculations are no more abstract than the typical linear regression model and yet are able to capture a much "wider range of values" (64). The key to successful application of this, or any other mathematical technique for that matter, appears to be resisting the temptation to merely "curve fit" existing models. Political scientist Courtney Brown (1995) elaborates on this point as follows.

> it is important to work from the perspective of social theory, not mathe-matical theory. Early catastrophe work was heavily criticized for loosely applying general catastrophe models to a wide variety of social processes. ... Thom suggested that all catastrophes could be identified from within a small set of canonical models. The problem in application occurred when theorists took this result too seriously, to the point of avoiding the theory construction enterprise entirely. (67)

In other words, model builders, of any bent, should focus on social processes first and then explore whether or not they might constitute algebraic structures that yield catastrophes second.

As it would turn out, catastrophes are now regarded as merely one of at least three types of "dynamical bifurcations" and not all that common. The other two are "subtle" (meaning gradual, like the famed Hopf bifurcation) and "explosive" (i.e., extremely rapid onset). Further explorations into these more common types of bifurcations became better known under the generic label *chaos theory.*

Chaos: The Seething Vortex of Nature

Given its close kinship to work in catastrophes, the designation "chaos" is perhaps only partially misplaced. However, since as alluded to earlier *chaos is really the quest for hidden order,* this misnomer is unfortunate, at best. At worst, it is misleading to the layperson. What is more important, perhaps, about this curious branch of applied mathematics is that a world full of this type of chaos is at once more orderly and yet more mercurial. In the words of the old Frankenstein movies, "it's alive." Viewing the world, especially the human portions thereof, as a living system may not seem all that novel. But as chaos theory's most popular proponent, James Gleick (1987), proclaimed, it consti-tutes "the making of a new science." What is essentially unique about chaos theory is its identification of complex and recursive dynamics as the heart of many orderly processes, thus bringing discontinuity and bifurcation from the wings to center stage.

Discontinuity and bifurcation become increasing important, because in a living-systems world, chaotic transformations characterize the processes at work between order and randomness (see table 4). In the past, if one wanted to describe something like a chaotic process, one would merely model it as randomness and/or conduct a laborious set of frequency calculations. Yet, by positing the possibility of a qualitative change in state, the process is described using a handful of equations. The keys to this simplification of complex dynamics are the concepts of *phase space* and *attractor.* As James Gleick (1987) points out, phase space is "one of the most powerful inventions in modern science" (134). Charting the phase space (on a phase plane) provides a road map of a system with moving parts. The phase plane is like a CAT scan, providing a cross-sectional snapshot of a dynamical process, where complex information is abstracted to a set of points (representing the entire system at a single point in time). History is added by projecting the orbit of the moving point through the phase space over time. Attractors, meanwhile, describe the movement of the points in terms of particular patterns. Attractors can be quite subtle. That is, they are often "fixed" or "cyclical," representing behaviors that are either steady state or continuously repeating. Recall that the early discontinuity studies focused on defining these smooth and continuous cycles. *Strange attractors,* on the other hand, are discontinuous, yet this aperiodic behavior can still be represented by a simple set of nonlinear equations that illustrates the convergence of trajectories within a phase space. An actual plot might appear as a bundle of spirals, yet using the phase plane knife, one can slice through and see that the lines do not intersect, nor points repeat.

TABLE 4. Between Order and Randomness

	Orderly	Chaotic	Random
Example	Planetary system	Weather patterns	The stock market?[a]
Predictability	Very high	Finite, short term	Little to none
Spectrum	Pure	Board	Noisy, very broad
Dimension	Finite	Low	Infinite
Control	Easy	Difficult, but effective	Very poor
Attractor	Point, cycle, torus	Strange, fractal	None
Effect of small changes	Small	Very large	Very small to none

[a]While most economists assume a "random walk," evidence is mounting that it is actually subject to periodic chaos and perhaps even "long way" cycles.

Bifurcations, or major changes in overall system behavior, generally in-volve a shift from one type of attractor to another (e.g., fixed to cyclical and/or cyclical to strange). However, they can also involve transitions from attractors to repellors (as in "Hopf bifurcation"; see Mandelbrot 1983). A *repellor* is another type of point, vital to topological explanations and oscillating phenom-ena. The easy way to describe a repellor is to visualize a watershed in which the attractor is one of the basins and the repellor is one of the sources. The zone between attractors and repellors is known as a *saddle.*

While it is an oversimplification, one way to view the contribution of chaos theory is that it deals with discontinuity problems of increasing complexity. Operationally these problems involve dynamical systems exhibiting behavior that is *nonlinear, aperiodic, and unstable.* In physics, chaos theory became a rallying point for those who wanted to break out of increasingly restricted paths to intellectual glory. Gleick (1987) explains that

> The mainstream for most of the twentieth century has been particle physics, exploring the building blocks of matter at higher and higher energies, smaller and smaller scales, shorter and shorter times. . . . Yet some young physicists have grown dissatisfied with the direction of the most prestigious of sciences. . . . With the coming of chaos, younger scientists believed they were seeing the beginnings of a course change for all of physics. . . . They believe in looking for the whole. (5–6)

In practical terms, the youthful zeal could be marshaled to address certain persistent problems for which classical physics had only partial answers, as well as opening entirely new domains for the theoretical applications. As is often the case, the real impetus for serious chaos work came initially by way of concrete applications, very far afield from theoretical physics.

The Beatific Butterfly

One of these early applications has to be one of the truly great stories in science. Meteorologist Edward Lorenz (1963) was experimenting with a simple mathe-matical model of atmospheric flow using a digital computer to perform the laborious manipulations required to capture the dynamic process. Returning from a coffee break, he noted a radically divergent outcome to a repeated sequence, which resulted from merely inputting a rounded version of the parameter from a previous run. Eventually, it would be realized that this particular complex, unstable behavior resulted from a "strange attractor." The Lorenz' attractor exhibited a double spiral shape (see fig. 2) and actually involved an attractor/repellor interaction. Mathematicians would later marvel that his fairly standard set of differential equations captured the complex interaction of temperature and velocity in the atmosphere. From a meteorological perspective this discovery of chaos dynamics (with its sensitive dependence on initial conditions) meant exact weather forecasting was and is doomed. Yet, predictable patterns may emerge. Lorenz coined the phrase "butterfly effect" to describe this curiousity (note the similarity to the plot). This notion that a butterfly flapping its wings in Brazil can cause a tornado in Texas became a powerful metaphor for the chaos movement in general.

While Lorenz was experiencing his revelations, physicists were reaching similar conclusions (probably less startling to them) regarding turbulent phenomena of more general varieties. In fact, Lorenz's original little model was fashioned on the hunch that atmospheric turbulence would behave a lot like ripples in water when it is brought to a boil. While physicists could represent these dynamics, they suspected that their explanations were incomplete, and

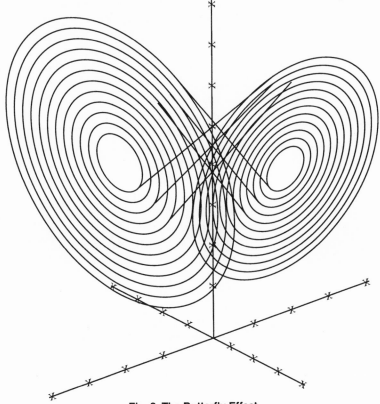

Fig. 2. The Butterfly Effect

again the mathematics were quite laborious. Therefore, chaos theory is used not only to expedite solutions but to fill in critical pieces of the puzzle of turbulence missing from classical physics. Fluid turbulence was especially puzzling. For example, why does oil start to slow down in a pipeline even as the pressure increases and the viscosity decreases? Stated simply, the turbulence causes the system to back up on itself. A better example, perhaps, is the much feared "wind-shear" effect in aerodynamics, where the turbulence over the wing disrupts the lift foil and, since planes do not really fly, they drop like a rock.

Knowing that turbulence exists does not make it easy to represent; that is, until the development of chaos models. One of the most important developments in this regard was the work of David Ruelle and Floris Takens (1971). Their model has a series of four "Hopf bifurcations," culminating in a solution dominated by a strange attractor. In other words, it demonstrates the transition from limiting cycles to chaos. Their *transitional model* has become a mainstay in physics as well as other chaos applications.

Another quite separate type of mathematical modeling that has fueled developments in chaos theory was Benoit Mandelbrot's work in *fractal geometry*. Fractals involve certain self-similarities at differing scales. By unraveling coils that bind around an attractor, a picture of a dynamic process is possible. Fractals depict the patterns that arise in chaos, and thus *fractal dimension* is another measure of the order within disorder. Mandelbrot, himself, believes that reality is fundamentally discontinuous, with the patterns yielding almost infinitely to a more "granular structure" at a higher level of magnification. This texture, within the texture, involves what he calls *multifractals*.

What is perhaps most interesting about Mandelbrot's work is that he arrived at this reconstructed view of the world while studying economic processes. Basically, he displayed, using real data, the essentially discontinuous nature of certain competitive markets (1963). In the process, he challenged the reigning paradigm of general equilibrium. Finding his own discipline less than congenial to these observations, he had to be content with merely becoming the darling of mathematics and remaining outside academia in his research post at IBM. Economic historian Philip Mirowski (1990), in his article on Mandelbrot, describes this situation as follows.

> Benoit Mandelbrot wrote several stunningly original papers in economics from roughly 1962–1972; and then, afterwards, he went on to become famous elsewhere. . . . Moreover, while it can be claimed that the work on economics was an important input into his later innovations concerning "fractals" which did make him famous, one can find no indication of how the connections might be made in the existing literature. (291)

This discussion will have more to say of this lacuna later. For now, suffice it to say that a prophet is never honored in his or her own land, especially when the prophet's message would mean the demise of the neoclassical hegemony in mathematical economics.

Another realm of application with perhaps the most far-reaching implications is that of population biology. Ecologist Robert May (1973) contends that biologists had been experiencing chaos in the ebb and flow of populations for some time (perhaps as early as the 1950s) but chose to ignore it. Using the rather crude tool of *logistic maps,* May (1976) began modeling ecosystem chaos in the early 1970s. What researchers were seeing in wildly fluctuating populations like the gypsy moth was the *period-doubling* phenomenon, which would later be captured more explicitly in Mitchel Feigenbaum's (1978) *cascade* or sequence model. Feigenbaum connected fractal geometry and nonlinear dynamics via simple logistic maps. The patterns of bifurcation he identified exhibited "scaler self-similarities," which define a fractal. For instance, for a given species with a constant of three (representing reproduction efficiency), the population would swing through regular "boom and bust" cycles; as the critical value increased, the oscillations would begin to double in magnitude. Yet at a certain critical threshold the population began to shift in a more erratic or "complex" pattern (see Davies 1987). In other words, certain populations experience a *cascade of bifurcations,* producing a doubling of the orbit period, just prior to the onset of chaos.

Similar processes might be at work in the social realm, ranging from transportation planning (see Cochrane 1993) to business cycles and stock-market "bubbles" (see Peters 1994) and bandwagon effects in politics (Brown 1995). Other patterns of social evolution may follow different paths toward and away from chaos. The literature of chaos (e.g., Goertzel 1994; Nicolis and Prigogine 1989) identifies at least four potential pathways, including the following: (1) periodic bursts at irregular intervals; (2) period doubling or cascades; (3) quasi-periodic; and (4) low-dimensional strange attractors. Of course, numerous other social discontinuities may not comprise a chaotic element at all. If no dissipation of energy or organization is involved, they might be described using basic Hamiltonian mathematics. However, if as the self-organization and complexity theorists suggest the potential for chaotic processes is a critical building block in living systems, then these models of nonlinear instabilities will increasingly become a vital element of any systematic analysis of social phenomena.

As will hopefully become increasingly evident subsequently, the growth, development, and change of all human systems are integrally linked to processes of nonlinearity, and these processes usually harbor potential instabilities. Hence as a process characteristic, the potential for chaos is as important as its actual presence. Much of the work in the social science applications of chaos theory has focused on locating specific instances of chaos, for example, finding a chaotic attraction in a sea of economic time-series data (note Brock, Hsieh, and Lebaron 1991). As with the physical sciences, this finding of an alien product is critical to understanding vital underlying processes. Unfortunately, a preoccupation with actual chaotic events, especially in the social sciences, may be missing the point. Having said this, precise measurement of chaos still remains essential to illustrating the larger meaning. Thus, this discussion now turns to a review of some of the more widely accepted elements of analysis.

From Measurement to Meaning

Measuring chaos is relatively straightforward, that is, if one remembers that one is looking for a relatively rare type of nonlinearity in a world normally measured completely in linear terms. The most widely accepted indicator of chaos was developed several years ago and is largely based on the stability calculations of the Russian mathematician A. M. Lyapunov (1857–1918). His work can best be thought of as a type of sensitivity analysis (see Lyapunov 1950) and is essentially a way of measuring the potential chaos exhibited in initial conditions. A Lyapunov exponential coefficient (LEC), or merely Lyapunov exponent, is a logarithm of the number representing how quickly the points diverge from a linear mapping. A positive exponent is usually indicative of chaos. A similar measure, known as the Lyapunov dimension, is used to indicate the *strangeness* of a given attractor (see Farmer, Ott, and Yorke 1983). A social scientist puzzling over a particularly rich but extremely messy scatter plot might be diverted from assuming randomness by a Lyapunov dimension and pointed in the direction of an astonishingly deterministic, albeit chaotic, path. By representing the level of displacement from a central point, the Lyapunov exponent can also be used to distinguish potential dissipation within previously conservative structure. To more fully grasp the significance of this contribution a comparison of major attractors might prove useful.

Major Types of Attractors

Fixed Point   Oscillations that return to an original position, usually associated with closed, linear systems.

Limit Cycle   Oscillations that *do not* come to rest at a fixed point but nonetheless, move within prescribed limits; usually associated with semilinear yet constrained closed systems, or energy-conserving systems, or Hamiltonian systems.

Torus Attractors	Oscillations involving the interaction of two or more limit cycles; can fluctuate like strange attractors but since they are largely energy conserving they are ultimately predictable.
Strange Attractor	Oscillations involving irregular, aperiodic, and unpredictable behavior or (once thought of as random) that arise in "dissipative" (nonenergy-conserving) systems. Exhibits noninteger or "fractal" dimensions with "trajectories" that *do not* close on themselves.
Chaotic Attractor	Oscillations similar to "strange attractor," highly sensitive to initial conditions, highly unpredictable; exhibiting rapid and exponential separation of trajectories.

Generally speaking, dynamical systems are characterized by one of these attractors. As alluded to earlier, historically it was believed that most dynamical behavior could be explained using the first two types. Early work in populations dynamics (i.e., predator-prey models) gradually pushed biology to embrace the third type (Lotka 1956). In fact, these simple logistic equations, originally developed by A. J. Lotka (1880–1949) and V. Volterra (1860–1940), remain a mainstay in the application of nonlinear dynamics.

It is, of course, the behavior associated with the latter two types of attractors that intrigues most chaosologists. Of particular interest are the so-called *strange attractors,* since they can display a wide range of behaviors, including very low-dimensional chaos. Detecting this attractor often draws upon earlier work in dynamic entropy theory, by the likes of Andrei Kolmogorov (1903–87) and Ilya Prigogine. The concept and methods of "Kolmogorov entropy" are still widely used in the designation of dissipative systems and are especially useful in determining the onset of chaos. Moreover, the modern day methodology of "algorithmic complexity," particularly the SKC (Solomonoff, Kolmogorov, and Chaitin) approach to establishing the minimum length of an algorithm for a complex data set, also relies upon this work (see Chaitin 1987; and for a much more accessible piece, see his 1988 article in *Scientific American*). The average rate of information loss in a system is defined in terms of exponential separation of trajectories in phase space.

To summarize the "tricks of the trade" for the typical chaos sleuth, one is generally trying to identify any number of the following necessary, if not completely sufficient, conditions.

- The system must be nonlinear, and its time series should be irregular;
- It can still have and probably should have random elements;
- The behavior of the system must be highly sensitive to initial conditions;

- The system should have strange attractors, which generally means that it will have fractal dimensions;
- In dissipative systems the Kolmogorov entropy should be positive; and/or
- Perhaps the most terse way of pronouncing a system to be chaotic is to determine that there are positive Lyapunov coefficients.

The purpose of these calculations is to isolate deterministic elements from an apparently stochastic world. Again, *chaos entails a curious blend of randomness and determinism.* Heretofore, stochastic processes were by definition a matter of *probabilistic parameters.* Pulling the deterministic thread from the bundle of probabilities normally involves the following types of procedures.

- Obtain a large amount of *time-series data;* if linear, then, by definition, no chaos exists;
- Check the scale to see linearity is authentic;
- If nonlinear, with an output signal that is larger than the input signal, check for patterns and/or look for chaotic dimensions;
- If chaotic dimension is suspected, then test for *algorithmic complexity;*
- One can also obtain a power spectrum and look for broadening via the *autocorrelation function;*
- If one identifies a noninteger or fractal dimension, a Poincaré map can be constructed by slicing through attractors and studying points in the phase space.

As most social scientists are already aware, good time series are scarce, and sufficient amounts to exhibit chaos are even more rare. While techniques such as ARIMA (interrupted time-series analysis) are useful in filling the holes in spotty measurements, their assumptions of linearity tend to complicate, if not obliterate, the search for chaos. A much more promising avenue is beginning to open up through the reemergence of a so-called narrative science, or "sensemaking," approach (note Weick 1995). Harkening back to earlier calls for the unification of qualitative and quantitative research (à la Polkinghorne 1988), it has been reinvigorated by recent computer applications (note Weitsman and Miles 1995). This new type of ethnographic research can convert individual and organizational "lived experiences" into data sets. Qualitative insights are clustered into "discrete events" through the aid of various clarifying software systems, such as Nud-ist (the nonnumeric, unstructured data indexing, searching, and theorizing system; see Richard and Richard 1991). Collections of events become a source of time series for otherwise standard linear regression. However, given that these events also often chronicle items such as radical organizational changes and/or other social turbulence, they also provide a source of nonlinear analyses. Unlike previous incarnations of historical analysis, which are geared to macroevents, these nonlinear time series can focus on microfluc-tuations using variable aggregations schemes (see Poole et al. 1997). Not only do these methods hold the promise of capturing greater levels of social non-linearity, they provide a conduit for bringing much of the complex contextual richness of qualitative studies back into quantitative research. As these methods become more widespread, entirely new examples of social systems chaos will join the mounting list of physical science discoveries. (For excellent anthologies of chaos in the social sciences, see Albert 1995; Kiel and Elliott 1996).

Ultimately however, whether or not social scientists locate chaos within a particular set of societal or organizational processes is not as important as the quest itself. Merely admitting the relevance of nonlinear dynamics (some of which result in chaos) is a significant watershed point in the annals of social inquiry. Moreover, as Kevin Dooley (1994) contends in his discussion of research techniques, the "methods stew" for "studying chaos and complexity" will continue to include approaches ranging from "case studies" and "metaphori-cal essays" to "simulations" and "time-series modeling." As long as the meta-phor is not too misplaced, social inquiry will continue to profit by applying the concepts of chaos borrowed from the physical sciences. With specific reference to the study of change in corporate settings, Dooley and Van de Ven (1998) take great pains to detect and distinguish forms of chaos from other forms of complex dynamics, especially randomness. For example, they distinguish "pink noise" (high-dimensional chaos with similar statistical characteristics to white noise, or randomness) from chaotic and periodic attractors. Moreover, they generate a number of extremely useful "propositions" (actually hypotheses requiring fur-ther testing) which relate these statistical features with particular organizational settings and management practices. In this way they demonstrate the centrality of the quest for chaos, as a modern (or postmodern) managerial prerequisite, even when actual chaotic attractors are not present in a relatively turbulent change situation. However they also allude to the fact the fuller impact will be more powerfully felt when seen through the lens of a larger frameworks of nonlinear dynamical systems. In short, acknowledgment of chaos portends a new era of social systems theory and application.

From Chaos to Complexity

Along with the discovery of social chaos, entirely new realms of inquiry have begun to emerge. A number of diverse problems, once regarded intractable, could now be explored in terms of simple dynamics. Collectively this realm is referred to as "complexity" (see Waldrop 1992). The study of complexity draws extensively upon earlier work in cybernetics and theoretical mathematics and has now become a watchword in social inquiry. As such, it is both a rallying point and a source of great confusion. Complexity has a rather discrete meaning in physics and mathematics, and this meaning is often lost in the various "sciences" that purport to explore complexity. As Daniel Stein (1989) explains in the introduction to the first volume of *Lectures in the Sciences of Complexity,* put out by the Santa Fe Institute:

> There is no universal agreement as to what constitutes a "complex system"; the term itself has been used in many ways by many people. Some use it to signify systems with chaotic dynamics; others refer to cellular automata, disordered many-body systems, "neural" networks, adaptive algorithms, pattern-forming systems, and so on. (xiii)

Some ambiguity, of course, is not necessarily a bad thing and may inspire diverse conceptual as well as methodological applications, particularly in the social sciences.

Unraveling Complexity

Confusion over the meaning of complexity is certainly understandable. As Mitchell Waldrop (1992) explains, it is "still so new and so wide ranging that nobody quite knows how to define it." Moreover, it "is trying to grapple with questions that defy all conventional categories" (9). It is also, like chaos, somewhat of a misnomer, since *complexity is really the quest for simplicity.* Furthermore, at a fundamental level, it is synonymous with nonlinearity, that is, a direct consequence of nonlinearity. While nonlinear systems occasionally yield chaos, they always breed complexity. Recursiveness, sensitivity to initial conditions, and weblike networks are inherent within the nature of nonlinear systems. These features are also the defining characteristics of complexity. In fact, it was the appearance of these convoluted causal paths that made these systems so intractable. Since complexity, by definition, also involves the participation of befuddling random elements, its close association with chaos is obvious. Similarly, complex systems are dynamic, in the sense that they evolve over time. Finally and most importantly, from an epistemological perspective (addressed in later chapters), *complexity entails a holistic perspective,* focusing on "emergent properties." In other words, "the whole is greater than the sum of the parts," because behaviors and/or properties emerge from the complex interaction that could not be predicted from focusing on the parts alone.

These defining characteristics, coupled with its inherent transdisciplinarity, not only make complexity a serious threat to remaining reductionist disciplines, they provide a conduit for the realization of earlier systems aspirations (see von Bertalanffy 1950). Complexity embodies the spirit of a unified science, as well as fulfilling many of its methodological imperatives. These elements will be explored at length in later chapters; at this point it is merely useful to observe that a viable mathematics of complex interactions was the major missing ingredient in past systems formulations.

To the extent that complexity carries forward the mantle of the living-systems paradigm, it represents the reenchantment as well as the redirection of science. As Peter Coveney and Roger Highfield (1995), respected scientist and distinguished science writer respectively, explain:

> we may draw strength from the ancient paradox that although the world is complex, the rules of nature are simple. The universe is populated by a rich variety of physical forms, from bacteria and rain forests to spiral galaxies, yet they are all generated and sculpted by the same underlying laws. Thanks to fast and powerful computers, biologists, physicists, and computer scientists pondering complexity can now explore complexity in its full glory, throwing light on questions that once lay exclusively in the province of philosophy and mysticism. (277)

Despite these lofty aspirations for a new complexity science, many if not most scientists actually doing complexity work tend to be carving out little niches for themselves at the margins of their particular discipline. This is especially true of social scientists, particularly economists. Of course, many scientists are far too busy and are generally oblivious to these larger epistemological issues. To the extent that they choose to label themselves, many still identify with the conventional designation of "nonlinear dynamics." By direct contrast, a few brave souls have chosen to affiliate themselves with a particular institute dedicated to the pell-mell pursuit of complexity. However, thus far these institutes have tended to specialize within specific domains (e.g., the Beckman Institute for Computational Biology). Even the more generic (from the perspective of discipline; e.g., the Sante Fe Institute for the Study of Complexity) have tended to isolate a common approach and/or delimit themselves to particular set of perspectives. Just as the choices of foundation and federal funding agencies have helped shape the course of science, these institutes, especially highly visible ones like Santa Fe, will exude an appreciable influence over the nature of this ongoing scientific revolution (or merely evolution). Hence it is worthwhile to outline in a bit closer detail their definition of the complexity enterprise.

The Santa Fe Express?

Despite the vast variety of research that might be construed as involving complex systems dynamics, several of the books written for a general audience tend to focus on a rather narrow band of activities (excellent exceptions, written for the semiscientifically literate, are Coveney and Highfield 1995; Capra 1996). In fact, the most captivating popularizations of complexity (e.g., Waldrop 1992) and several of tracts for the layperson, written by accomplished scientists (e.g., Gell-Mann 1994; Holland 1995; Kauffman 1995), deal primarily with a rather circumscribed set of perspectives. These perspectives, in turn, can be ascribed to the Sante Fe Institute (SFI).

SFI, founded in 1984, is a private independent research and education center; however it does receive significant government funding. In the words of its web page, it is dedicated to

> creating a new kind of scientific research community pursuing emerging science. Operating as a small, visiting institution, SFI seeks to catalyze new collaborative, multidisciplinary projects that break down the barriers between the traditional disciplines, to spread its ideas and methodologies to other individuals and encourage the practical applications of its results.

From the perspective of scientific organization, SFI seeks to unleash the same type of nonlinear evolutionary dynamic that they study in natural and machine systems. Yet, just as in nature, whether or not a particular novelty thrives is extremely problematic, and their attempt to create a hybrid with conventional science may prove daunting. Daniel Stein (1989) describes this goal as follows.

> Its primary concern is to focus the tools of traditional scientific disciplines and emerging new computer resources on the problems and opportunities that are involved in the multidisciplinary study of complex systems—those fundamental processes that shape almost every aspect of human life. Understanding complex systems is critical to realizing the full potential of science, and may be expected to yield enormous intellectual and practical benefits. (iii)

The key phrases are "tools of the traditional scientific disciplines" and "multidisciplinary" (rather than interdisciplinary) as well as "may be expected."

Under the leadership of Nobel physicists Murray Gell-Mann and Philip Anderson (as well as Nobel economist Kenneth Arrow), SFI has created an odd amalgam, which while never quite jelling, clearly exhibited a particular methodological undercurrent. This may not have been their original intent. Yet while diverse in discipline, they all pretty much share a passion for computation. Stein (1989) observed when speaking of the first generation of complexity, "in much of this research, computer simulations have proved more important than analysis" (xiii), and this emphasis on simulation for its own sake seems to continue.

Among the social scientists associated with SFI, this bias is even more pronounced, limiting involvement to a small band of disenfranchised mathematical economists or similarly oriented political scientists. It is interesting to note that mainstream work in these realms, in particular, is less easily reconciled with the larger epistemological implications of complexity. Thus the combined effect of these elements tends to maintain the focus on arcane modeling and "toy" problem solving.

In following chapters much more will be said about the role of computational approaches, especially simulation, in the development of nonlinear social inquiry. At this point suffice it to say that as a result of this emphasis, the Santa Fe express has been sidetracked somewhat. Despite its tremendous potential, without more widespread application its influence may be truncated. Just as the earliest version of the personal computer created in nearby Albuquerque required a "killer app" (significant business application) like "spreadsheet" in order to move beyond the isolated world of hobbyists and hackers, the simulation tools developed by folks associated with the Santa Fe Institute need to find their killer apps. The ongoing program to generously distribute the experimental software SWARM (Langton et al. 1995) is certainly an important step in this direction.

Complexity in Broader Context

To the extent that the analogy is appropriate, the processes of scientific discovery are nearing a critical bifurcation point, very far from conceptual equilibrium. In this context, the Santa Fe Institute or similar centers throughout the world are especially well situated to serve as radical initial condition. However, the resulting transformation can and will manifest itself in an expansive array of possible network combinations. Relatively few of these emergent properties of the new scientific estate will bear a direct resemblance to a simulation laden model of complexity. The Santa Fe perspective with its heavy reliance on *cybernetics* and advances in "artificial intelligence" will obviously play a major role, but it may not necessarily dominate. Nonlinear evolution is full of surprises. Thus, it may be useful to visualize complexity from the broader perspective of generic nonlinear science.

The Cybernetic Connection

While not widely acknowledged, much of the work currently going on in places like Santa Fe has its origins in the cybernetic theories of Claude Shannon (note Shannon and Weaver 1963), Norbert Wiener (1948), and John von Neumann (1958). The contribution of these extremely forward-looking scientists was itself a branch of larger systems research. Thus, the cybernetic approach to nonlinear processes, while significant, is merely a portion of the story of complex systems. Like their closely associated colleagues in the general systems movement, early cyberneticians lacked the high-speed computational tools to make their view of complexity fully operational; however, they were very nearly there. Complexity studies of the sort envisioned by these early pioneers were not really possible until 1970s, and by then cybernetics was pretty much absorbed into a larger biological and social systems context. This broader view of complexity is well represented in a piece written by Ilya Prigogine and Peter Allen (1982) entitled "The Challenge of Complexity," which served as an introduction to a collection of applications of self-organization/dissipative structures to diverse phenomena, including human systems (Schieve and Allen 1982). This was followed by a complete text on the subject of complexity by Prigogine and his old collaborator Gregoire Nicolis (Nicolis and Prigogine 1989). For them, the two major disciplines of "nonequilibrium physics" and "dynamical systems" have contributed the most to understanding complexity (ix). In this context, complexity is merely the study of self-organizing systems. In their chapter entitled "The Vocabulary of Complexity," the subtitles include the terms *dissipative systems, bifurcation,* and *symmetry breaking* (45–78). While they take some pains to distinguish *complex behaviors* from *simple behaviors* in physics and biology, they maintain that most *open systems* involve the interaction of both.

In the more diffuse literature of discontinuity, the term *complexity* pops up from time to time, often in very different contexts. Yet generally (particularly in the more recent literature), it is used to designate a threshold point where the curious dynamics of nonlinearity take over. Moreover, in a handful of places, it appears as a synonym for chaos. Some chaos theorists, especially the mathematicians, associate complexity with the use of *complex numbers* (i.e., those that arise on a plane with imaginary parts; see Gleick 1987, 215–20, 226–32).

In order to clarify and combine these various perspectives, physicist Ali Çambel (1992, 3–4), provides the following shopping list of complexity characteristics. To paraphrase:

1. Complexity can occur in all systems, including social systems.
2. Complex dynamical systems come in various sizes and cooperate across component levels.
3. The physical shape may be regular or irregular.
4. The more parts in a system, the more complexity.
5. Complexity can occur in both energy-conserving and dissipating systems.
6. Complex systems exhibit both determinism and randomness.
7. Complex systems experience nonproportionality in regard to cause and effect.

8. Complex systems are synergistic.
9. There is positive or negative feedback.
10. The level of complexity depends on the environment and the patterns of interaction.
11. Complex systems are open to their surroundings (they exchange material, energy, and information).
12. Complex systems often involve irreversible processes.
13. Complex systems entail dynamic nonequilibrium and thus are more about processes and less about products.
14. Many complex systems frequently undergo sudden changes, and functional relations are often not differentiable.
15. Paradoxes are normal for these systems (they often combine fast and slow events, regular and irregular forms, and organic and inorganic bodies).

Çambel himself is primarily concerned with chaos theory and sees it as the primary window on complexity. However, noting that chaos is a specific "condition," he recognizes that "not all complex systems are chaotic." Moreover, all chaotic systems involve nonlinear dynamics, but not all nonlinear dynamics produce chaos (14–17). Similarly, "not all complex systems are self-organizing, but most self-organizing are complex" (20).

Since, as alluded to earlier, this discussion is primarily concerned with living systems, and such systems tend to exhibit both chaos and complexity in the context of self-organization, it may provide a useful benchmark. Çambel reminds one that much of the work in dynamical systems involved "conservative" (Hamiltonian) and/or closed systems, "which experience no energy loss"; but, as "most real-life situations are dissipative" (systems that must exchange energy and information), self-organizing dynamics are more indicative of living systems. Applying this broader view of complexity one can return to the work of SFI associated scholars and develop linkages between simulated reality and real reality.

From Simulation to Assimilation

The mathematical expression of living systems is not without its hazards. However, complexity applications ranging from the simulation of biological processes known as *artificial life* and *adaptive agents* to *organizational learning* provide a virtual cornucopia of useful insights into the functioning of social systems. Perhaps the most interesting work along these lines was done by University of Michigan psychologist and computer scientist John Holland back in the early 1970s (reprinted in 1992). Holland was primarily concerned with simulating the behavior of "complex adaptive systems." According to Holland, his notions apply to systems ranging from the human brain and immune system to ant colonies, political parties and scientific communities. With global economic development as a case in point, he (see Holland 1988, 117–24) sees the following dynamics at work.

1. Dispersed units, agents, networks acting in parallel and interdependence;
2. Controls are provided by mechanisms of competition and coordination between units, mediated by *operating procedures,* assigned roles, and shifting associations;
3. Units at each level serve as building blocks for units at next higher level, and these are recombined and revised continually as the system accumulates experience and adapts;
4. The arena in which the economy operates is typified by many *niches* that may be exploited by particular adaptations; and niches are continually created by new technologies and governed by ecological principles, such as parasitism and symbiosis; and
5. The entire system "operates far from an optimum (or global attractor)," and thus there is *no* equilibrium; rather there is *perpetual novelty.*

What makes Holland's work so interesting is that it dovetails with past attempts to operationalize a general model of adaptive systems for social inquiry.

Holland's characterization of the economy as an *adaptive nonlinear network* is a great deal like Edgar Dunn's (1971) social-learning model for economic development, as well as other work in adaptive systems and social ecology (e.g., Emery and Trist 1973). Holland's unique contributions are his development of the *genetic algorithms approach* and his concept of *perpetual novelty* (an alternative to Darwinian natural selection). However, his use of simple Markov chains to represent probabilities in the learning process harkens back to Ashby's use of "Markovian machines" (see Ashby 1955). While simple, these "hunt and stick" processes can add an element of adaptability not currently appreciated in models of social dynamics.

Another stream of work emerging from the merger of natural systems and "machine models" of the brain is Christopher Langton's (1989) megaconcept of *artificial life* (or "A-life"). In the tradition of Norbert Wiener (1948), Langton literally sets out to create ecosystems in a computer. This work actually conducted with the U.S. Department of Energy (DOE) researchers in nearby Los Alamos may serve as the hallmark of the Santa Fe perspective. Essentially, it directs research on chaos away from the realm of energy transformations and toward the evolution of information systems (including genetic information).

As Langton observes: "the edge of chaos is where information gets its foot in the door in the physical world, where it gets the upper hand over energy" (Lewin 1992, photo insert, 7).

The major contribution of Langton and his colleagues may well be as a spur to others' use of simulation as a primary research tool. Under a grant from the Office of Naval Research and the O'Donnell Foundation, SFI developed a relatively "user-friendly" software called *SWARM* (see Langton et al. 1995). This software facilitates the simulations of multiagent complex systems via an architecture of "concurrent objects," which can be "continuously active" and thus interactive. SWARM is not only a mechanism for simple simulation of complex interactions; it may also provide a focal point for larger experiments in "distributed parallel processing." Since it establishes an intermediate level of virtual processing machinery, open to a broad range of execution platforms, it can be used to orchestrate a huge network of parallel processors. In this regard, SWARM can escape many of the limitations of standard digital computation. For example, by adopting the discrete approximation of time, synchronicity can be defined for a particular set of agents and their communications networks, while asynchronous messaging can be maintained for isolated agents. This represents a rather novel feature with regard to concurrent object systems. Unlike some of its counterparts, SWARM includes both discrete events and periodically synchronized global time. Thus, a variety of "coarse-grained agents" can be simulated along with the presence or absence of dense connections.

SWARM has undergone a number of applications to a wide range of phenomena, from bacterial colonies and chemical reagents to "flexible manu-facturing" and "global supply-chain management" (see Lancaster 1998). These later domains are particularly noteworthy. For example, SWARM has been used to demonstrate the utility of "decentralized control in discrete part manufactur-ing" (Fulkerson and Staffend 1997) and in determining the impact of "informa-tion sharing" in "divergent differentiation supply chains" (Strader, Lin, and Shaw 1998). While as much about people as they are about machines, many of these operations and production management applications are misperceived as pure engineering. Hence like simulation more generally, these nonlinear simu-lations have yet to make substantial inroads into the larger social science community.

Readily available software and admonishments for social scientists (espe-cially economists) "to get A-life," have caused the simulation of "artificial adaptive agents" (see Arthur 1991) to grow by leaps and bounds. However, this approach to growing complex systems from simple algorithmic agents has thus far generated more adherents in Europe and Australia than in the United States, despite the much larger academic market. Game theoretic economists continue to question the value added by all this additional work. It has taken political scientists like Joshua Epstein and Robert Axtell (1996), using their own software and gaming method called *Sugarscape,* to demonstrate the value of a nonlinear approach. Using simple behavioral assumptions and rules of interaction, these scholars can literally "grow" complex societal processes on a computer. Joshua Epstein is quoted as saying that such studies will revolutionize the way in which warfare, trade, and other strategic processes are studied and will "fundamentally change the way social science is done" (Horgan 1995, 107).

A couple of additional examples of adaptive systems have also found their way to Santa Fe. Stuart Kauffman (1993, 1995), physician turned computer alchemist, has focused on the role *self-organization* plays in biochemical evolution. In his opus *Origins of Order* (1993), Kauffman demonstrates the validity of many of Erich Jantsch's (1980) speculations regarding the centrality of self-organization. In essence, the "origins of the species" is much more a story of cooperative "coevolution" than it is a model of Darwinian competition. The current configuration of creatures would be an astronomically "long shot" if systems evolved without this ability to discover their own order. In his earlier work on "Boolean networks," Kauffman (1993) called this phenomenon *order for free* and *antichaos*. Kauffman (1995) has also interpreted a number of other arcane notions for the educated layperson (e.g., "fitness landscapes," see 166–68), thus his work can be seen as aiding in the conversion of tools (e.g., "simulated annealing," see 248–52) for more general-purpose (especially social) inquiry.

By way of a footnote to these grand applications, Per Bak's (Bak and Chen 1991) work on *self-organized criticality* illustrates that complex systems "naturally evolve toward a critical state in which a minor event can lead to a catastrophe." Bak, a Danish physicist employed by the U.S. Department of Energy Brookhaven Laboratory, contends that his theories have applications to topics ranging from earthquakes to stock-market crashes to entire ecosystem transformations. Essentially, self-organizing systems are pro- as well as anti-chaos, and successful evolution may occur at the very cutting edge of extinction. His earlier work on the dynamics of forest fires produced results that tended to reconfirm earlier real-world studies of *resiliency* (see Holling et al. 1978). Beyond these natural systems studies, Bak believes that the most profound impacts of work on self-organization will probably be felt in the social as well as biological sciences. He is quoted as saying that it "will bring about a revolution in such traditionally soft sciences as economics, psychology and evolutionary biology. These things will be made into hard sciences in the next years in the same way that particle and solid-state physics were made hard sciences" (Horgan 1995, 107–8).

Conclusion

If social scientists fail to accept Bak's challenge of nonlinearity, then there are certainly a number of natural scientists willing to step into the void. As John Brockman (1995) observes, there is a growing *Third Culture,* made up of scientists who bridge the gap between their estate and the realm of literary intellectuals. He adds that by bringing their arcane concepts down to the layperson level, they are "taking the place of the traditional intellectual in rendering visible the deeper meaning of our lives, redefining who and what we are" (17). Brockman actually chronicles a couple of the complexity theorists, in this regard, and would probably consider most of the physicists, biologists, and so on, who pass through Santa Fe as members of this new culture. Hence, even with the fruition of Bak's prognostications, the study of complexity will generate insights into the human condition. Imagine how much more insightful social inquiry will be if it develops its own unique understandings of complex systems.

Generally speaking, chaos, complexity, and associated concepts (such as self-organization) are merely pieces in the larger puzzle of natural and human systems. Complexity might actually be thought of as a synonym for systemic interaction beyond a certain intensity threshold. Collectively these concepts, which are the hallmark of postmodern science, represent a focus on critical process dynamics. While these dynamics may have been only partially captured (especially in terms of tools) in the past, they were certainly anticipated. Moreover, their theoretical relevance might have been more fully appreciated. Thus, in the coming chapters several antecedent elements will be reintroduced. Ultimately, even if chaos and complexity remain isolated and/or are co-opted by existing paradigms, their repercussions will still eventually topple the nineteenth-century notions of stability and change. In the process, they will unleash a virtual intellectual chain reaction of epic proportions.

CHAPTER 3

Undercurrents, Crosscurrents, and Corresponding Concepts

The emerging sciences of nonlinear dynamical systems have widely and wildly diverse origins. Besides well-established branches of physics, chemistry, and biology, a number of crosscutting disciplines have contributed to the study of nonlinear dynamical systems. As one might suspect given the delimiting effects of conventional disciplines, many innovators were academic orphans and/or merely transdisciplinary scholars (known to many but claimed by few). Some even came from beyond the cloistered walls of academia. By way of analogy, Albert Einstein was working in a Swiss patent office when he formulated his general theory. The world might never have heard of him had he been doing the mundane work required for tenure in a university. Nearer to this discussion, the father of fractal geometry, Benoit Mandelbrot, originally worked in economics but did not find a home there.

Having duly noted that nonlinear science is inherently a transdisciplinary enterprise, it is essential to further note that not all excursions into chaos and complexity are equally suited to social science applications. This is especially important in light of ongoing metaphorical abuse. Some lines of inquiry are obviously more promising than others in terms of illuminating the evolution of human artifacts and institutions. While what follows in this chapter is a smattering of diverse pursuits, most of them fit within the general rubric of what is now being called the *cognitive sciences* (itself an amalgamation of communications, psychology, neurobiology, systems engineering, and computer science). In toto the implications of these diverse yet related realms of inquiry are immense for social inquiry generally. Moreover, their impact is likely to be more immediate and more readily accessible to a range of applications. Reasons for this "ready to wear" status are multiple but generally relate to the following four items. First, as suggested previously, while much of this work preceded the formal designation of "complexity," often by decades, its highlighting by the Santa Fe Institute and other funding agencies (e.g., the National Science Foundation) has given it a certain primacy. Second, while these pursuits rely heavily on models and methods from the physical sciences, they remain at least intellectually connected to the social sciences (e.g., psychology). Third, the emphasis in psychology on *the individual* is, at least at first blush, compatible with the reigning social science paradigm with its emphasis on methodological individualism. Fourth, and perhaps most importantly, the promise of unlocking some of the mysteries of the human mind is, in itself, compelling far beyond the boundaries of psychology.

It is worth noting that this great promise is not without potential pitfalls. Most noticeably, the mixture of specific concerns within the composite field of cognitive science harbors the prospect of epistemological confusions. Just as the problem of isomorphism (the one-to-one correspondence) plagued earlier systems' theoretics, the issue of using a "machine model of the brain" looms large. When those striving to build machines that think like humans and also those who study actual brain biology begin to use similar terms and methods, the confusion is compounded. Rather than making more humanlike machines, they may merely be making humans more machinelike. This discussion deals only tangentially with these larger issues, particularly the one of whether artificial intelligence (AI) will ever simulate human thought precisely. It is unlikely that this type of issue will be resolved any time soon. However, physicist Roger Penrose (1989) makes a fairly convincing case that mathematical replication will be confounded evermore by Gödel's Paradox Theorem (also see Haugeland 1985 and Churchland 1990). This having been said, most machine simulations are simplifications and approximations and need not be exact duplications to be illuminating. The science of complexity is predicated upon the notion that, at the level of underlying processes, such simplifications are often extremely instructive. Moreover, if the brain is the result of multiple nonlinear processes, then its exact configuration will almost always be in flux. Nonetheless, the brain as a metaphor produces many a useful method.

Another danger, more germane from the perspective of this discussion, is again the issue of techniques being taken out of context. Several devices emerging from the study of complex thinking patterns are finding popular applications, well beyond the design of computer intelligence. These pop applicators, in turn, may obscure the general epistemological concerns that prompted the technical development in the first place. For example, the notions of cellular automata and neural networks have roots in the foundational formulations of information theory and cybernetics. Similarly, the recently popularized idea of "fuzzy set theory" may go back even further to the evolutionary musing of early systems theorists. In other words, there is much old dogma in these new tricks.

Old Dogma, New Tricks

While extremely diverse in content and application, many of the recently emerging (or reemerging) tools and concepts have an amazingly shared heritage.

For the most part, they find their origins in the pursuit of cybernetics and general systems theoretics of past generations. The exact character of this genealogy will become clearer in coming chapters. What is important here is establishing some common tiles from the larger mosaic. What is missing from the current incarnation of these systemic tools is the rebellious indignation of a serious intellectual challenge. Many of the current generation of scholars seem to merely assume that all these battles have already been won. In point of fact, they were either lost or postponed. While some of these dogmas are better left sleeping, some will obviously be awakened, especially in the next chapter. For now, it is useful to explore a few of the possible sources of renewed confrontation. Perhaps their long awaited popularity will inspire a more decisive outcome this time around. Hopefully this review of origins and key ingredients will reestablish a certain level of epistemic intent. Two highly divergent approaches that exemplify these earlier imperatives are cellular automata and fuzzy sets.

The Automata Empire

A simple numeric device for dealing with simultaneity and graphically exploring dynamic processes is the *cellular automaton.* Essentially, cellular automata involve cells, arranged in a lattice (for one-dimensional) or grid (for two-dimensional) systems, which are transformed through a simple set of rules. The rules usually establish a homogeneous, deterministic system, limited to local interactions (within a "neighborhood"). That is to say, the values within cells experience transformation depending upon the values in adjacent cells. The best-known example of cellular automata is John Horton Conway's "game of life" (see Gardner 1983). This two-dimensional checkerboard device provides a simple yet instructive simulation of an evolutionary system. Each cell or square is either alive or dead (on or off, white or black). Using a "Moore neighborhood" (made of all eight adjacent squares), the rules of the game are threefold: (a) if exactly two neighbors are alive, then the cell maintains its present state in the next period; (b) if exactly three neighbors are alive, then the cell will be alive in the next period, irrespective of its current state; and (c) if any other number of neighbors is alive, then the cell is dead in the next period. The logic is that a cell thrives in a lively neighborhood up until it gets overcrowded, suffocates, and dies. What is so interesting is that over time a unique menagerie of "life-forms" emerges (see fig. 3).

While such devices may seem exceedingly simple, the underlying ideas of cellular automata are quite rich. Cellular automata provide a model of *parallel processors* and have been used to address a number of complex calculations. For example, hydrodynamic flow problems have been addressed using "lattice gas" (a type of cellular automata) models (see Wolfram 1986). Cellular automata

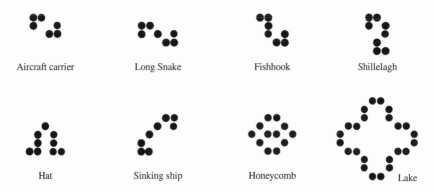

Adapted from Gardner 1983.

Fig. 3. Life Forms

can also facilitate the graphic display of evolutionary dynamics (e.g., self-organization). As John Casti (1989) explains:

> This view of the evolutionary behavior of an automaton allows us to make contact with the issue of dynamical systems involving the structure of the attractor set for a dynamical process, as well as certain questions centering upon self-organization. (59)

As with so much of modern-day applied mathematics, *cellular automata* is usually credited to John von Neumann. However, Toffoli and Margolus (1987) chronicled its origins in Konrad Zuse's work on "computing spaces" in the early 1940s, as well as later work by Stanislaw Ulam (one of the inventors of the Monte Carlo method). Yet, it was indeed von Neumann who anticipated its current use for simulating complex and *spatially extended structures* (see Wolfram 1986). While remaining quite simple, these "cellular computers" have become a valuable research tool in diverse scientific realms.

Social science applications of cellular automata remain relatively rare but are growing rapidly. In the vanguard is John H. Miller (1988, 1989). Miller (1989) combines a basic cellular automata approach (known as "Moore machine") with elements of *genetic algorithms* and *game theory* to "mathematically represent a system which responds to discrete inputs and outputs" (4). Actually Miller is far too modest; his model adapts and learns, develops novel strategies, and does everything except the laundry. Plus, it illustrates the nonlinear evolution of strategic choice. As Miller elaborates,

> techniques that allow carefully controlled experimentation with the model under a variety of situations will not only increase our current knowledge

about the game's characteristics, but also expand the possible set of applications. A key to maintaining this generality is finding a convenient yet flexible representation for the strategies of the game. While a variety of possibilities exist, the use of finite automata for this purpose appears promising. (3)

He outlines possible extensions of this approach, including "the impact of changes in information levels and symmetries, population sizes, innovation rates, pay-off structures, etc." (21). This capturing of some of the critical ingredients of *systemic choices* will be discussed at greater length later. For now suffice it to say that cellular type simulations, while simplistic, provide a vital link to the evolution of "cooperative" institutional structures.

Another example of the potential of cellular automata is provided by Barry Singer (1994). Singer develops a number of potential management applications, which are perhaps more in keeping with its origins in systems theory. In particular, he focuses on how various integral "organizing processes" evolve over time or become "emergent" via certain internal dynamics. Singer's check-erboards have rules associated with different colored squares. Thus he refers to his approach as "colors." He explains the uniqueness of this approach and of complexity studies generally as follows.

Complexity reverses the explanatory direction, explaining the large phe-nomenon as a function of the small rule. Also rather than elegant formal equations from which instances can be calculated and new findings derived, complexity offers simple and unimpressive local variables and rules, from which elegance emerges. (6)

As Singer describes, the crux of applied cellular automata is the demonstra-tion of how "analytic" and "managed" processes continually interact with "synthetic" and "self-organized" processes (1994, 27). In this particular appli-cation he explores group formation dynamics that account for many of the "networks" and "subcultures" so critical to corporate performance. Specifically, he makes a number of potentially robust observations about the role of "attrition" within the natural "annealing" processes of complex organizations (i.e., the processes by which unique domains are blended into cooperative synergy).

More extensive applications of this technique are likely to emerge. Hope-fully in the process, the unique conceptual features derived from self-organizing systems theory will not be lost along the way. Stephen Wolfram, best known, perhaps, for the software program *Mathematica*, contends that a new generation of cellular automata might save complexity studies from what he perceives as the excesses of the Santa Fe Institute. He explains that, while not necessarily a "theory of everything," this work may well be "as important as, say, Newton's discovery of calculus" (see Horgan 1995, 108).

Cuddly Concepts as Technique

Another extremely rich set of concepts in danger of being reduced to mere technique is those associated with the notion of *fuzzy sets*. A fuzzy set, as opposed to a standard set (the customary designation of a similar class of items in mathematics), involves membership that is not simply a matter of yes or no, A or non-A. Thus, the mathematics of fuzzy sets entails states that cannot be captured by simple binary values of true and false. Rather, truth values are usually represented by probabilities. The basic concepts of fuzzy logic actually date from the early 1900s. Referred to with terms such as vagueness and/or multivalence, the notion implied that either set membership or level of truth was problematic, or both (see Black 1937).

The first scholar to appreciate the implications of "vagueness" for systemic formulations was the prophetic South African statesman *Jan Christian Smuts* (1870–1950). When he wasn't carrying out his prime ministerial duties, contributing to the formulation of the League of Nations, or battling the Axis powers, this Cambridge-educated visionary worked diligently on an integrated theory of holism and evolution for artifactual as well as natural systems (Smuts 1926). Smuts maintained that the concepts of *vagueness* and/or *shadings* were vital to animating an otherwise dead world of nineteenth century science. He elaborates as follows.

> Situations were not envisaged as a whole of clear and vague obscure elements alike, but were analyzed merely into their clear, outstanding, luminous points. A "cause," for instance, was not taken as a whole situation which at a certain stage insensibly passes into another situation, called the effect. . . . This logical precision immediately had the effect of making it impossible to understand how the one passed into the other in actual causation. . . . We have to return to the fluidity and plasticity of nature and experience in order to find the concepts of reality. When we do this we find that round every luminous point in experience there is a gradual shading off into haziness and obscurity. A "concept" is not merely its clear luminous center, but embraces a surrounding sphere of meaning or influence of smaller or larger dimensions, in which the luminosity tails off and grows fainter until it disappears. Similarly a "thing" is not merely that which presents itself as such in clearest definite outline, but this central area is surrounded by a zone of intuitions and influences which shades off into the region of the indefinite. The hard abrupt contours of our ordinary conceptional system do not apply to reality and make reality inexplicable, not only

in the case of causation, but in all cases of relations between things, qualities, and ideas. (16–17)

These earlier conceptions of "fuzziness" were substantially recast and made more coherent by the modern-day father of *fuzzy set theory*, Lofti Zadeh (1965). Zadeh, an Iranian, was born in the former Soviet region of Azerbaijan and received advanced education in the United States (obtaining a master's degree in electrical engineering at MIT in 1946 and a Ph.D. in applied mathematics from Columbia in 1951). Perhaps it was his cross-cultural origins, or the fact that his student Rudolf Kalman had pretty much cornered the market of the mainstream information theory (e.g., probabalistic) with his famed "filter" (a Gaussian-type device used in navigation and computer systems), that caused Zadeh to rekindle the unorthodox concern for vagueness. No matter; Zadeh became the modern father of fuzziness. His primary contribution was the characterization of systemic reasoning involving "fuzzy rules." Fuzzy rules are the relational processes between fuzzy sets. For example, Japanese washing machines use control mechanisms that might involve the interaction of water temperature (warm rather than a particular degree) and level of agitation (medium rather than a particular speed); and the rule might be "when the water gets warm, switch to medium."

At its core, fuzzy logic provides a vital learning device. As Bart Kosko (1993) points out, "everything is a matter of degree" (2). Yet, "fuzziness" means much more than that. It means that most items are relational (Zadeh 1965). For example, a set of all tall men includes some shorter men, as the set of short men includes some taller men. The average NBA guard (at well over six feet) is tall in public but a midget on the court. In other words, these smaller players still "participate" in *tallness*. Kosko suggests that this represents "the whole in the part" (chap. 3). He also takes great pains to explain that fuzzy set theory is not merely a matter of probabilities, since as precision increases so does fuzziness. He describes the level of fuzziness in a fuzzy set as its "fuzzy entropy" (126–35), and contends that it mirrors entropy in thermodynamics and information theory (i.e., noise). As such, it also corresponds to notions of nonlinear learning, albeit machine learning. Kosko maintains that most machines are fuzzy machines (38) and that most adaptive systems are fuzzy systems (see his chap. 11). He elaborates as follows.

How do you make a machine smart? Make it FAT [Fuzzy Approximation Theorem]. Put some FAT in it. In theory a FAT enough machine can model any process. . . . A FAT theorem shows why fuzzy systems have raised the machine IQ of camcorders and car transmissions and helicopter stabilizers and why future fuzzy systems can raise MIQs even higher. (157)

By 1991, Japan had already achieved over a billion dollars in sales of fuzzy products ranging from consumer electronics to elaborate manufacturing systems.

Thus far, fuzzy logic has found only a few applications in social inquiry. Nevertheless, the fact that it provides a better approximation of human intelligence should make it useful not only in artificial systems (note Grossberg 1982) but in institutional design as well. For example, Rod Taber (1991) uses the international cocaine trade as a test case for "fuzzy cognitive maps." Eventually, fuzzy thinking, or something with a less pejorative designation, should become a mainstay of mainstream research methodology, especially as learning processes are incorporated into models of social choice. Apparently, fuzziness has captured something essential about the way most systems learn, create their own rules, and adapt. As Earl Cox (1993) explains, "adaptive systems" using fuzzy logic

> not only adjust to time-phased or processed-phased conditions, but they also change the supporting system controls. This means that an adaptive system modifies the characteristics of the rules, the topology of the fuzzy sets, and the method of defuzzification based on predictive convergence metrics. Adaptive systems usually work like back-propagation neural networks by examining a solution with a target result. Some recent adaptive work has produced a few surprisingly robust systems that also perform in an unsupervised mode. (27)

If only metaphorically, the ways in which fuzzy sets and "smart machines" using fuzzy logic derive their own rules should be highly instructive to those who want to design smarter institutions. Kosko (1993) maintains that fuzzy logic is so useful in clustering data into rules, it will be used to grow systems in realms of high uncertainty. He contends that one could use "fuzzy sets to model events in politics and history and medicine and military planning" (221–22).

From Artificial Intelligence to the Real Thing

While the logic of nonlinear systems is useful in building smarter machines, the application of this new machine logic to human interaction may well be a form of reverse anthropomorphism. As critics of early systems theories contended, a mechanistic metaphor only takes one so far. However, there are at least two major differences in the current generation of systemic formulations: (1) The new nonlinear systems theories are much less wedded to mechanistic or even biological metaphors, and (2) machines themselves are constantly striving to more nearly approximate human processes. Of course, this may be of little comfort to those who see the entire enterprise of AI as an elaborate rubber chicken and egg problem. Yet, current critics appear to be preoccupied with the issue of whether computers will ever duplicate human intelligence (note Haugeland 1985). Of greater interest here is whether humans will ever be able to understand their own artifacts and institutions sufficiently to make them work more like their smarter (i.e., adaptive) machines. Given the convoluted nature of emerging interdisciplinary fields such as cognitive science, answers to the second inquiry may well emerge from the first. Certainly two broadly defined domains, neural networks and parallel processing, at least harbor clues to both how humans think and how they might design institutions as if that thinking could be used to better serve the commonwealth.

Neural Nets

An extremely intriguing nonlinear dynamical device arising out of the confluence of informational theory and neurobiology is the *neural network* (or net). A neural network is by definition a system that attempts to pattern information in close approximation to the complex processes of neurons and synapses within the human brain. The brain, of course, is made up of tens of billions of neurons and nearly a trillion of the tiny connecting synapses. Further, exact circuitry of the brain is somewhat enigmatic. However, this labyrinthine network of networks may be the ultimate complexity problem—ergo, "the brain" as the archetypal metaphor of postmodern science.

The basic notion of neural nets actually has its origins in an earlier epoch of systems research. The brilliant cybernetics pioneers Norbert Wiener (1894–1964) and Claude E. Shannon developed the mathematics of neural and parallel networks back in the late 1930s. Shannon, who is famous for his notion of "informational entropy," was instrumental in the specification of the logic of switching circuits. As a result, he set the stage for the application of Boolean algebra to the development of so-called *thinking machines* (see Riordan and Shannon 1942; Shannon 1949). Shannon also provided basic foundational constructs, which included various "bistable states" in which a system can be either x or y or both. These characterizations allowed simple logical truth tables to be converted into elaborate circuitry maps. Following the path blazed by Shannon, information theory quickly emerged as the practice of computer science.

Other early icons of information theory included W. S. McCulloch, Oskar Morgenstern, Walter Pitts, and, of course, John von Neumann, according to the chronicle provided by Jugjit Singh (1966). In general, these innovators used "the brain" as their role model. McCulloch and Pitts, for example, differentiated between *receptor and effector* neurons and demonstrated that any level of complexity can be captured within a particular network configuration, given sufficient specification (see Singh 1966, 150–53). Meanwhile, von Neumann illustrated various probabilities for transmission malfunction over multiple strand nerve fibers. He suggested that a critical threshold of fibers is necessary for successful transmission (e.g., von Neumann 1958).

Among the current generation of scholars who use the term *neural nets,* a primary focus of inquiry is a curious dynamic of *associative memory,* in systems ranging from rats to robots. Of particular interest is the nonlinear logic of machines that can learn and adapt, in addition to merely engaging in pattern recognition (Thaler 1996). The core of these explorations is the specification of various *feedforward* and recursive mechanisms, as well as conventional feedback systems. While much debate has transpired over issues such as the computational efficiency of various algorithms (e.g., "the Perceptron"), the basic approach of nonlinear networks has added considerable richness to the study of intelligence, artificial and otherwise. Mitchel Waldrop (1992) describes this potential, in the context of complexity research, as follows.

> If a programmer has a neural network model of vision, for example, he or she can simulate the pattern of light and dark falling on the retina by activating certain input nodes, and then letting the activation spread through the connections into the rest of the network. The effect is a bit like sending shiploads of goods into a few port cities along the seacoast, and then letting a zillion trucks cart the stuff along the highways among the inland cities. But, if the connections have been properly arranged, the network will soon settle into a self-consistent pattern of activation that corresponds to a classification of the scene: "That's a cat!" Moreover, it will do so even if the input data are noisy and incomplete—or, for that matter, even if some of the nodes are burned out. (289–90)

Meanwhile, those who study the actual brain have become increasingly fascinated with the power of these nonlinear systems. For instance, Nobel prize-winning neuroscientist Gerald Edelman (1989) believes that the neural nets may hold the key to human evolution itself. He explains that

> the brain is dynamically organized into cellular populations containing individually variant networks, the structure and function of which are selected by different means during development and behavior. The units of selection are collections of hundreds to thousands of strongly interconnected neurons. (4–5)

As a metaphor for self-learning mechanisms, neural networks may make substantial inroads in terms of practical management. For instance, William Perry (1994) maintains that once a neural model is "trained and validated" it can be used to augment any number of "management decision-making" processes, "as long as final data values are associated with the process" (12). Applications ranging from credit markets (Jost 1993) and stock choices (Kryzanowski, Guller, and Wright 1993) to marketing (Venugopal and Baets 1994) and finance (Perry 1994) have already been explored. One of the more novel applications is to the prediction of bank failures. Kar Tam and Melody Yan-Kiang (1992), using actual default data, specify a neural net model that demonstrates greater "predictive accuracy, adaptability and robustness," when compared to conventional "linear classifiers."

The Parallel Paradigm?

One particular technical development with potential implications for the study of complex systems is the advent of *parallel processing.* Parallel processing literally involves connecting multiple, independent CPUs (central processing units) to conduct numerous independent calculations simultaneously rather than serially. By linking numerous microprocessors, computer designers can achieve the power and speed of a supercomputer (e.g., a Cray), at a fraction of the cost. This concept has also been known as *connectionism* (see Bechtel 1991). Under the auspices of David Rumelhart and his colleagues at the University of California–San Diego, this computational technique became a model of human cognitive processes (see Rumelhart 1986) via the more elaborate designation of "parallel distributed processing" (PDP). Moreover, some scholars found extensive epistemological implications in these breakthroughs (note Moore 1990; Taylor 1993; Shane and Connor 1993). In short, parallelism has been viewed as an alternative approach to applied social inquiry. While actually a subset of nonlinear dynamical systems theory, it does introduce some unique and important methodological features. As Barry Shane and Patrick Connor describe, escaping from the bounds of sequential processing opens up the following research domains:

- evolution: as in complex adaptive systems;
- collectivity: as in interactive systems; and
- anticipation: as in adaptations in advance of external stimuli.

Moreover, they highlight a number of clear utilities, made possible through the use of parallel computing, including the following: (1) graphic presentation, (2) field representation, and (3) developmental computation (4–8). At a glance, one can represent multiple interactive activities within a complex evolving system. Examples given of these capabilities are the "lattice gas algorithm" and "genetic algorithm" techniques used by "complexity" researchers (see below). Both lattices and genetic algorithms, of course, also date back to early work in cybernetics. Moreover, parallel processing, in particular, has been a cornerstone of operations research and industrial engineering (especially multistage flow problems) for some time (note Shetty 1990).

Widespread social science applications have yet to fully emerge and remain, for the most part, more metaphorical than methodological. Nevertheless, the potential of representing a diverse array of qualitative distinctions in algorithmic form is compelling to say the least. For example, they could be used to consolidate and provide systematic representation to diversely textured observations such as those that motivate organizational development (e.g., to model approaches such as "total quality management" [TQM]). Their elements are nearly isomorphic to *team design dynamics.* As Glen Taylor (1993) maintains, "parallel processing is a design principle for system-side total quality management" (99). What is so interesting is that the actual hardware of a connectionist or PDP system requires distribution of knowledge just like the semiautonomous realms of TQM. Knowledge is represented by "patterns of network activation" across several processing units instead of within individual nodes. It is this feature of "distributed processing" that allows paralleled mechanisms to simulate organizational learning. Patterns of activity can be readily adapted in response to experience and produce novel behaviors in the system as a whole. Much more will be said about links between TQM and nonlinear methods elsewhere. For now suffice it to say that parallel processing provides a powerful tool for representing newly emerging theories of organization and that those theories, in turn, are closely tied to nonlinear logic. While this argument is somewhat circular, the strings that run completely through will become more apparent as these various approaches are more thoroughly unraveled.

Evolution on Demand

The early architect of artificial systems tended to look to biological evolution as the key to the basic processes such as the brain. These observations when combined with contemporary genetic understandings paint a modified picture of the complex internal dynamics of human evolution. The evolutionary significance of the brain, in turn, spawns powerful implications regarding macrosocietal dynamics. By implication, these nonlinear dynamics also stir the pot of evolution from protozoa to pan-national institutions. Until very recently this "grand view" of self-organizing, evolutionary dynamics was limited to a handful of radical intellectuals such as Erich Jantsch (1975). As he elaborates:

> A broad evolutionary view provides us with a basis of principles which are at work at all evolutionary levels, including the level of the systems in which and through which human life evolves and organizes itself. This important aspect has been generally emphasized by evolutionary thinkers

through the ages. The dynamic situations governing the evolution of form in the physical and biological domains are basically the same which govern the evolution of man, society, and culture. (51)

Once one accepts an evolutionary ethos as a fundamental property of social systems, the types of simulation devices developed in brain and biological studies take on much greater centrality in the battery of viable social research methods. In particular, genetic algorithms that illuminate these fundamental processes should have immense pedagogic value and may ultimately hold the secret of survival itself.

Algorithm and Blues

A primary device for simulating evolution at both the microlevel and macrolevel is the *genetic algorithm.* Essentially, it is an evolution on a computer. Genetic algorithms can trace their origins to R. A. Fisher's work (1930) *The Genetical Theory of Natural Selection* and the mathematical brain theories of M. A. Arbib (1964). They have been popularized through the innovative work of scholars at the University of Michigan, particularly John Holland (1992, 1995). Meanwhile, John Koza (1992, 1994; Koza et al. 1996) and colleagues at Stanford have developed new programming models that "genetically" grow algorithms for use in a variety of applications, ranging from problems in biology and chemistry to business and government (see Koza et al. 1996).

Generally speaking, complex adaptive systems are represented by simple lines of codes that act like living organisms. Search and selection rules are modeled as a particular element (e.g., "chromosomes") containing many of their salient characteristics. A population of these elements is allowed to evolve via a simple three-stage breeding process (i.e., evaluation, selection, and recombination). Random populations of individuals or units can be created, each of them represented by a chromosome (a string of genes that characterizes the unit). The population is exposed to an evaluation function that plays the role of the environment. This first stage serves as fitness function with usually the best-fitted units being allowed to progress. The second step, selection, is carried out by eliminating low-fitness individuals from the population, and inheritance is added by making multiple offspring or copies of high-fitness units. The third stage applies a particular set of rules that determines the process of recombination.

It is this final stage of greatest interest to students of social evolution, for as Holland (1992) maintains, different systems imply different rules of recombination. For example, Darwinian dynamics of random mutation rarely applies above the very basic levels. AI systems evolve through recombination or "crossover" rules of the learning variety, and most social systems are of the latter type. That is, they search, learn, and adapt rather than following the processes characterized in standard economic models (i.e., optimization). Similarly, the performance measures associated with more complex social systems may even escape the *survival of fittest* concepts of other evolutionary processes. As Holland illustrates at the AI level, performance is relative, and collective improvement may suffice.

From Brain Salad to Social Systems

As alluded to previously, the model of intelligent machines or even the human brain, while extremely instructive, is only a partial explanation of evolution in societal macrosystems. Selection for incremental improvements characterizes, perhaps, what is truly unique about social networks, but humans also participate in all the other evolutionary dynamics as well. Many systems, even the most sophisticated human institutions, are still governed by Darwinian dynamics from time to time. However, what makes humans truly unique is their ability to intervene in their own evolution, often overriding biological determinism. Moreover, as humans begin to explore the critical systemic interactions between body chemistry, physiology, and psychology from the perspective of nonlinear dynamical systems even more powerful avenues of intervention will emerge. Recent studies of basic development physiology tend to illustrate how even basic "motor skills" development is governed by self-organizing dynamics, and may have larger cognitive feedback components than imagined. As Linda Smith and Esther Thelen (1993) observe, most developing organisms are "dynamic, open, contingent systems." Since the state of the system is determined by the state of the organism "within its total context, there can be no logical distinction made between the organism and the environment as the cause of behavior and its change." Thus they add that linear cause/effect has no meaning since agency resides outside the organism. State-space is visualized as the possible "parameters of the cooperating components" and the viability of the system is interactive. Smith and Thelen believe that

> developmentalists will be receptive to dynamic systems because we come face to face with complexity, nonlinearity, and context dependency every day. When dealing primarily with infants and children—or with aging, handicapped, or disadvantaged populations—the real complexity of subjects' lives cannot be avoided through clever experimental design. (xiii)

AI models of complex systems may produce insights for other branches of psychology as well. Heretofore intractable processes such as intuition and human creativity may ultimately be captured in terms of innovative search algorithms (see Simon 1987). These insights, in turn, may have profound implications for the design of learning systems at both the level of the individual and the level of institutions. Here again, complex dynamics are both a process and a product. Psychologist Mihaly Csikszentmihalyi provides a glimpse of an expanded notion of social-psychological complexity in his work on *The Evolving Self* (1993). "Complexity" he defines as a healthy psychological state that blends *differentiation* (e.g., individual autonomy) and integration (social responsibility). For example, "a complex family" provides "freedom and stimulation" while also being "supportive and harmonious" (172–73). Complexity is less a natural state of affairs than a set of processes that one should consciously pursue so as to further one's own evolution. However, like natural systems, striving for complexity involves delimiting entropy. In this case, entropy involves the breakdown of productive social order.

At the microlevel, Csikszentmihalyi's notion of psychological complexity combats the biological reductionism of conventional evolution. While humans continue to carry a great deal of biological and cultural baggage, they are also capable of creative actions that overcome these deterministic impulses. His theory sees "creative individuals" prevail against "instinct and worldly wisdom" by visualizing the freedom and happiness of others. He believes that "free will is a self-fulfilling prophecy." In his (1993) view:

> Chance and necessity are sole rulers of beings who are incapable of reflection. But evolution has introduced a buffer between determining forces and human action. Like a clutch in an engine, consciousness enables those who use it to disengage themselves occasionally from the pressure of relentless drives so as to make their own decisions. (15)

In nonlinear systems, the weak pull of causality is exactly what makes human freedom more robust. Contrary to popular misconception, choice is more compatible with adaptability than predictability.

More Fun and Games

Perhaps one of the more compelling conceptual devices for bringing the insights of nonlinear science to bear in the social domain is that of *game theory*. Thus, it warrants detailed discussion. While John von Neumann and Oskar Morgenstern (1944) expressly designed this tool for economists back in the 1940s, it really did not catch on until the 1970s. However, after this somewhat laborious beginning, games are now a mainstay of microeconomic theory (see Gibbons 1992). Leading microeconomics textbooks (e.g., Kreps 1990) now spend a substantial number of pages on the subject. One might say that game theory, with its much modified notions of equilibrium, has actually saved neoclassical economists, as well as other social scientists, from their methodological malaise.

Moreover, after initial misgivings (Postrel 1991; also note Saloner 1991), game theory recently emerged as a mainstream management tool (see Dixit and Nalebuff 1991; Brandenburger and Nalebuff 1996). Consulting firms like McKinsey have created entire bureaus dedicated to its application to choices of competitive or *co-opetitive* (the term given to cooperative competition) strategy.

By game theory, one is referring to any number of concepts that involve two or more agents interacting in pursuit of their interests. The *interdependence of interests* is the crux of the game approach. Economists and decision theorists maintain a distinction between cooperative and noncooperative games. Furthermore, the decision theory approach generally entails discrete probability appraisals of noncooperative interdependence. However in many cases these subtle distinctions are blurred in actual applications. In particular, noncooperative games still require a measure of cooperation between the players. Even fierce competition must follow basic rules of interaction, and as industrial organization (IO) economists are well aware, fierce competition is relatively rare. In fact, state-of-the-art IO game-theory applications usually include characterizations of "comparative advantage" and ecological niches (à la Porter 1985). These realizations notwithstanding, game theory provides economists with a convenient retreat on issues ranging from rationality to "general equilibrium." As a business reporter (*It's only a game* 1996) put it:

> Stripped to its essentials, game theory is a tool for understanding how decisions affect each other. Until the theory came along, economists assumed that firms could ignore the effects of their behaviour on the actions of rivals, which was fine when competition was perfect or a monopolist held sway, but was otherwise misleading. (57)

Also he adds that "managers have much to learn from game theory—provided they use it to clarify their thinking, not as a substitute for business experience" (57).

Bounding Rationality

As originally conceived by von Neumann and Morgenstern (1944), game theory incorporated a form of "bounded" or constrained rationality. They describe the constraints imposed by this interactive system as follows.

> Every participant can determine the variables which describe his own actions but not those of the others. Variables cannot, from his point of view, be described by statistical assumptions. [Their] actions will be influenced by his expectation of these [variables], and they in turn reflect the other participants' expectation of [their] actions. (11–12)

To deal with these constraints, strategies were conceived in terms of minimax solutions that sought to minimize constraints while maximizing utility. This approach, however, was quickly overtaken by John R. Nash's famed solution, known as *Nash equilibrium.* Nash (1950) defined a system in which the mixed strategies of one or more players are accommodated to the mixed strategies of the others. More recently, decision theorists have focused on the "structural uncertainty" imposed by "incomplete information" (Luce and Raiffa 1957) and other factors. Also they apply probabilities to strategic elements. John Harsanyi (1967–68) visualized these probability problems in terms of *Bayesian distributions.* Others have viewed these processes in terms of *sequential equilibrium* (note Fudenberg and Tirole 1991). More recently, games have been reconfigured to account for processes of "signaling," "reputation," and all manner of *informational asymmetries* (for an overview see Gibbons 1992). Despite all these modifications, certain problems persist. Rational-choice sociologist Michael Hechter (1990) contends that certain core assumptions—infinite iteration, perfect information, and multiple equilibria—make game theory less applicable to "real world collective action problems" (also note Postrel 1991). Moreover, Hechter's "modest proposal" regarding the need for more focus on "external" and/or contextual elements (known as the *contractarian* or *microconstitutional* approach) is certainly a point well taken. Culling out and explicating various institutionally embedded processes is an extremely useful enterprise, and a handful of scholars, especially political scientists, has made significant contributions to both game theory and social inquiry generally, along these lines (e.g., Bendor and Mookherjee 1987; Heckathorn and Maser 1990) Yet it is well to note that the faulty assumptions Hechter lists have been substantially adjusted as a result of increasing encounters between hard-core game theorists and these types of empirical inquiries and by the conceptual modifications alluded to earlier. Like any good science, game driven studies tend to thrive in a sea of disconfirming results. The increased imposition of "real world" constraints such as discounting of the future, other information or transaction costs, and "imperfect monitoring" (e.g., "principal-agent" problems) bedevils the intellectual enterprise. Furthermore, incorrect conclusions often emerge. For example, Roy Radner and his colleagues (Radner, Myerson, and Maskin 1986) demonstrated that not only do such constraints often produce multiple equilibria but in some cases these equilibria are not "Pareto optimal." That is, they could not make anyone better off without making someone else worse off; hardly an encouraging basis for collective action. As this type of inconvenient evidence, and associated alterations, continues to accumulate, one may wonder at what point the edifice will crumble. Yet unlike the sand piles used to visualize "self-organized criticality," paradigmatic shifts may be far less dramatic. Game theory's only partial parentage in economics and its proximity to other avenues of systems research may provide entirely new vectors of possibility. The most promising of these avenues appear to be those that develop direct linkages between game theory and the evolutionary dynamics of nonlinear systems. This path will further divorce these endeavors from conventional economic thinking, however. This great divide will be explored at length in later chapters; for now suffice it to say that nonlinearity wreaks havoc on cherished economic notions such as equilibrium. Yet, this tread has already grown increasingly thin, as multiple equilibria problems continue to be resolved by the positing of elaborate search selection assumptions.

The Evolution of Evolution within Games

These assumptions regarding various auxiliary activities (such as learning, adaptation, or merely selection) that go on between the periods of multiperiod games are the major missing link between game theory and reality. Of course, additional ecological assumptions (e.g., shared beliefs, size of groups, distribution of resources, and so on) that usually appear in an elaborate list of "priors" (or preconditions) are also used to shore up these mathematical simplifications of complex strategic events. Like the famed "desert island joke," if one assumes a can opener, as well as assuming the contents of the can will evolve through mutual agreement into a seven-course meal with sufficient portions for all, then the castaways have no problem. Actually, this assumptive sleight of hand, is not unlike the types of imaginative machinations that appeared while quantum theory was catching hold. In fact, certain game-theoretic dilemmas might be thought of as Schrödinger's cat in reverse. Basically, the heart of the matter was the problematic translation from a quantum theory item (a single ion) to a classical theory item (the cat). Game theory involves the opposite scale problem. In essence, classical (or neoclassical) ingredients work well at the microscale, but as the size of the group (and associated differentials) goes up, the theory breaks down. For example, Robert Boyd and Peter Richerson (1988) illustrated how group size influences the "evolution of reciprocity." In other words, for game theory to realize greater potential, transformational devices are needed that mediate between individual and systemic levels. One source of these devices may be the newly emerging studies of cooperative dynamics.

Early in the annals of game theory, Duncan Luce and Howard Raiffa (1957) described a type of "quasi equilibrium" appearing in repeated games, in which a "positive sum" strategy emerges over time. They hypothesized that this prudent cooperation might overcome the short-term profitability of a "nonconforming strategy" (1). Yet, more important, they maintained that this "stability" might be only temporary.

The issue of strategic stability took center stage following the development of the best-known game, the *prisoner's dilemma* (see fig. 4). With this clever little invention, Anatol Rapoport and Albert M. Chammah (1965) inspired a wide range of social scientists to explore experimentalism. Stated simply, this game involves two "partners in crime" being subjected to the stereotypical police questioning. Cooperation equates to *not* "ratting" on one's comrade and thus both being released; the defection of one means the other goes to prison. However, if both defect, then both go to prison. Interestingly enough, if one follows strict economic notions of self-interest and rationality, then double defection (D, D) is the only Nash equilibrium. This "paradox of uncooperation" is not only counterintuitive, it defies a good deal of actual experience—ergo the initiation of a serious social scientific dilemma. Armed with this simple puzzle, investigators began the quest for more robust explanations of basic human cooperation in earnest. However, it took a biologist, John Maynard Smith (see Maynard Smith and Price 1973; Maynard Smith 1982), to show social scientists how games should be played—that is, to describe an "evolutionary stable strategy." Maynard Smith speculated about competition with mutations within a given animal species and suggested that balanced strategy (between confrontation and submission) would extend the survival capabilities of the entire species. Political scientist Robert Axelrod (1984) used this conceptualization as the basis for his experimental approach to the "evolution of cooperation." Therefore, it was not economic constructs or static equilibria that Axelrod sought to confirm but rather his own notions of *viability* (the successful invasion of a mutant strategy) and *robustness* (the cooperation of multiple strategies within the same population). Axelrod and his colleagues at the University of Michigan sponsored two computer-assisted tournaments, involving a diverse array of players (psychologists, computer scientists, and so on). They were invited to attempt robust solutions to a repeated prisoner's dilemma (RPD) game. At one of these tournaments, Anatol Rapoport offered up the famed "tit-for-tat" strategy. Essentially this strategy involves the following.

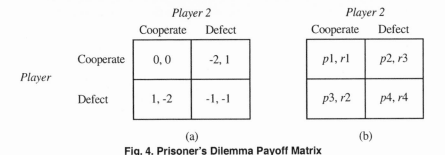

Fig. 4. Prisoner's Dilemma Payoff Matrix

1. One should cooperate as long as one's partner does;
2. One should only retaliate in kind in response to an unprovoked defection;
3. One should forgive one's partner following retaliation; but
4. One should always be clear about the conditioned basis of cooperation.

This strategy, especially the part about expressing one's intent (what economists call "signaling"), provides a basis for learning and adaptation. Axelrod (1984) discovered that given these rules, relatively stable cooperation evolves as the game proceeds. Hostile players are eventually deterred, just as mutant species are either absorbed or destroyed. Yet, it is well to note that some especially hostile mutants may actually overwhelm their parent species, particularly if assisted by extreme environmental turbulence. Thus, the question still arises about how sustainable this robust cooperation is in the long run. Moreover, is this essentially Darwinian characterization valid?

In light of these inquiries, and from the perspective of nonlinear dynamical systems, Axelrod's pathbreaking work is yet incomplete. Recalling the scale issues alluded to earlier, certain missing concepts become more apparent as one moves from RPDs to actual collective choices. Yet, one can see some conceptual gaps emerging even at the level of simple games. For instance, in another microsituation known as the *diner's dilemma,* Natalie Glance and Bernardo Huberman (1993; for a more accessible version see 1994; also note Schuessler 1990) demonstrate the nonlinear ebb and flow of cooperation. In this situation, friends who have been agreeably splitting the bill equally become disaffected when, for whatever reason (e.g., a diet), someone decides that he or she does not want to have an expensive meal. Similarly, academic departments often become hostile when the distribution of responsibilities and rewards becomes inequitable. Applying concepts and methods of "statistical thermodynamics" (i.e., self-organizing system), Glance and Huberman describe the evolutionary process in terms of "outbreaks of cooperation." One might also observe that this notion corresponds to new non-Darwinian characterizations of biological evolution (à la Kauffman 1993, 1995). As paleontologist Stephen J. Gould (1989) contends, Darwin's notion of natural selection does not explain the "fits and starts" exhibited in the fossil record.

Another expansion of game theory arising from advanced computational realms (i.e., quantum computing) is physicist David Meyer's (1999) notion of "quantum strategies." By using algorithms derived from quantum mechanical theories of brain, strategies can be represented that are neither "pure" (deterministic) nor "mixed" (probabilistic). Also, unlike classical game theory, they need not be in equilibrium in order to increase expected payoffs. However, Meyer's thought experiment requires that one imagine processes of coin tossing with neither heads nor tails. In order to actually enter this strategic nether land, one needs additional tools of the nonlinear variety.

Nonlinear Games

If one approaches game theory with nonlinear notions of evolution in mind, then the processes of adaptation take on a vastly more creative character. Simulations of these processes, using *genetic algorithms,* introduce a variety of novel strategies into otherwise quickly collapsing cooperation. John H. Miller's dissertation (1988; also note 1989), in which he applied John Holland's (first published in 1975, reprinted in 1992) type of "classifier system" to the prisoner's dilemma, is an excellent case in point. His genetically evolving game generates a variety of flexible strategies through the use of finite automata. In this way, he could actually observe the processes of creative learning and innovation. *Genetic algorithms* depict the interaction of strategies and their environment. In other words, this device "manipulates the population in order to produce a new population that is better adapted to the environment" (Holland and Miller 1991, 367). Miller (1989) adds that automata have emerged as a tractable way to model bounded rationality considerations in the theory of games (6). Beginning with four "internal states" and thirty "randomly generated structures," an "environmental test" quickly creates a new population of twenty fitful structures and "ten new structures via crossover and mutation" (7). As this nonlinear evolutionary process is repeated to see what types of strategies emerge, a key feature of this approach is that memory of the entire history of the game is embedded in the automata's internal states. A simple "tit-for-tat" (TFT) strategy only remembers the last period. In this case, the initial TFT quickly evolves into a unique offspring that punishes twice for possible defections (see fig. 5). This propagation of new strategies is reflected in simple binary code changes. Much like the DNA of a given offspring, these algorithms represent the experimentation with new strategies over time.

A *crossover* point is randomly selected within the parental codes to present the offspring's inheritance (see fig. 6). For example, the hybrid strategy that emerges from the mating of TFT and punish twice might be a bit strange from a logical standpoint and yet prove environmentally robust. Unlike simple game solutions and/or optimal choice calculations, these genetic algorithms may not always exhibit the "best" structures, but they are likely to be more durable across a broader range of possible environments. This feature, known as *genetic drift,* may not only represent the real world more accurately, it might suggest mechanisms for exploring institutional constraints. K. A. DeJong (1975), in another Michigan dissertation, explored a number of "appropriate parameter settings" and concluded that (1) larger populations move more slowly, but produce better long-term performance; (2) higher mutation rates produce only better short-term performance; (3) higher crossover rates produce lower character loss but slow initial performance. Similar studies might test other elements of the institutional ecology. John Miller (1989) maintains that "automata can be used as a model of networks, thereby allowing an analysis of the evolution of organizations" (21). He has focused his empirical analysis (thus far) on issues directly relevant to game theory. For example, he more or less confirms what others had concluded about imperfect information, payoff structures, and cooperative reciprocity (note Bendor 1993; Linster 1992). However, his assessment of information in terms of "noise levels" has more extensive implications. For instance, systems of verifiability may be more instrumental than simply addressing asymmetries. More important, since noise levels exhibited "definite phrase transitions," models that fail to account for possible discontinuities will obviously miss the mark.

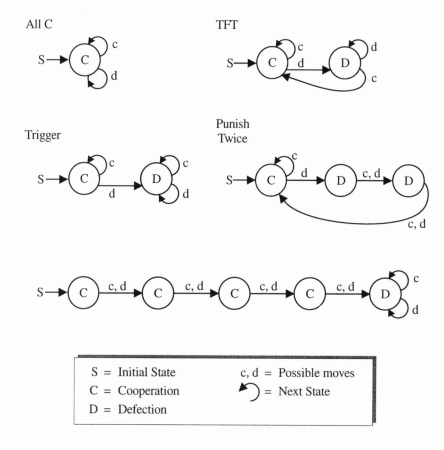

Adapted from Miller 1989, 5.

Fig. 5. Possible Automata

The problem with nonlinearity and periodic discontinuities is that they not only introduce disequilibrium to the game, they require a new type of interactive (not merely bounded) rationality. For example, Christos Papadimitriou (1992) explains how an infinite RPD can be "bounded" into a nearly cooperative equilibrium (C^n, C^n), using automata and a *polynomial device* (compare with Linster 1992). Yet, he doubts that this process actually captures "bounded rationality" since the state bounds (represented by the polynomial in n) really act upon the *implementation* of strategy, not the *design* of strategy. He goes on to demonstrate how complexity at the level of design and complexity at the level of implementation "interact in an unexpected way" (123). Using concepts derived from computational complexity and solving the problem "in parallel" rather than polynomial time, he is able to locate an optimal state-bounded response pattern that is cooperative. But his Hamiltonian assumptions, which automatically impose a "limit cycle" upon discontinuities, may or may not be relevant to the "real world."

Even when modeling relatively mechanical problems, the polynomial approach to complexity reduction often "overfits" the data. In other words, it rather arbitrarily selects models "that cannot adequately represent the underlying function or, worse yet, one that primarily fits the noise" (Buescher and Kumar

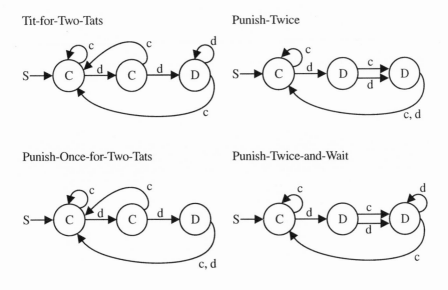

Adapted from Miller 1989, 9.

Fig. 6. Crossover

1993). Noisy or "learning problems" demand selection techniques of a more "natural" variety, which include a detailed characterization of creative adaptation.

What makes the nonlinear games approaches so promising is that it is a tool for scholars to play with the parameters that establish the processes through which systems learn. Furthermore, these process understandings may ultimately be crucial to the design of more sustainably cooperative institutions. Nonlinear games not only provide a more accurate characterization of these curious cooperative dynamics, they provide a critical transformation between individual space and social space. Whenever markets clear the way models say they should, or some other predictable pattern of aggregate behavior emerges, it is not because of the magic "invisible hand." Rather, thousands of institutionally prescribed transactions (not to mention hundreds of altruistic as well as antisocial ones) coalesced through nonlinear mechanisms of coordination and cooperation. *This should be the heart and soul of economic analysis—the design of institutions that support sustainable cooperation.* As the wind tunnel is to aircraft and now to automotive design, nonlinear games could provide the simulated environment for testing alternate designs. More importantly, since they attempt to represent in microcosm both neoclassical patterns and nonlinear processes, they constitute a transformational nexus. By providing experiments analogous to Schrödinger's box in reverse, they illustrate the ionic qualities of the cat's world—that is, a world in which infinitesimally small changes (i.e., the unprovoked defection or institutionally inspired acquiescense of a single free agent) can dramatically alter the already oscillating pattern of cooperation.

Concluding Observations

It is, of course, this "toy" aspect that is both the blessing and the bane of game theory. The seductiveness of its mathematic elegance often blinds scholars to the fact that these are still highly stylized choices made in a test tube. These microobservations must be reinterpreted in the light of macrounderstandings and vice versa. In nonlinear perspective, any one of these micropatterns might be "the butterfly" that generates dramatic changes in the macrostructure. Yet, for this insight to emerge, scholars must be able to appreciate the large within the small. How much more plausible might various game theoretic explanations be if they were more nearly informed by larger systemic or ecological observations? As nonlinear researchers apply adaptive algorithms to fill the gaps in the procedural record, they cannot operate in a contextual void. In the piece of fiction that made *chaos* a household word, *Jurassic Park,* Michael Crichton's (1990) dinosaur regenerators use fragments of frog DNA, along with computer simulations, to augment broken strands. This analogue, among other events and self-organizing dynamics, allowed the giants to escape intended biological and ecological boundaries. Lessons regarding the hubris of microconstitutional design are myriad, especially if one ignores the ever present potential for qualitative state change.

In the final analysis, evolution is a truncated and often catastrophic process. The value of computer simulations is that they provide not only ample time but a safe distance. To the extent that social scientists wish to address evolution (even at the level of the "self") in a meaningful way, the tools and concepts of artificial systems will be instrumental. Whether one chooses a ready-made method for representing complex reality or designs one's own classifier system and/or set of genetic algorithms, the issues of isomorphism and/or correspondence persist. This is not necessarily a bad thing. Hopefully as these techniques become more widespread, scholars will not lose track of these fundamental issues. In fact, they should be a central ingredient of any research enterprise. Whether or not the model fits the reality is always germane, even if the reality itself is quite fluid and otherwise intractable. The value of simplifying heuristics notwithstanding, it may be better to let sleeping dogma lie, rather than replace the old clockworks with new oversimplifications. Nevertheless, if one realizes that the only universal properties are process dynamics, and that the products of these processes vary widely depending upon time and context, then perhaps the applications will exhibit greater care. Such care is especially vital when normative use is to be made of the simulated results—that is, if the rules that set the boundaries of a particular game will eventually be reflected in policy. This is an especially tenuous process, particularly when the rules have not been sufficiently self-written by the game itself and if the game is not behaviorally and systemically actuated. This systemic reality is the topic of the chapter that follows.

CHAPTER 4

Systems Thinking Revisited

Many themes developed in the literature of chaos and complexity have direct antecedents in the *systems theory movement* of several decades ago. While comprised of extremely diverse factions, this movement was generally unified in the belief that both natural and social systems shared certain common patterns of interaction. As a paradigm of social inquiry generally, systems approaches have been in decline in the United States since the late 1960s. In the rest of the world, its influence has been more or less suspended (perhaps a bit more enthusiastically in Europe). However, certain isolated and largely unacknowledged elements of systems thought continue to undergird diverse disciplines. *With the recent rise of interest in nonlinear social inquiry, systems theory should experience a significant revival.* Systems theorists were the first to recognize the importance of patterns and processes now being embellished through the sciences of chaos and complexity (note von Bertalanffy 1950). In many ways, these early systems advocates fully anticipated the development of tools designed to unravel these complex patterns of interaction. Yet, development of these tools would await recent advances in machine intelligence and computational skills. Thus, systems theory provides an extremely useful conduit for conveying the importance of nonlinear processes. For systems thinking to play this vital role, it must first be revitalized as a central paradigm of social inquiry.

Key Thoughts and Thinkers

As with any paradigm, even a paradigm in exile, there is some measure of confusion about what constitutes systems thought. This confusion is likely to grow as its conceptual influence reemerges. It is important to note that growing interest in systems applications does not necessarily equate to understanding let alone acceptance of the basic paradigm. Hyperspecialization (the hallmark of the last few decades), coupled with the often subliminal character of systems concepts, has produced a panoply of partial paradigms. Moreover, the general tendency of disciples to jealously guard their turf and reinvent their own unique concepts has militated against early systems theory's emphasis on cross-disciplinary effort. Widely shared computational devices have only moderately ameliorated this tendency. As figure 7 indicates, current applications represent, at best, a loose-knit confederation of systems concepts. Hence before proceeding further it may be useful to briefly review the basic tenets of systems thought.

Back to Basics

The basic elements of systems thought are quite simple and straightforward. *Webster's New Dictionary* (1997) defines a system as a "complex whole" and that which "stands together" (339). In other words, *a system is any given entity that exists through the complex interaction of its parts.* That is, a system maintains its existence through the mutual causal interplay of various elements. Hence the central contribution of systems thought is a shift in focus from the parts to the whole. This basic premise, the source of much intellectual controversy, is the least methodically reconciled. Later, this contentiousness will be explored at length; for now, suffice it to say that this element is so critical to systems thought that it would not be such without it. In essence, a system is a whole that is greater than the sum of its parts. This increase in substance is a function of the organizing processes that the system provides, and these organizing relations and their emergent properties cannot be discerned from the parts.

Another core feature of systems thought is the belief that *insights about critical process dynamics apply across a variety of systems.* It was this belief in the possibility of a set of "least-common denominators" that provided the primary motivation for the *general systems theory* movement (see von Bertalanffy 1968). Despite this generality, systems thought is also *highly contextual in orientation.* Phenomena are usually explored in terms of a unique set of environmental contingencies, as well as institutional factors that are relatively isolated. It is this focus on contextual richness, coupled with postpositivist sentimentalities, that directly links systems thought to various branches of *critical theory* and associated qualitative approaches. However, it is systems theory's emphasis upon quantitative commonalities that provides a hedge against certain levels of epistemological relativism present in many critical approaches.

In classic systems theory and its associated sociological formulations, every structure represented a particular set of functions (see Parsons 1951). In modern or postmodern systems thought, *all structures represent underlying processes,* but since many of these processes are manifestations of self-organization, much of the functionalism (overstated in previous epochs) is substantially reduced. The emphasis on structures, especially emergent structures, remains and is much enhanced through the current emphasis on nonlinear dynamics. One particular instance of this mutual conceptual enhancement involves the *definition of boundaries.* By isolating the processes of *emergence,* where novel behaviors

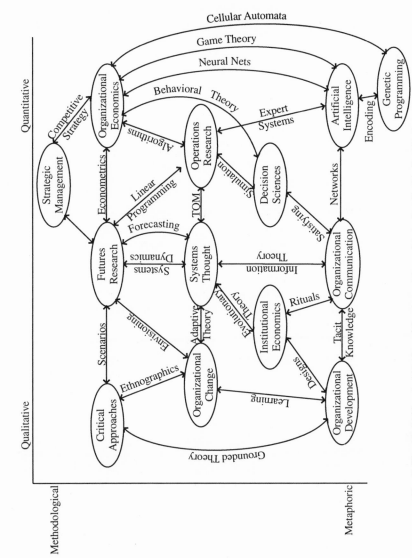

Fig. 7. The Multi-Headed Hydra of Systems Thought as Applied to Institutional Inquiry

and structures are engendered, the dimensions and density of a given network can also be characterized. Using these network mappings as a surrogate, persistent problems regarding analytical boundaries can be addressed. Back in the 1970s, applications of systems theory were widely criticized for creating vast webs of causality spinning off in all directions (Roos 1972; Berlinski 1976). The question arose as to how one begins to define the operational boundaries of a given problem, in other than arbitrary, idiosyncratic, and ultimately unwieldy terms. For example, a systems analysis of a new airport on an estuary in New Jersey might entail a look at the entire New England fishery, or the entire BOSWASH (Boston to Washington, D.C. transportation corridor). In actual practice, however, a "soft systems" approach arose that focused upon smaller patterns of interaction and defined boundaries in terms of a collection of elements exhibiting the same emergent properties (Checkland and Scholes 1990). Since nonlinear mathematics can more nearly capture the process of emergence, boundaries can be even more tightly circumscribed.

Next to holism, the most critical element in systems thought is the *focus on feedback*. Feedback is the process by which systems outputs return as inputs. Moreover, it implies *that information about the results of a given process is used to change that process.* This simple notion provides the bulwark for cybernetics and computer science and is applied in evolutionary theories from single cells to social networks and societal learning. Feedback, with its loops of causality, is the essence of nonlinearity. Negative or "self-balancing" feedback can produce relatively predictable decreases in the direction of change. Positive or "self-reinforcing" feedback are relatively indeterminate, as they can quickly amplify increases in the direction of change. This process of amplification can allow faint signals or nearly random events to take on critical causal significance. In other words, feedback (especially positive feedback) is the central mechanism of complex and chaotic phenomena.

Icons and Embellishments

Systems thought can actually be traced back to the ancient Greeks. Yet in the configuration just summarized, it is very much a modern or perhaps postmodern pattern of thought. It clearly rejected the clockwork worldview inherited from Newton and Descartes. Like earlier systems process understandings emerging from quantum physics and cell biology, social systems theorists maintained that the interaction of individuals and their institutions could not be described with the concepts of mechanistic science. Strangely enough, systems thought itself would soon be condemned as too mechanistic. Early excitement quickly gave way to widespread derision. Currently however, the precipitous rise and fall of the systems paradigm is being supplanted by a somewhat reluctant resurrection.

As with any intellectual tradition, it is useful to review some of its icons as well as a few of their obscure offspring.

Modern systems thinking can probably be traced to the brilliant Italian social theorist Vilfredo Pareto (1848–1923). Pareto's creative conceptualizations of dynamic social systems have been influential in fields ranging from sociology to production management (see Pareto 1935). The "Pareto optimal" (an equilibrium point where it is impossible to make one group better off without making another group's plight worse) remains a benchmark in welfare economics, and "Pareto charts" (with their linkages to statistical quality control) remain a mainstay in operations research.

It was Pareto's popularity among sociologists at Harvard during the 1930s that did the most to spur fully formed theories of social systems. One of the first of these formulations was undertaken by Lawrence Henderson (1878–1942), a biochemist turned sociologist. He extrapolated from his studies of "self-regulating" and equilibrium processes in medicine and suggested a crude mathematical approach to social systems (see Barber 1970). Henderson not only drew upon the work of Pareto but also on the thermodynamic studies of Willard Gibbs (a forerunner of Prigogine's breakthrough).

Henderson's colleague Walter B. Cannon is also recognized as an early systems thinker. In his *Wisdom of the Body* (1932) Cannon extended earlier work in biological systems into a universal concept of *homeostasis* to explain the ways in which various systems maintain a balance (e.g., blood sugar, temperature, etc.). Moreover, in his final chapter, he argues that these "general principles of stabilization" might be applied to organizational and societal systems as well.

Despite these important precursors, the father of modern systems thinking is usually thought of as Austrian-born biologist Ludwig von Bertalanffy (1901–72). In the early 1930s, his basic conceptualizations were taking shape (1933), but they did not gain widespread recognition until his *Science* article in 1950. At that point the movement that he called *general systems theory* (GST) began to gather momentum. Von Bertalanffy's central concept was the distinction between *open and closed systems*. Open or "living" systems, according to von Bertalanffy, experience both "positive and negative entropy." Open systems take in complex organic molecules and give off simpler by-products; in this way, they avoid the full impacts of energy loss. In other words, open systems evolve toward higher levels of complexity at the expense of "energy-yielding processes" in the environment (see von Bertalanffy 1950). In a later compilation of his work (1968), he sets forth the basic mission of the systems approach as follows:

> The 19th and first half of the 20th century conceived of the *world as chaos* [his emphasis]. Chaos was the oft-quoted blind play of atoms, which, in mechanistic and positivistic philosophy, appeared to represent ultimate

reality, with life as an accidental product of physical processes, and mind as an epiphenomenon. It was chaos when, in the current theory of evolution, the living world appeared as a product of chance, the outcome of random mutations and survival in the mill of natural selection. . . . Now we are looking for another basic outlook on the world—the world as organization. (187–88)

Von Bertalanffy also believed that GST would ultimately lead to a sweeping reunification of the sciences. This theme in particular has remained moribund until very recently. Only iconoclasts, such as E. O. Wilson (1998), have argued for a reversal of intellectual fragmentation. Wilson, who is best known for his biological reductionism (see 1988), has eloquently argued for *consilience* or the "unity of knowledge" along "ecological" lines in order for scientific enterprise to progress in the twenty-first century.

Another major proponent of GST was economist Kenneth Ewart Boulding (1910–93). After an award-winning early career in mainstream economics, Boulding would move so far beyond the pale that his significant body of work is virtually unknown to his parent discipline. While teaching labor economics at Iowa State in the 1940s, he came to realize that economic concepts were inadequate to understanding evolutionary dynamics at work in labor markets (Boulding 1950). Upon moving to the University of Michigan in the 1950s, he taught a seminar on the integration of the social sciences and cofounded the Society for General Systems Research. He went on to be president of the American Association for the Advancement of Science.

Boulding's contributions have been myriad; however one worth special note in this brief chronicle is his designation of five distinct "classes of systems" (1985). These include the following: (1) *Parasitic* (i.e., ones that exchange negative for positive resources); (2) *Prey/Predator* (e.g., rabbits and foxes); (3) *Threat Systems* (e.g., arms race); (4) *Exchange Systems* (i.e., "the market"); and (5) *Integrative Systems* (e.g., cooperatives). Unfortunately, these and perhaps more insightful conceptualizations failed to achieve even a modicum of recognition as social inquiry drifted into the doldrums of atheoretical empiricism during the late 1970s.

Many authentically systemic approaches were sustained, and a few have even evolved into more powerful conceptual foundations. Perhaps the best example of a present day benchmark, is the work of Harold A. Linstone (summarized in his 1989 piece). His "multiple perspectives approach" is derived from an array of cases on how systems analyses actually proceed. He illustrates how those relying primarily upon the "technical" aspects while ignoring "organizational" and "personal" elements quickly go awry (also see Mitroff and Linstone 1993). However, the intellectual fragmentation of the 1970s (which reinforced artificial disciplinary boundaries) combined with the ideological backlash to banish systems to a handful of enclaves in the United States. Numerous systems theory units survived in Europe, of course; yet, in toto few of these generic programs have thrived and most paled in comparison to successful mechanical or "closed systems" applications, in fields such as engineering. For many reasons, generally much more ideological than epistemological, GST had been pretty much abandoned as a basic research paradigm by the late 1960s. Systems theory was largely displaced by reductionistic and positivistic approaches that grew out of the era of behaviorism and/or atheoretical empiricism, and so it is very curious indeed to see systems theory being lumped with these antithetical elements by the end of the positivistic era. Postpositivists and various "interpretive" theorists have tended to associate systems theory with its more successful yet far-removed offspring (e.g., systems analysis and systems engineering). Again, these various offspring are a manifestation of closed (nonliving) systems thinking. In fact, GST was more concerned with *open systems* and was clearly a type of *pre-postpositivism* (see Wilson 1980; Daneke 1992). As David Wilson maintains,

> though it shares the same scientific attitude, it is profoundly different from the physicalism, reductionalism, one-way causality, and "truth" of logical positivism and empiricism. By investigating organized wholes of many variables, system epistemology requires many new categories of interaction, transaction, organization, and teleology, as well as a view of knowledge as an interaction between the knower and known. It is thereby dependent on multiple biological, psychological, cultural, and linguistic factors. (135)

This original orientation seems to have been overlooked during the postpositivist muddle of the late 1980s. Robert Backoff and Barry Mitnick (1986) analyzed various factors including "definition integrity, holism, isomorphism, and problem solving" and concluded that its untimely demise was ideological rather than methodological.

An important tangent to early general systems theorizing was the development of the *systems dynamics* approach (see Forrester 1961, 1968, 1973). Developed at MIT in the 1950s, it has experienced a resurgence of late, both as a modeling technique (see Richardson 1991; Kirkwood 1992) and as a multipurpose managerial metaphor (Senge 1990). The central feature of this approach is the study of complex interactions of heretofore isolated variables. In other words, a web of interconnected nodes and associated feedback loops is used to explore how changes in the levels and rates of one variable accumulate across an entire system. While greatly oversimplified, these interacting algorithms provide a useful heuristic in fields ranging from urban and industrial design (Forrester 1961, 1968) to corporate problem solving (Kirkwood 1992). These models are used to test causal assumptions when the exact path of causality is indeterminate. In other words, they can be used to explore nonlinear relationships. Unfortunately, the entire enterprise of systems dynamics was held up to public ridicule during the 1970s, when MIT researchers were commissioned by the Club of Rome to address the issue of global resource depletion (note Meadows, Meadows, and Randers 1972). Given a vast number of simplifying assumptions and what many economists claimed were insufficient substitutions via new technology, the exercise painted a fairly gloomy future. Economists, generally, like to think of the pie infinitely expanding so as to avoid difficult questions of how to redistribute the slices. This inborn tendency, along with associated economics versus environment issues, made the *Limits to Growth* report synonymous with doomsaying. Interestingly enough, reassessments have only slightly altered their original predictions (see Meadows, Meadows, and Randers 1992).

This well-publicized debate has little to do with the basic viability of the tool, however. Certainly if humankind continues to exhibit total disregard for its impact on the natural environment, the consequences would be devastating, and this warning should be taken seriously. Yet, given the fact that such forecasts cannot pinpoint when this seriousness will arrive and how human creativity will open a new path of adaptation (let alone account for chaos in advance), all such prognostications are severely handicapped from the outset. Nonetheless, this is not sufficient reason to reject the basic methodology.

Despite these setbacks, systems dynamics remains a valuable decision tool, especially when time and complexity are more tightly circumscribed. Furthermore, the widespread availability of the basic model—originally called "Dynamo"—in various microversions (one of the more user-friendly software packages is "Vensim") should enhance its acceptance as a problem-solving instrument. Increased utilization, in turn, should engender greater appreciation of the systems perspectives generally. Some, however, will continue to misperceive the approach as delimited by previous grandiose or merely mechanistic applications.

Lost Tribes of the Intellectual Diaspora

Even in Europe, where intellectual heterogeneity has allowed many more types of systems theory to be sustained (see Jackson et al. 1991), the closed systems tail has tended to wag the general systems dog. Furthermore, remaining generic programs have largely failed to deliver on their considerable promise. While some would argue for further patience, it is not highly probable that the current generation of systems concerns in Europe will yield a worldwide paradigm shift. This is not so much a case of "arrested development" as it is intellectual ethnocentrism. Yet, both elements, plus others, are certainly present. The largely mythical scientific hegemony of the United States, while more manifest in the physical sciences, has had its impact in the social sciences as well. In fact, if paradigmatic progress has been retarded (see Daneke 1988), then it was more pronounced in the United States. While Europeans were developing elaborate challenges (such as critical theory, postmodernism, deconstructionism, and so on), the United States was engaged in protracted battles with logical positivism (e.g., Campbell 1979; Cronbach 1982). Most of these challenges were ignored in the rush to embrace the neoclassical economic paradigm throughout the social sciences. This emphasis was also present on the continent, yet given the coexistence of many other economic concepts (e.g., Marxian, Austrian, etc.), Europe tended to maintain a much more mixed approach. In the United States systems elements were isolated in obscure pockets of intellectual activity.

Alive and Living in Europe

Within this mixing of schools in Europe, systems thinking more or less endured, yet it may be its durability that hindered its development. In addition to systems theory being embodied in various operations research and/or engineering departments as it was in the United States, many European universities developed various systems science and/or applied systems theory units. This consolidation of systems in particular cubbyholes appears to have been a mixed blessing. These transdisciplinary departments were automatically divorced from mainstream disciplinary work. From this position they tended to merely replicate and reinvent well-worn wheels rather than advance their own unique pursuits. Moreover, although they were obviously preaching to the choir (via their own journals, seminars, and professional meetings), they continued to beat the long-dead positivist horse as well as repeat perennial criticisms of neoclassism. These critiques are usually accompanied by arcane self-reflection and theoretical hairsplitting, rather than practical demonstrations. When the main topic of discussion is systems thinking itself, it appears that lots of intellectual energy can be wasted in elaborate theoretical refinements. Consider, for example, the raging debate over the appropriate level of integration between "critical theory" and systems thinking in the pages of the journal *Systems Practice* (e.g., Payne 1992), a title that belies its primary focus on theory (also note Tsoukas 1992). Since these discussions are so esoteric, it might be more useful to return the basic elements from the original theories, to develop perspectives on paradigmatic progress.

Other Remnants Worth Reformulating

Many remnants from early GST are worth reformulating. Beyond the obvious contributions of von Bertalanffy (1968), a few additional and rather obscure systems thinkers provide a foundation for reformulation of the basic paradigm. These include Stephen Pepper, Walter Buckley, and Edgar Dunn.

Stephen C. Pepper (1891–1972), a philosopher, was perhaps the most obscure of systems thinkers. Pepper saw in early systems theory an emergent paradigm that would combine and overcome various metaphysical epochs and reconcile their basic "root metaphors" (1942, 1966). His metaphors, which he also called "world hypotheses," included *mysticism, dogmatism, formism, mechanism, contextualism, organism,* and *selectivism.* His formulation of this last worldview, *selectivism,* anticipated many latter developments, not the least of which was Herbert Simon's notion of "human design" processes (see Simon 1969, 1985). Selectivism combines elements from contextualism and organism in an almost dialectical fashion. It extends contextualism to include the dynamic evolution of human intelligence and choice. For Pepper, selectivism provides a nonteleological approach to the issue of purposeful structures within "self-regulating systems." He describes how physiological, normative, and social/cultural dispositions and entities interact to mediate between values (both individual and social), choices, and behavior. Pepper illustrates how certain selective systems and values combine to establish "lines of legislation" (1966, 552). This conceptual restoration of human agency within complex, coevolving systems and structures was certainly well ahead of its time.

Walter Buckley, a sociologist, also attempted to illustrate the role of humans within complex systems and in the process added many far-reaching conceptual advances to the basic paradigm (note 1967). Unfortunately, his book, *Sociology and Modern Systems Theory,* was not published until the late 1960s. By then, sociologists had already become disenchanted with systems thinking through Talcott Parsons's more laborious development of "structural functionalism" (1937). Buckley rejected the static equilibrium approach that formed the basis for closed systems applications. He suggested that neither the mechanical nor the organismic elements of systems theory are useful to the study of society. He envisioned a much more dynamic process that is more akin to communications theory. Plus, his approach was highly contextual in orientation. He also anticipated some of the advances in evolutionary theory by rejecting the Darwinian model and describing processes of social entropy and evolution through institutional innovation.

Buckley's primary focus was the ties between goal seeking, self-awareness, and self-direction within complex organizations. Buckley firmly believed that, as social researchers began to develop these linkages, they would, in turn, develop new analytical tools that would replace the quantitative techniques of correlation and factor analysis. Along these lines, he developed his own concept of "mutual causality," which, for him, freed systems theory from its limited notions of equilibrium and one-way feedback. Moreover, his characterizations of evolutionary dynamics anticipated many of the current advances in nonlinear systems. As he (1967) contends:

> Only a modern systems approach promises to get at the full complexity of the interacting phenomena—to see not only the causes acting on the phenomena under study, the possible consequences of the phenomena, and the possible mutual interactions of some of these factors, but also to see the total emergent processes as a function of possible positive and/or negative feedbacks mediated by the selective decisions, or "choices," of the individuals and groups directly or indirectly involved. (79)

In sum, Buckley's reformulation of GST to suit the needs of sociologists provides a useful framework for social inquiry in general. Thus, his outline of its central elements remains instructive to this day. These elements include:

- A common vocabulary unifying the several behavioral disciplines.
- A technique for treating large complex organizations.
- A synthetic approach where piecemeal analysis is not possible due to the intricate interrelationships of parts that cannot be treated out of context of the whole.
- A viewpoint that gets at the heart of sociology because it sees the sociocultural system in terms of information and communication nets.
- The study of relations rather than entities, with an emphasis on process and transition probabilities as the basis of a flexible structure with many degrees of freedom.
- An operationally definable, objective nonanthropomorphic study of purposiveness, goal seeking, system behavior, symbolic cognitive processes; consciousness and self-awareness; and sociocultural emergence and dynamics in general. (39)

Edgar Dunn, like Buckley, was so far ahead of his time that his ideas have gone largely unnoticed. Moreover, because of the fact that he was an economist (actually an agricultural economist), his leanings toward GST were regarded as complete heresy among his peers. Dunn (1971) had set out to describe the processes of economic development in systemic terms. Dunn derived from systems thinking a framework of sociocultural evolution through adaptive learning and therefore found himself fascinated with many epistemological controversies. In this regard, he began raising issues that would later be echoed, albeit not acknowledged, by the postpositivist and "design science" advocates. For example, he differentiates his notion of design from both the physical science and standard social science methods as follows.

> Classical experimental physical science takes place at two levels: analysis and system design. At the level of system design, these relationships or laws are applied to the design of deterministic systems like machine systems . . . the social system experimenter is not exogenous to the system. . . . He is the agent of social learning—a purposive, self-actuating, but not fully deterministic process. . . . It can be characterized as evolutionary experimentation. (240–41)

Dunn also saw implications for social inquiry emerging from the quantum revolution in physics, beyond Heisenberg's "uncertainty principle." He felt that an integrative discipline was needed that could facilitate these types of multiple "portals." For example, Dunn invokes Neils Bohr's "notion of complementarity" and suggests that it "can be extended to assert the complementarity for both physiological and psychological theories in human science, both human system and social systems theories in social science, and both steady state and social learning theories in social change" (267). In essence, just as wave and particle theories are incomplete unless combined, deterministic and indeterminate social explanations must be integrated. Unfortunately, by the time Dunn was raising these concerns, only the rather narrow systems subfield of cybernetics was addressing them.

Cybernetics: The Art within the Science

Cybernetics, literally "the art of steersmanship" (from the Greek), had its origins in the early communications theory and fledgling computer sciences of the late 1940s; however, it emerged as social theory in the turbulent 1960s. The theory was generally regarded as a branch of GST, and its successful applications sustained it well beyond the half-life of early systems formulations. In fact, much of the work currently being conducted under the label *complexity theory* (e.g., Kauffman 1993; Holland 1992) is directly linked to cybernetics and its near cousin "cellular automata."

Generally speaking, cybernetics is concerned with the internal workings of the system, especially *feedback* and processes through which systems create *emergent properties* and *adaptive behavior* (see Ashby 1956, 1960). Like quantum physics, it was not necessarily concerned with material objects but rather with the interrelation between objects. Moreover, since most systems are only partially observable, the science of cybernetics has tended to focus on the *couplings* and *transformations* that occur between systems and the *properties* that emerge from these interactions. In fact, for cybernetics, the term *system* refers less to a specific set of items and more to the patterns of interaction. In this regard, early cyberneticians anticipated the current preoccupation with postpositivist epistemologies in that cybernetics actually allowed for the inter-action of the observer and the observed. As W. Ross Ashby maintained, science should be less concerned with discovering what a system contains and more concerned with coordinating the various discoveries of diverse observers, each of which is only a partial reality, at best (1956, 110–17). While cybernetics has a rich array of contributors, only a sample of its more influential thinkers is discussed here. These include Norbert Wiener (1894–1964), W. Ross Ashby (1903–72), and Gregory Bateson (1904–80).

Norbert Wiener, a founding father in the field, is perhaps its most obscure figure to the world at large. Yet, when his work is considered in the light of current activities at places like Santa Fe, he was truly a visionary and a significant contributor. Wiener realized that just as physics had replaced the deterministic world with the probabilistic one, social sciences, too, would have to begin to apply the insights of Boltzmann and Gibbs (e.g., entropy). In fact, he suggested that Gibbs's message was that *order is far less probable than chaos.* The purpose of cybernetics, according to Wiener (1954), is in explaining the islands of order upon which life thrives, within the sea of chaos (20–22). These insights into the nature of reality were largely lost in the rush to develop practical applications. Most notably, feedback, adaptive response, and other communication dynamics were quickly incorporated into the burgeoning science of computer design. Meanwhile, Wiener's more philosophical writings (e.g., *God and Golem, Inc.* 1964) were considered extremely speculative in their time. Yet today, his ideas about machines that simulate life are commonplace. Less appreciated, perhaps, are his observations about the interaction between *ontogenetic* (individual) and *phylogenetic* (entire species) learning and evolution.

Given his bold pronouncements regarding "lawlike" patterns in human interaction, W. Ross Ashby is, perhaps, the most flamboyant of these somewhat eccentric thinkers. His major tracts, *An Introduction to Cybernetics* (1956) and *Design for a Brain: The Origin of Adaptive Behavior* (1960), went a long way toward establishing the "machine model" of human behavior. Yet, it is essential to note that his categories were usually *process* dynamics rather than *product* determinations. Drawing upon Claude Shannon's (1949) mathematical theories of communication processes, Ashby sought to derive formal laws of *information and control.* But, in this context, control relates to the reception of the signals that trigger systemic response. By focusing upon the canonical *transformations,* snapshots of an entire system could be obtained, even if individual functioning of parts were ill understood. For very complex systems, functions could only be approximated statistically.

Beyond suggesting a link between cybernetics and *game theory* (strategic decision dynamics), Ashby's major contribution was the "law of requisite variety" (1956, 204–12). This basic concept, which has been the source of much confusion, deals with processes by which systems regulate *disturbances* (e.g., by limiting the flow of variety from the environment to essential variables). In his gaming characterization, regulators must counter variety with variety to reduce the flow. This concept has been used to illuminate many social processes (e.g., emphasis on redundancy in Japanese firms; see Nonaka 1990), as well as applied to the basic design of communication networks.

Ashby believed that these types of laws from cybernetics would find universal application in controlling variation from economics to epidemiology and from sociology to psychotherapy (1956, 244). But of course, missing elements in early cybernetic thinking proved this hubris was merely that. As Gregory Bateson observed:

> Cybernetics is the biggest bite out of fruit of the Tree of Knowledge that mankind has taken in the last 2000 years. But most of such bites out of the apple have proven indigestible—usually for cybernetic reasons. (quoted in Brand 1974, 26)

Bateson's own approach was at once more modest and yet more expansive than Ashby's in terms of applications. His classic *Steps to an Ecology of the Mind* (1972) provided a vital benchmark for a cybernetics of larger societal dynamics. The key to Bateson's approach was to extend the logic of natural systems to the interface between human and natural systems. His marriage to famed anthropologist Margaret Mead and his work as a mental health professional gave him a lifelong appreciation of how individuals interact within complex systems of mores and mental images. As Bateson pointed out,

> Mere purposive rationality unaided by such phenomena as art, religion, dreams, and the like, is necessarily pathogenic and destructive of life; its virulence springs specifically from the circumstance that life depends upon interlocking circuits of contingency, while consciousness can only see such short arcs as human purpose may direct. (Brand 1974, 10)

It is also interesting to note how Bateson used the terms of social psychology to describe biological phenomena: for example, "If Lake Erie is driven insane, its insanity is incorporated in the larger system of thought and experience" (Brand 1974, 10). Overall, Bateson believed that cybernetics would remain a subpar discipline as long as it ignored the "two-way feedback" between humans and their environment. He argued that only with this renewed power might it address the critical evolutionary problems posed by the urban ecosystem (1972, 502–13).

Cybernetics as a generic approach to social inquiry has *not* been widely sustained. As mentioned earlier it underpins numerous efforts such as artificial intelligence, neural networks, and algorithmic complexity; however, as an overarching applied paradigm its manifestations are highly scattered. Perhaps the most prominent remaining paradigmatic efforts are those of Stafford Beer and his disciples, labeled the *viable systems model* (note Espejo and Harnden 1989). Beer is by far the most tenacious scholar in his attempts to have the work of Ashby and other cyberneticians applied to management and manufacturing (among others see Beer 1959, 1979, 1985). For the most part, this work is European-style operations research (remembering its associated eclecticism). However, at another level it is highly innovative in its balancing of control theories and interpretive analyses. Unfortunately, this blending has produced the same type of epistemological debate that European GST scholars have found so debilitating.

Self-Organizing Systems

Perhaps the greatest conceptual advance in systems thinking is that of *self-organization*. Actually a small bundle of concepts, at the core it refers to *the processes by which order arises out of disorder* or fluctuation. As the preceding discussion suggested, self-organization has been an underlying theme in systems thinking and other domains for over thirty years, yet of late its position has become more central given the mathematical elaboration of nonlinear dynamics. Eugene Yates (1987), in the preface to his huge volume on self-organization, admits that attempts to define it are plagued by imprecision. Part of this imprecision stems from the fact that self-organization has emerged in many research streams. Moreover, like complexity and other paradigms in progress, it has been sustained by widely disparate disciplinary and substantive applications. Nevertheless, it is possible to distill from these a set of common characteristics. Before attempting such a distillation, it may be useful to review some of the more insightful developments.

Ideas akin to self-organization are probably traceable all the way to Immanual Kant's attempt to provide purposefulness to nature and Adam Smith's notion of the "invisible hand" in economics. However, modern formulations began in the 1960s through a few related but rather distinct research programs. The earliest and most comprehensive effort was that of Heinz von Foerster (von Foerster and Zopf 1962) and his colleagues at the Biological Computer Laboratory at the University of Illinois. Von Foerster's physical descriptions of information dynamics were unique in holding that order automatically increases in systems whose capacity for disorder is greater than the disorder in their environment. According to von Foerster, order emerges through the interaction of processes he labeled *order from noise* and *order from order*. Via the noise route, a system selects a certain level of environmental turbulence for incorporation into its structure. But this process is balanced against instances in which the system expands by incorporating new structural elements. Meanwhile, Manfred Eigen was developing a similar set of ideas and experiments for what he called *hypercycles* in the evolution of biological macromolecules (1979). Eigen's early formulations involving complex nucleic acids and proteins are seen as the key to larger *autopoietic* (self-reproducing) and *autocatalytic* (reinforcing) processes. In another hemisphere, a couple of Chilean biologists, Humberto Maturana and Francisco Varela (1975, 1992), were formulating full-blown theory of autopoiesis in which ontogeny serves as a source of structural change as well as renewal, since transformational routes are genetically encoded.

Perhaps the most prominent pillar of this paradigm is Illya Prigogine. For over thirty years he concerned himself with the self-organization appearing in the realm of thermodynamics. In classical equilibrium thermodynamics, fluctuations play a very minor role, and Boltzmann's famed constant prevails. Yet, Prigogine studied chemical systems far from equilibrium, where fluctuations accelerate and generate changes in the spatiotemporal structure (see Nicolis and Prigogine 1971, 1977, 1989). In these realms *symmetry-breaking bifurcations* occur. These events were labeled *dissipative structures* and defined as *order through fluctuation* (see Nicolis and Prigogine 1977). His work in clarifying these dynamics of ill-understood *phase transitions* was recognized by the Nobel prize in chemistry in 1980. Prigogine not only forced a reassessment of the second law of thermodynamics (entropy), but his ideas have been combined with various advances in mathematical biology (such as those alluded to earlier) to forge a dramatic new conception of evolution. This conception, in turn, has broad implications for sociocultural and biological systems. In the late 1970s, he began suggesting how these same dynamics may prevail for social systems (see Prigogine and Allen 1982), therefore this discussion will have much more to say about his ideas subsequently.

A similar tangent emerged from Hermann Haken's work on lasers at the Bell Laboratory in the 1950s. Haken generated an elaborate system that he called *synergetics* (1978) initially to explain the dynamics of monochromatic light. Yet, it quickly became clear that these self-organizing processes had analogues in many other domains, such as the problem of morphogenesis in biology (Haken 1983). Of course, these various contributions to the self-organization paradigm drew upon numerous other conceptual innovations, such as the models of predator-prey dynamics (see Lotka 1925); C. S. Holling's studies of *ecological resilience* (see Holling 1973); and Maturana and Varela's (1975) clarification of autopoietic systems.

As Erich Jantsch (1980, 7) points out, harbingers of these insights can also be found in classical cybernetics and other elements of *general systems theory* (GST), especially the work of those who emphasized *positive feedback* and *destabilization* in the development of new forms. However, it is relatively clear that self-organization provides a distinct demarcation point between the old and the new cybernetics. Generic applications of self-organizing systems were not taken seriously until the previously mentioned physicists and chemists showed an interest. Moreover, inroads in biology also set the stage for sociocultural applications.

The upshot of self-organization research has not only been to rejuvenate various systems theoretics but to serve as a framework through which currently popular pursuits such as chaos and complexity can be given paradigmatic significance. *In essence, self-organization constitutes the inner workings of living systems.* Its critical elements might be summarized as follows (paraphrased from Jantsch and Waddington 1976, 6–7).

1. A necessary *nonequilibrium* is maintained between a system and its environment.
2. *Structure* and *functions* are mutually causal and complementary.
3. *Deterministic* and *stochastic* (random) features involve interdependent processes.
4. The system can undergo *qualitative change* when switching between *multiple stable regions.*
5. Evolution implies an ordered *succession* of such *transitions;* autocatalysis at many levels seems to be a principal "driving mechanism."
6. *Resilience* is highest near the boundaries of *maximum sustainable nonequilibrium* and lowest near the boundaries of stability.
7. The thrust of evolution seems to further *flexibility* of the individual system at all levels; this implies that the long-term capability to deal with the unexpected is favored over short-term efficiency and productivity.
8. By virtue of this flexibility, the evolutionary processes work through *evolutionary experimentation* at many levels of an open learning hierarchy—testing directions, not places, and finding confirmation, not certainty and prediction.
9. The result of evolution is a *progressive correlation between genotypes and physical, social, and cultural environment,* characterized by an increasing emphasis on epigenetic group processes, mainly intersystemic exchange, which in the human world come to dominate over linear genetic processes.

10. A basic principle of this correlation is *symbiotization of heterogeneity.*
11. *Resilience through fluctuation* may be assumed to imply viability *through transformability.* A "healthy" system both resists and copes with qualitative change.
12. Evolutionary process implies *openness as self-transcendence* and thus *imperfection, courage, and uncertainty*—not the perfectionistic, static security and certainty inherent in the traditional orientation.

Advocates of self-organizing systems have also forged links to the larger postpositivist-methodological movements (see Krohm, Gunter, and Nowothy 1990). Moreover, basic notions of self-organization have even found their way into mainstream economics (see Krugman 1996). However, these applications remain relatively selective. More critically, modern-day economists, by and large, apply self-organization without reference to its origin or its larger systemic implications.

Holism and Other Epistemological Hang-ups

Several reasons for the intellectual gulf between systems theory and the reigning economic theory have been alluded to previously. Many points of contention are mere matters of misperception and/or ideological bias. Nonetheless, a few are more fundamental. Primary among the more authentic controversies is holism versus reductionism and the associated issue of methodological individualism (i.e., maintaining the sole rational actor as the unit of analysis). This apparent disagreement may not necessarily prove as ironclad as one might think, however. There are perhaps ways to reconcile these divergent epistemological perspectives. If so, both traditions could achieve greater explanatory power. Ultimately, the future progress of the systems paradigm may rest upon its level of integration with existing methodological imperatives. One such reconciliation will most probably entail a concept of rational choice that appreciates the interplay of systemic processes. *Holism is simply the position that systems cannot be understood merely by looking at the parts individually.* Synergistic and/or coevolutionary dynamics often makes the "whole greater than the sum of its parts." *Reductionism,* by contrast, maintains that one can understand the whole by studying the parts. Apparently those working in chaos and complexity are not nearly as concerned about these distinctions as various philosophers of science (see Bechtel and Richardson 1993) think they should be. Essentially, it seems that many of those who actively pursue nonlinearity believe that their studies will simply render these issues moot (see Waldrop 1992). While it may be obvious that focusing on the dynamical patterns and/or processes as units of analysis makes reductionism ridiculous, unbridled holism may be equally de-limiting.

Those who assume that the holism issue has somehow already been resolved still continue to maintain a rather vague methodological position. As Daniel Stein (1989) suggests in the introduction to a collection of *Lectures in the Sciences of Complexity* (1989), "holism" is one of the few things that the various approaches to complexity have in common, yet is rarely explicated. He suggests that

> At the heart of many of the problems discussed herein is some kind of non-reducibility: the behavior we're interested in evaporates when we try to reduce the system to a simpler, better-understood one. . . . The systems presented here all show surprising and unexpected behavior that somehow seems to be a property of the system as a whole. (xiii–xiv)

Similarly, Ali Çambel (1993) maintains that there is something inherent in the nature of complex systems that makes them holistic phenomena. This, however, is a partially tautological argument, that is, simply true by definition. But, Çambel takes some pains to make it less so. Initially, he argues for the peaceful coexistence of reductionism and holism, while contending that "it is doubtful that the reductionist approach *by itself* will be fruitful in understanding complex systems" (22). Furthermore, he distinguishes this detente across levels of inquiry that include the following: (a) hierarchical, (b) geometric, and (c) algorithmic. The *hierarchical approach* goes the farthest in maintaining the integrity of the individual disciplines and constituent elements. In other words, it is reductionist at its root. The *algorithmic approach,* on the other hand, which is the least concerned with disciplinary boundaries, is the one that typifies current complexity studies, especially those at the Santa Fe Institute. In fact, one might argue that this algorithmic uniformity is a new form of reductionism. William Bechtel and Robert Richardson (1993) take a bit different cut at these issues, adding the categories of (a) mechanistic explanations, (b) decomposition, and (c) localization. However, they seem to acknowledge that complexity studies can vacillate between these categories. Thus, once again, actual studies of complex systems tend to defy being pigeonholed into either extreme.

A more useful approach, perhaps, is provided by Stephen Kline (1994). In his opus *The Logical Necessity of Multi-disciplinarity,* he displays the untenable character of both reductionism and holism. (His definition of the "bottom-up" vs. the "top-down" approach creates a bit of a "straw man" in this regard.) His purpose is to develop a full-blown methodology for determining the level of integration and/or aggregation, which he calls the *consistency* principle. While this is essentially a hierarchical approach to complexity, it uses the types of criteria generated by the *algorithmic approach* (what he calls *integrated-control-information*). According to Kline, *consistency* involves asking the following questions (1987, 19–20).

- How many levels are there in the system structure?
- How many degrees of freedom in each level?
- How many of these degrees of freedom are constrained from levels above and below, and how many are left open to independent action, thoughts, choices?
- Which are the levels of control, and are controls open or closed loop, rigid or flexible?

While somewhat laborious, these types of decompositional analyses may allow the new generation of social systems researchers to avoid past pitfalls and potential blunders.

Another aspect of Kline's analysis worth highlighting is his curious maintenance of a "top-down–bottom-up" dichotomy, since his criteria facilitate starting in the middle, as it were. Apparently, this methodological caricature is being used to supplant the old individualism versus holism polarization. For example, Epstein and Axtell (1996) self-describe their approach to nonlinear dynamics as *social sciences from the bottom up* in the subtitle of their book. For them, the distinction is critical, since it allows them to demonstrate their allegiance to "agent-based" theory while moving "beyond methodological individualism" (16–17). Moreover, since they emphasize "growing collective structures" rather than modeling them directly, the point is immensely important. However, their casting all macrodynamical models as somehow defective top-down reasoning tends to distort nonlinear reality. Neither the behavioral proclivities of autonomous agents nor the resulting systems are the appropriate focal point. Rather, it is the patterns of interaction that matter most, and these patterns are neither the product of the parts nor purely the purview of the whole. Recognizing this conundrum logically commits one to the search for intermediating constructs. In the context of the dominant social paradigm of "rational choices," and for lack of a better designation, one such construct might be a notion like *systemic choice.*

Having paid what is hopefully sufficient homage to early innovators of systems thinking and recognizing that many ideas are being replicated today, it becomes necessary to generate a bit of distance from the basic paradigms of cybernetics and general systems. A new systemic science of human institutions would be substantially different from previous attempts at social and/or human ecology. These differences stem not only from recent advances in the understanding of complex systems but also from a reconfiguration and rechanneling of concepts from earlier efforts. What is more important, perhaps, is that this redirection also attempts to incorporate many conventional and nonsystemic research traditions, such as neoclassical and neoinstitutional economic theory. It is the advent of nonlinear systems that makes this curious recombination possible. It not only rejuvenates systems theory, it reifies elements of methodological individualism. *In essence, nonlinearity is the missing link between individual choices and systemic imperatives.*

The Individualistic Imperative

Individual choice, even if irrational or merely "bounded" (via Simon 1957, 1982), is such a pivotal idea in the annals of contemporary social inquiry that unless ecological approaches can somehow reconcile the agent and the system, paradigmatic development will be mired for many years to come. An authentic representation of systemswide decision dynamics must not only strive toward reconciliation, but it also must restore a notion of human purposefulness. As suggested earlier, the systemic elements inherent in most social phenomena (amplified by recent work in complexity) are at marked odds with the prevailing paradigm of social inquiry. This paradigm derived from neoclassical economic theory has individual rationality as a methodological imperative. This imperative is manifest not only in economics but in several other disciplines as well (particularly sociology and political science) and is especially entrenched in professional fields such as business and public administration. The hostility between systems and rational-choice approaches may have even intensified in light of the reemergence of systems concepts such as self-organization (note Aranson 1990; Buchanan and Vanberg 1990). In the inaugural issue of the sociology journal entitled *Rationality and Society,* James S. Coleman (1989) manifests this latent hostility as follows.

> It [the Journal] sacrifices disciplinary comprehensiveness for theoretical coherence; it explicitly espouses methodological individualism, with the theory of rational action serving as the microlevel foundation for explanation of systemic functioning. It does not find congenial work that is methodologically holistic, floating at the system level without recourse to the actors whose actions generate that system. (6)

It is noteworthy that few systems theorists actually remain "floating" in a way that is totally "without recourse" to individual behavior; they merely maintain that such behavior is shaped by systemic interactions. These types of straw-man dichotomies are, however, increasingly common.

The battle between systems and rational choice theories is probably as much ideological as it is methodological. Systems thinking is mistakenly associated with totalitarianism and rational choice with democratic capitalism. This intellectual non sequitur is even more curious when one considers that current accounts of rational choice actually place severe constraints on human agency. From a philosophical standpoint, it is really in their best interest for rational choice advocates to accept a certain level of behavioral variability at the individual level despite the havoc it will wreak upon their tidy mathematic models. Without such variability, choice is rendered moot. If rationality is complete, then choice becomes mere stimulus and response. For example, Alan Blinder (1984) contends that such variability might be advisable at the aggregate level as well, if economics is to avoid a fundamental denial of "free will." As George Shackle (1961) observed some time ago:

> Conventional economics is not about choice, but about acting according to necessity. Economic man obeys the *dictates* of reason, follows the *logic of choice*. To call this conduct choice is surely a misuse of words, when we suppose that to him the ends amongst which he can select, and the criteria of selection, are given, and the means to each end are known. (272–73)

Challenges to rational choice rarely come at this philosophical level. Rather, empirical evidence of how individuals actually make decisions has been the basis of refutation. The narrow notion of rationality that associates human action with simple utility maximization has taken a beating over the years, and significant modifications have emerged. As a result, the exact nature of rationality has become increasingly problematic. Beginning with Herbert Simon's (1957, 1982) formulation of "bounded rationality," the work of decision scientists (e.g., Tversky and Kahneman 1986) and so-called behavioral economists (note Hogarth and Reder 1986) has become less and less peripheral in recent years. Anomalies such as the "framing effect," "sunk cost problem," and "preference reversal phenomena" combine to characterize decisions that are *quasi-rational* (see Thaler 1991) at best.

Many economists, however, do not want to forsake their basic intellectual infrastructure. Some maintain that these psychological *processes* that interfere with pure rationality are compensated for in the aggregate *products*. This argument, however, conflicts with studies that show that under certain conditions (e.g., governmental regulation) anomalies are actually exacerbated through aggregation (see Frey and Eichenberger 1989). As James March (1986) once observed, economists have been trying to "have their cake and eat it too." He explains that

> pure models of rational choice seem obviously appropriate as guides to intelligent action, but more problematic for predicting behavior. In practice, the converse seems closer to the truth for much of economics. So long

as we use individual choice models to predict the behavior of relatively large numbers of individuals or organizations, some potential problems are avoided by the familiar advantages of aggregation. Even a small signal stands out in a noisy message. On the other hand, if we choose to predict small numbers of individuals or organizations or give advice to a single individual or organization, the saving graces of aggregation are mostly lost. (143)

Could it be that the type of rationality with which economists are concerned is incongruent with methodological individualism? No less a figure than Nobel economist Kenneth Arrow (1994) appears to promote just such a conclusion. He contends that

> Social variables not attached to particular individuals are essential in the studying of the economy or any other social system and that, in particular, knowledge and technical information have an irremovably social component, of increasing importance over time. (14)

In this context, Arrow points out that methodological individualism is "not very compatible with neoclassical paradigms and particularly not with rational choice" (14). This seems a curious admission, but perhaps James March (1986) can help in making sense of it. March draws a key distinction between *calculated* and *systemic* categories of rationality. Among the calculated are those types where most of the economists and their decision science critics have focused, including "limited" (or bounded), "contextual," "game," and "process rationality" (148). In the systemic category the following types prevail (149):

- *adaptive rationality:* emphasizing "experiential learning by individuals and collectivities";
- *selected rationality:* emphasizing "the process of selection through survival or growth"; and
- *posterior rationality:* emphasizing "the discovery of intentions as an interpretation of action rather than prior position."

March describes these systemic processes as follows.

> Suppose we imagine that knowledge, in the form of precepts of behavior, evolves over time within a system and accumulates across time, people, and organizations without complete current consciousness of its history. Then sensible action is taken by actors without comprehension of its full justification. (149)

Are these not the types of rationality that economists generally associate with their aggregate assessments? For much of the behavior of interest to economists (e.g., markets) and other processes of collective action (e.g., politics), if models of choice are appropriate at all, then they would be models of *systemic choice.* Economist Armen Alchian (1950) recognized this situation nearly a half century ago, but it was a realization that has remained underappreciated, to say the least. Political scientist Terry Moe (1984) is one of the few to recognize Alchian's departure from orthodoxy. Moe maintains that

> In a fundamental sense, Alchian's theory of economic organizations is different from those of Coase or Simon. He disavows an explicit model of individual choice . . . and . . . offers a system-level explanation of organizational emergence, structure, and survival that is largely independent of decision making at the micro level. . . . Alchian's logic of natural selection, when grafted onto either approach, provides a powerful means of deriving and integrating expectations about individuals, organizations and systems. (746)

In contrast to Alchian's model, the notion of systemic choice forwarded here is driven by self-organization rather than natural selection. This provides a more viable characterization of the complex individual and institutional interactions (such as coevolution). Plus, systemic choices are much more compatible with conventional ideas of *human agency.* As Prigogine and Allen (1982) elaborate:

> intrinsic nonlinearities, in dialogue with fluctuations, result in the self-organization of the system, so that its structures, articulations, and hierarchies are the result, not of the operation of some "global optimiser," some "collective utility function," but of successive instabilities near bifurcation points. . . . [I]ndividuals acting according to their own particular criteria may find that the resulting collective vector may sweep them in an entirely unexpected direction, perhaps involving qualitative changes in the state of the system. (37)

Beyond Equilibrium

Unfortunately, models of choice predicated upon nonlinear perspectives would demand significant modifications in economists' cherished notions of *general equilibrium,* and these might prove difficult. *General equilibrium theory* has become more than theory over the years. It is canon law; and as such it is a basic unquestioned principle that supports many questionable concepts. As Sidney Winter (1989) suggests, the integrity of "rational choice" relies upon an elaborate self-equilibrating model. That is, macroequilibrium depends upon micromaximization behavior (individuals' and/or firms') and vice versa. George Akerlof and Janet Yellen (1985) contend that "small deviations from rationality" (like the anomalies alluded to previously) can, under certain circumstances, make "significant differences to economic equilibria." Moreover, if the general equilibrium should fail, rational choice, even of the learning variety, would stand on shaky ground indeed.

Having been the sacred temple of neoclassical economic theory, general equilibrium fostered its own elite priesthood, in which mathematical defenders of the faith are held in extreme reverence (and rewarded with Nobel prizes, and so on). The high priest was Leon Walras (1954), who mounted the first axiomatic defense, thus removing general equilibrium from the fray of empirical verification (see Ingrao and Georgio 1990). Even Joseph Schumpeter (1934), who was hardly a defender of faith, described Walras's static system of equations as the "Magna Carta of economic theory" (242). Essentially, Walras posited the mythical mechanism of the all-seeing "auctioneer" who only allows trades to occur when a simultaneous equilibrium of supply and demand is achieved (see Walras 1954, 172). This notion, known as *tatonement,* is still invoked by public-choice theorists who strive to establish a "unanimity rule" for voting situations (see Mueller 1989, 49). For these "frictionless" auctions to actually have meaning, economics would have to remain in a contextual void, like a vacuum in laboratory physics.

Over the years, of course, great theorists have substantially enhanced the logic of Walrasian equilibrium (e.g., Hicks 1939; Debreu 1959; Arrow and Hahn 1971); however, the emphasis remains highly formal and largely out of touch with social reality. Sidney Winter (1989) describes the problem as follows.

> The allocations of intellectual resources in economic research is warped by the widespread uncritical acceptance of a particular mathematical aesthetic of theory construction, involving the familiar linked commitments to modeling optimizing actors in equilibrium situations. Theorists who adhere to this aesthetic are acclaimed by their fellows for aesthetically pleasing treatments of toy problems—and sometimes, fortunately, for aesthetically satisfactory treatments of substantial problems. . . . Portions of the real subject matter that are highly significant but intractable or messy from the approved aesthetic standpoint tend to get neglected, distorted, or relegated to an atheoretical limbo for examination. (357)

However, certain branches of economics have already begun to reformulate their prevailing notions of equilibrium. Driven mostly by work in industrial organization (IO) economics, a revival of "game theory" has led to the widespread acceptance of *Nash equilibrium,* or the "strategic profile" that corresponds to the best responses to other players' strategies (see Kreps 1990, 402–12). Work in this realm also accepts the existence of multiple equilibria that do not quite fit within the "closed system" mechanical world of Walras. In much the same way as certain neoinstitutionalists (e.g., Williamson 1985) have shifted the unit of analysis to the "transaction" or "contract," this addendum subtly shifts its focus from the individual to the process of strategic interaction. If, in turn, these interactions are studied a bit more carefully, it may become apparent that under many circumstances the true dynamics are more of the self-organizing than the self-equilibrating variety.

From the outset of the modern era, mathematical refurbishing has harbored subtle modifications. Leon Walras and his set of algebraic equations that established the original linear model of supply and demand would quickly be converted with the application of calculus by Wilfred Pareto (1909); however, Pareto added his notion of optimality as a needed addendum to competitive equilibrium. In order for Kenneth Arrow (see Arrow and Debreu 1954) to develop more fully mathematized proofs of general equilibrium, assumptions regarding convexity (e.g., continuities in preferences) had to be added to the mix, and the existence of these assumptions became the source of many challenges and clarifications (e.g., Marshall 1920; Baumol 1972; Rand 1976). Alfred Marshall's early speculations about the possibility of multiple equilibria that drift between stable and unstable conditions later gave rise to explorations of "nonconvex preferences" (Rand 1976) in which bifurcations and discontinuities (e.g., "the cusp") emerge. Admitting that at least one actor may exhibit suboptimal behavior (e.g., addiction) opens a Pandora's box of multiple equilibria. Moreover, if preferences are cyclical and income elastic, then chaos dynamics may appear over time (see Benhabib and Day 1981), and if this occurs then equilibrium is a chimera.

From the Garbage Can to the Participatory Imperative

A contemporary classic in the debate over the exact nature of collective and/or organizational choice is Cohen, March, and Olsen's (1972) "garbage can model." While initially a critical departure from conventional economic notions of choice, it has now been thoroughly absorbed, especially in the behavioral and neoinstitutional circles (discussed at length in the next chapter). This innovation goes a long way toward characterizing the idea of systemic choice advocated here; however, it does not quite reach sufficient velocity to escape the inertial pulls of the neoclassical paradigm, nor facilitate a full-scale exploration of nonlinear dynamics.

In fairness, James March and his students were focused on a fairly narrow set of organizational constraints. The garbage can model characterizes the type of rationality that emerges within organized anarchies (e.g., universities). Its key features include the following.

1. They operate on the basis of a variety of inconsistent and undefined preferences. It can be described better as a loose collection of ideas than as a coherent structure; it discovers preferences through action more than it acts on the basis of its preferences.
2. They have fluid participation. Participants vary in the amount of time and effort they devote to different domains; involvement varies from one time to another.
3. They have unclear technology. Although the organization manages to survive and even to produce, its own processes are not understood by its members. (11)

In other words, the boundaries of these particular types of organizations "are uncertain and changing" and "the audiences and decision makers for any particular kind of choice change capriciously." Consequently, the model can be applied to processes with decisions whose interpretations continually change during the process of resolution. Problems, choices, and decision makers can arrange and rearrange themselves. During these rearrangements the meaning of a choice can change several times (see Cohen and March 1986). The "garbage can" analogy comes into play as follows.

> To understand processes within organizations, one can view a choice opportunity as a garbage can into which various kinds of problems are dumped by participants as they are generated. The mix of garbage in a single can depends on the number of cans available, on the labels attached on the alternative cans, on what garbage is currently being produced, on the speed with which garbage is collected and removed from the scene. (Cohen, March, and Olsen 1972, 2)

The implications of this model are extensive, far beyond merely giving the phrase "this is garbage" a new meaning. Initially the lessons for university presidents and similar "leaders under ambiguity" were most in evidence (Cohen and March 1986), yet other applications, such as accounting (March 1987) were developed. These follow-up studies were particularly insightful in demonstrating that real world decisions dynamics are not merely a matter of organization constraints upon economic style rationality but rather vice versa. In essence, if homogeneous decisions manage to emerge, then these are the result of the prevailing chaotic process being constrained or accommodated. Attractors and/or "rules of thumb" can, of course, result from constraints other than those imposed by conventional rationality. In other words, it is the ignorance that is bounded, not the rationality. Funtowicz and Ravetz (1990) observed this type of phenomenon that they called "bounded ignorance" as it related to issues of scientific uncertainty in global environmental models. They call for a "second-order science" or contextual approach. However, their garbage comes from the external environment. It is not necessarily generated internally.

Another way of looking at these dynamics is that one person's garbage is another's systemic choice. While not using this particular frame of reference, critics of this model who come from an artificial intelligence (AI) perspective make a very similar argument (Masuch and LaPotin 1989). Their major criticism of the garbage can model is that it merely assumes that somewhere in the organization an individual decision maker is playing the appropriate role and therefore this critical role is exogenous to the model. As they suggest, AI models of choice include these interacting agents in their simulations. Moreover, they assert that "garbage cans represented organizations on high levels of aggregation and ignored the complex interaction patterns between individuals to generate plausible patterns of behavior" (38). What complexity approaches to choice begin to reveal is that human agency is a systemic process. In fact, the *imperative of widespread participation* is a synonym for complex systems. As John Casti (1994) observes, simple systems are ones in which a few decision makers control most of the power. He cites political dictatorships, privately owned corporations, and the Catholic Church, with their patterns of low interaction between the lines of command, as examples of simple systems. Furthermore, it is easy to trace the effects of central authority. *Complex systems, on the other hand, exhibit more diffusion of authority.* While such systems often appear to have a central leader, Casti explains that

> in actuality the power is spread over a decentralized structure. Actions of a number of units then combine to generate the actual system behavior. Typical examples of these kinds of systems include democratic govern-ments, labor unions and universities. Such systems tend to be somewhat more resilient and stable than centralized structures because they are more forgiving of mistakes by any one decision-maker and are more able to absorb unexpected environmental fluctuations. (272)

In other words, the choice dynamics that economists associate with individual autonomy are very often the result of irreducible complexity, and such complex-ity is inherently systemic in nature.

Conclusions

In the final analysis, whether or not systems theory can be fully reconciled with neoclassical economics could be a moot point. Systems concepts, reconciled or not, will continue to grow in explanatory significance. For ideological or equally irrelevant reasons, elements may be reinvented and/or bear little resemblance to earlier efforts at forging a general systems paradigm, even if the conceptual issues remain similar. The conceptual potential of systems theory has obviously been substantially enhanced by recent computational advances, especially the rise of nonlinear mathematics. These new tools and methods not only enliven traditional systems pursuits, they greatly expand their conceptual reach. Moreover, these new devices arise just at a point in time when social and institutional turbulence are laying waste to conventional mechanistic policy and management approaches. Already, a number of managerial "best-sellers" have begun to extol the virtues of a systems approach (Senge 1990; De Geus 1997). One in particular, written by former Dutch Shell executive, Arie De Geus (1997), describes how adaptive, long-lived companies recognize the need for systems features such as "sensitivity to the environment," "cohesion and identity," "tolerance and decentralization." He contends that a "living-systems" approach is the key to corporate life extension. In the following chapters these practical applications of systemic wisdom will be explored in much finer detail. At this juncture it is sufficient to recognize that systems thinking is in the midst of a significant resurgence and that advances in nonlinear methods have greatly contributed to this turn of events. Recall that it is the purpose of complexity research to discover the simple rules at work in complex behavior. These rules, in turn, govern the processes that direct, without necessarily dictating, the patterns of interaction. In other words, they provide the parameters of systemic choices. In conventional economics, these rules are usually characterized as "bounds" upon individual rationality. However, as this discussion maintains, these characterizations do not account for the full range of the interaction, learning, and adaptation that often supersede individual aspirations and activities. Even if individuals met the psychological prerequisites for rational behavior, the buffeting of other agents and institutions would certainly conspire to subject outcomes to strategic negotiations. These negotiations do not necessarily follow a swift equilibratory path of the Nash-like game solution (see chap. 3). Negotiations themselves experience a nonlinear ebb and flow or "outbreaks of cooperation" (see Glance and Huberman 1993). From this perspective the *processes* by which individuals participate in the evolution of cooperation may be more important than the *products* being pursued by particular individuals. While it may seem self-evident, managers and policymakers who wish to build systems of more *sustainable cooperation* should seek to design institutional processes that enhance the spectrum of involvement, as well as make allowances for nonlinear patterns and systemic influences. Hopefully, this participatory imperative will go a long way toward reducing the fear that a systems approach to social inquiry will somehow fuel the rise of a technocratic elite. If the participatory nature of rationality is not enough, the realization that other aspects of nonlinear dynamics virtually guarantee that centralized plans will swiftly go awry might help. Systemic choices can be aided by analysis, but they cannot be supplanted. From ecological perspectives, the process dynamics of human systems embody their own wisdom, and this is the heart of systematic choice.

CHAPTER 5

Toward an Institutional Ecology

The basic aim of social systems theory, both past and present, is the development of ecological understandings. A typical dictionary definition of *ecology* is "the science of the relationships between organisms and their environments." Since institutions are the central mediating mechanisms among individuals and between individuals and their environments, many of the elements of critical concern to social scientists can be characterized as *institutional ecology*. This current incarnation of an ecological perspective shares several elements with previous attempts to fashion a transdisciplinary discipline. In particular, it is primarily focused upon the evolutionary dynamics. However, given recent advances in nonlinear science, both evolutionary ingredients and associated systemic processes are viewed quite differently. Beyond the pivotal role that individuals play in the creation and evolution of institutions and vice versa, the actual processes of societal adaptability can now be studied in complex co-evolutionary terms. As a result, it should be possible both to more carefully study and more artfully design resilient institutions. Yet, before these new ecological understandings can be generated, the theory and methods of complex systems must become more judiciously diffused within as well as between the various disciplines that guide practical policy and management, especially economics. To promote this diffusion of the tools of knowledge, it may be useful to assemble an array of possible entry points.

From Neoclassical to Systemic Economics

The current theoretical hegemony enjoyed by neoclassical economic theory does not necessarily imply a completely static discipline, despite its affection for relatively static models. Over the years many theoretical challenges have arisen. Some were designed to challenge the basic approach (e.g., Austrian and institutional economics). Others were designed to avoid confrontation by developing unique elements, generally based in a disparate discipline (e.g., economic psychology). Generally speaking, these alternate approaches tended to discount the power and sophistication of neoclassicism. Moreover, they underestimated its ability to absorb diverse elements. With growing popularity of nonlinear science, it would seem that economists would quickly co-opt the loose-knit confederation of tools and concepts. While eagerly experimenting with the tools, they have yet to embrace the concepts. As alluded to earlier, various deeply ingrained ideological as well as methodological biases make this conversion less than complete. Canadian economists Murray Frank and Thanasis Stengos allude to this approach/avoidance problem as follows.

> At times particular branches of mathematics have sparked interest amongst economists. Game theory, catastrophe theory and the theory of fuzzy sets come to mind. In each case, there was some initial excitement due to the potential for constructing theoretical models. In each case, initial excitement dissipated as the new theory turned out not to be a miracle cure. Interest revived in game theory a couple of decades later, and it may yet do so for the other examples. Is chaos likely to follow the same pattern? To some extent the answer is inevitably yes. Initial enthusiasm inevitably grows more temperate as the work gets more difficult. However, we would suggest that chaos is not quite of the same ilk as these others. The reason is that chaos also provides empirical tools. If these empirical tools prove fruitful in unearthing otherwise unsuspected structure in real data, then chaos may be expected to take a permanent place in the box of tools that economists employ. (128)

Despite the presence of provocative "tools," the ultimate attractiveness of a given theoretical domain may also be contingent upon its compatibility with existing imperatives. In systems terms, the economics profession is not completely open to the exchange of intellectual energy. However, if it is to avoid the inevitable entropic fate of all closed systems, economics will eventually have to incorporate many highly conflicting notions. In fact, *entropy* itself is one of the more important of these neglected items. As economic historian Philip Mirowski (1989) explains, economists have

> appropriated the mathematical formalisms of mid-nineteenth-century energy physics, which for convenience we shall refer to as "proto-energetics," made them their own by changing the labels on the variables, and then trumpeted the triumph of a truly "scientific economics.". . . The neoclassicals had neglected to appropriate the most important part of the formalism, not to mention the very heart of the metaphor, namely, the conservation of energy. This little blunder rendered the neoclassical heuristic essentially incoherent. (91)

Meanwhile, of course, physics moved on to demonstrate that the mechanical world that economists adopted applies to only a small set of primarily nonliving systems. While human institutions may indeed impose a set of dampening *limit cycles* on an otherwise oscillating environment, the behavior of these institutions must be given a full accounting. Anthropologist Mary Douglas (1986) describes these institutional preconditions as follows.

> Equilibrium cannot be assumed; it must be demonstrated and with a different demonstration for each type of society. . . . Before it can perform its entropy-reducing work, the incipient institution needs some stabilizing principle to stop its premature demise. That stabilizing principle is the naturalization of social classifications. There needs to be an analogy by which the formal structure of a crucial set of social relations is found in the physical world, or in the supernatural world, or in eternity, anywhere, so long as it is not seen as a socially contrived arrangement. (48)

Economists, and other social scientists, have made a number of earnest attempts at incorporating various institutional and evolutionary elements into their enterprise over the years. Some of these attempts are quite instructive and when combined with the logic of nonlinear systems provide a clearer picture of the ecology of human artifacts and hence a more effective guide to social enterprise. In other words, this broader framework or *institutional ecology* not only appreciates the nonlinear dynamics, it adds flesh and bones to "homo-economus" (the economic person).

Institutional and Evolutionary Antecedents

Back around the turn of the last century, Thorstein Veblen (1898) addressed his colleagues in the fledgling American Economic Association with the query, "Why Is Economics Not an Evolutionary Science?" The question is still cogent today. This is not to say that economics has not come a long way and developed various representations of evolution (e.g., Boulding 1981; Nelson and Winter 1982). However, the impact of these various evolutionary perspectives upon mainstream thinking has been fairly low (particularly Boulding). Most models are relatively static, and nearly all involve equilibrium (for a few exceptions, see Quandt 1988). Moreover, to the extent that evolution is dealt with at all, it is usually pictured in traditional Darwinian terms (see Rothschild 1990).

Evolutionary thinking, in general, dates back to the ancient Greeks. Heraditus, who lived around 500 B.C., is well known for his claim that "all is flux" and his statement that it is "impossible to step in to the same river twice." Nearly all the major social thinkers from Aristotle to Rousseau to Hegel forwarded elaborate evolutionary theories. Of course, evolution was introduced in biology with Darwin's *Origin of the Species* in 1859 and did not catch on until the turn of the century. At about the same time, it was banished from much of social inquiry. That is, evolutionary dynamics have been pretty much excluded since the synthesis of classical economic theory and marginalist methodology (or utility theory) in the late nineteenth century. As Dorfman (1969) describes:

> During the 1870s and 1880s in both Europe and the United States, the marginal utility theory of demand was systematically developed and became in effect an extension of classical economic theory. By the 1890s the work of synthesizing the two had been completed. The result was what came to be known as neo-classical economics. Its followers generally speaking saw in it a complete explanation of the workings of the economic system, a fully integrated model of an idealized, frictionless, automatic system. Being mainly concerned with statics, they deemed historical and statistical research as at best of secondary importance. (44)

Given its formal/mathematical sophistication this small branch of economics quickly grew in size and prestige and by the mid– to late twentieth century had displaced most other schools of thought, at least in the United States. One of the displaced schools was the *institutionalist movement.* Institutionalism, also known as *evolutionary economics,* rejected the antihistorical, static equilibrium models of the neoclassicists and sought initially to remake economics more along the lines of biology than physics. U.S. institutionalist thought actually had its origins in the German historical philosophers but consolidated its own unique perspectives as a challenge to the rise of marginalism. Its most outstanding originators were Thorstein Veblen, Wesley Mitchell, and John R. Commons.

Thorstein Veblen (1857–1929), in addition to wanting to make economics an evolutionary science, was a pioneer in the application of cultural anthropology to contemporary economic issues. The focus of these applications was the processes that produced the modern corporation and its interdependence with technological innovations (see 1919, 1934). This work clearly influenced the more orthodox Austrian economists (especially Joseph Schumpeter), but given his hostility to marginal utility, Veblen's views have had little impact on mainstream economics. For Veblen the demand for a particular good was not merely a function of rational market forces. Rather, it was a complex process often involving emotions and institutionally induced impulses. Hence, these processes could only be understood using historical and statistical analysis.

One scholar who took Veblen's admonitions quite seriously was W. C. Mitchell (1874–1948). Mitchell applied elaborate historical data to the investigation of a number of institutionally bound dynamics, such as the monetary system. Mitchell is best known for his work on *business cycles* (1913), and his detailed understandings of the interplay of social conventions and external forces became the basis for a number of direct governmental interventions into the macroeconomy just prior to the popularity of Keynesian economics. As the founding director of the National Bureau of Economic Research, Mitchell performed landmark empirical studies of capital formation and consumer credit. These were combined with his development of macroeconomic indices (e.g., the price index) to provide a benchmark for the era of modern economic policy.

Another institutionalist who combined scholarship with activism was John R. Commons (1862–1945). Commons became the father of labor economics, and his innovative studies of the jurisprudential system and the trade union movement provided the basis for social legislation in his native Wisconsin. His later studies of monetary problems led to his involvement in designing a major policy role for the Federal Reserve Board (via the *Strong Act of 1928*). His synthesis of law and economics and his concern for integral social dynamics not only expanded institutionalist tools and concepts, they provided the groundwork for a diverse array of studies of "collective action." In fact, it was Commons who defined "institutions" as "collective action in restraint, liberation, and expansion of individual action" (1961, 73). Moreover, he invented a version of institutional analysis that focused on"working rules." These rules convey what

> individuals *must* or *must not* do (compulsion or duty), what they *may* do without interference from other individuals (permission or liberty), what they *can* do with the aid of collective power (capacity or right), and what they *cannot* expect the collective power to do in their behalf (incapacity or exposure). (1968, 6)

While Commons's work has found a wide spectrum of applications, the more general tradition of institutional thought has languished somewhat. One would think that the model of clear minds and dirty hands would have burgeoned in an activist discipline such as economics; however, the pull of pure science set up a curious bifurcation between theory and practice. Hence, it was institutionalism's more arcane cousin, neoclassicism, that grew in power and influence over the past century. Despite the significant contributions of modern day institutionalists such as Ayres (1944), Galbraith (1973), and Boulding (1981), and even a Nobel prize for one, Gunnar Myrdal (1960), as an intellectual enterprise it has been relegated to the status of a second-class subculture.

Despite this status problem, the basic paradigm of institutional economics provides a useful guidepost en route to a more scientifically based approach to social inquiry. Jerry Petr (1984) describes the basic elements of institutionalist thought as follows:

- value sensitivity;
- process orientation;
- Deweyist instrumentalism;
- technologically focused;

- factually based;
- methodologically holistic; and
- support of democratic ideals. (8–10)

Essentially, institutionalism is concerned with a real world where habit and ritual are as important as reason in describing economic behavior. This behavior is primarily pragmatic (à la John Dewey; see Eldridge 1998) yet often experimental and/or merely mistaken about consequences. Nevertheless, it is self-correcting over time. This instrumentalism must constantly negotiate between the "ceremonial" and "technological" in order to secure "institutional progress," and this mediation of priced and unpriced values is more easily facilitated in "democratic" systems, according to institutionalists (see Gruchy 1987). Their commitment to evolution is exemplified in the name of their leading professional organization: the *Association of Evolutionary Economics.*

Despite certain attractive elements, institutionalism remains pretty much a tangent to mainstream economic thinking. In fact, to the extent that institutional thinking influences the larger discipline, it is more often than not of the neoinstitutional variety. *Neoinstitutionalism* represents the incorporation of a handful of behavioral and institutional elements into the neoclassical framework. While this work is interesting in its own right, it does not necessarily share the aims discussed earlier. Moreover, its applications have been narrowly defined. One hallmark of neoinstitutionalism is the idea of "transaction cost" (see Coase 1960; Williamson 1975, 1985). This notion that originated with Commons (1950) is used to explore how various hierarchies tend to displace markets and how legal institutions shape markets in the first place. Neoinstitutionalism generally has had more influence among economic historians (e.g., North 1990) and in sociology (especially the subfield of organization studies) than in mainstream economics.

Organizational and economic sociologists have also done the most in terms of restoring the original intent of the earlier institutionalist movement (see Granovetter 1985; March and Olsen 1989; Zukin and DiMaggio 1990; Perrow 1991; Powell and DiMaggio 1991). Richard Swedberg, Ulf Himmelstrand, and Göran Brulin (1990) draw key distinctions between the sociological view of economic activity and the reigning paradigm of neoclassical theory. Key distinctions include alternative views of actors, actions, time, and objectivity, as well as basic method. In essence, starting from the viewpoint of society rather than the transaction, economic sociology strives to develop a more holistic view of economic activity. It is not ideologically wedded to a particular set of institutions since it accepts Karl Polanyi's (1957) view that mechanisms, such as "the market," merely denote particular historical epochs.

A similar yet more orthodox tangent to neoclassicism is the so-called behavioral economics movement (for an excellent overview, see Eggertsen 1990). Its principal point of demarcation was Herbert Simon's work on "bounded rationality" (1957), which was eventually embraced by a range of economists and awarded their Nobel prize in 1978. In fact, a select group of economists and associated social scientists has made a career out of modifying neoclassical theory in a way that allows for rather extreme limitations on human reasoning (e.g., Heiner 1983; Hogarth and Reder 1985; Machina 1989). An excellent example is Richard Thaler's collection of these diverse modifications, appropriately entitled *Quasi-Rationality* (1991).

These modifications were driven and substantially augmented by the empirical research of psychologists (also called decision scientists) who focused on actual decisions under conditions of uncertainty and risk (see Kahneman, Slovic, and Tversky 1982). In a practical sense these observations establish a contextual view of decision dynamics. Schneider and Ingram describe these contextual elements in terms of the following heuristics.

1. Recognition: An opportunity for decision must arise, and the opportunity must come to the attention of a person before he or she is even aware that a decision situation exists.
2. Framing: Framing refers to the definition of the situation or problem confronting the individual. The way in which the problem is framed has substantial implications for the response.
3. Search: Search involves scrutiny of large stores of information stored in memory, or search for new information, to identify ideas or approaches to the problem.
4. Crafting: Crafting refers to the means/ends reasoning, simulations, and other strategies used to design a possible course of action.
5. Choice: The choice of a course of action may not be based upon selection from among alternatives but may involve choosing the only alternative identified.

Behavioral economists not only accept these decision parameters, they explore how these individual "anomalies" impact the aggregate outcomes within economic institutions (e.g., Frey and Eichenberger 1989). Yet, here again, some of the most insightful work on the nature of limited rationality has been done by noneconomists (note Cook and Levi 1990). Amartya Sen (1979) points out that the foundations of neoclassical theory lack sufficient structure to comment on much beyond the behavior of "rational fools." What apparently remains lacking is an effective operationalization of what Neil Smelzer and Talcott Parsons labeled *communal rationality* (see Smelzer 1978).

Some branches of economics (such as industrial organization), however, have added a more fluid or interactive type of rationality via *game theory*. Despite its protracted adoption, these cybernetic concepts might be credited with saving neoclassical economic theory from a number of its major conceptual limitations, especially those related to "multiperson competition problems." Game theory has been applied in situations involving strategies and bargaining in fields ranging from labor economics to industrial organization and "international trade" (see Gibbons 1992). In fact, the once obscure field of industrial organization (IO) economics moved to the cutting edge of microeconomic theory through its development of games (see Milgram and Roberts 1991; also note Kreps 1990). As suggested previously, the major theoretical element of games is the substitution of strategic or negotiated equilibrium for conventional general equilibrium (see Nash 1950). Starting with simple "prisoner's dilemma" type games, game theory has moved from static/complete information to dynamic/incomplete information and from single-period to multiperiod situations. Yet, the most interesting work involves assumptions about "learning" and/or "signaling," which goes on in the void between periods (for an overview see Gibbons 1992, chap. 4). These elaborate presumptions (about learning, communication, and coordination) often assume away a variety of institutional interactions, yet they at least allude to their importance. Ultimately, however, game theory, as applied by neoclassicists, is designed to simplify, formalize, and gloss over complex systemic interactions. According to Jack Hershleifer (1982) games also serve to reduce convoluted evolutionary phenomena to a set of discrete decision frames. While mathematically elegant, these characterizations can produce distortions. Charles Dyke (1988) notes that while game theory is useful in "converting bookkeeping dialectically to explanation," it has certain limitations when it comes to "evolutionary dynamics" (44–50). For example:

> evolutionarily important events could have the consequence of ending the competitive relationship between "players," rendering them oblivious to one another, or even landing them in positive mutuality. If, when, and where this occurs is clearly a matter for concrete research, not *a priori* theorizing. (50–51)

Since game theory forms a formal bridge between individual decisions and certain stylized settings, it may eventually span the gulf between institutional dynamics and rational choices. However, the most promising work in this regard is being done by complexity theorists, such as John Miller (see 1989), who uses genetic algorithms and elements from cellular automata to allow games to encompass various systemic patterns (e.g., "informational coevolutions"). One might readily note that this new strain of game theory gradually leaves the bounds of methodological individualism. Moreover, while these systemic elaborations are useful in characterizing the texture of choice, they still tend to blur many important institutional influences. Last, to the extent that these simplifications remain anchored in antiquated notions of evolution (largely Darwinian) they may find it increasingly difficult to accommodate the curious process dynamics of cultural change. In order to more nearly approximate these important variables, additional ecological elements are needed.

Societal Science?

If it were possible to aggregate the various elements of economic inquiry outlined in the preceding, the resulting socioeconomic mosaic would still lack a few critical conceptual elements. Foremost among these missing ecological elements is one that facilitates the integration of diverse societal motivation. This is not just a matter of "unpriced values." Rather, it relates to the residual effects of linking economic theory with "free market" ideology in such a way that economic activity is viewed in isolation from other integral societal processes. This isolation, often manifest via artificial distinction such as public versus private, is especially acute in the United States, where so many economics departments reside within business colleges. Such distinctions are less useful if one wants to fashion a science of society to which economists once aspired. Thorstein Veblen (1898) concluded that

> There is no neatly isolable range of cultural phenomena that can be rigorously set apart under the head of economic institutions, although a category of "economic institutions" may be of service as a convenient caption, comprising those institutions in which the economic interest most immediately and consistently finds expression, and which most immediately and with the least limitation are of an economic bearing. (77)

With specific regard to the social conventions known as corporations, it is well to note that it is impossible to remove business from a larger set of societal obligations. Sociologists Robert Bellah et al. (1985) quote business historian Alan Trachtenberg in this regard.

> The word [corporation] refers to any association of individuals bound together into a *corpus,* a body sharing a common purpose in a common name. In the past, that purpose had usually been communal or religious; boroughs, guilds, monasteries, and bishoprics were the earliest European manifestations of the corporation form. . . . It was assumed, as it is still in nonprofit corporations, that the incorporated body earned its charter by serving the public good. (289)

In sum, even if various economic institutions behaved in the mechanical ways that mainstream models depict, their actual meaning would still be a function of ecological forces. In essence, competitive markets result from a range of societal collaborations and conventions. From a nonlinear dynamics perspective, while certain institutions can certainly set up rather severe limit cycles, they are still subject to periodic oscillations. The business cycle itself is obviously one of these more radical, albeit constrained, swings of the pendulum out into social complexity. An ecological perspective, anchored in these new insights into complex systems, would pick up where earlier efforts at fashioning an integrative discipline left off. While less ambitious than the so-called social ecology movement of twenty years ago, it would have as its central focus the ecosystems that give rise to human institutions. It is well to note that when economists speak of "institutional arrangements" they imply everything from simple unwritten rules to multinational agreements and all of the organizational structures in between.

Origins of an Ecological Vision

Like so much of the current thinking about the complexity of social systems, an ecological viewpoint is hardly novel. It is, however, relatively unheralded. The basic concept of an *ecology* originally stems, of course, from the physical and biological studies of populations. These studies essentially focused on the relationship of plants and animals with their environments. Ecology was also a synonym for environmentalism during the 1960s, but this was often misleading. The basic aim of ecological studies generally was the integration of a range of disciplines focusing on critical interactions between species (including humans) and their environments. They identified various links, such as food chains and cyclical processes (e.g., the nitrogen cycle, the carbon cycle, and so on) that connect levels and sustain the entire system. The systems ideas were, in turn, quite mechanistic and homoeostatic. Thus, the idea of environmentalism came through the realization that humans introduced highly disruptive changes into these otherwise stable (self-regulating) processes.

When the term ecology began to appear on a more or less regular basis in social applications during the 1950s and 1960s, it already had multiple meanings. Even among the relatively mild-mannered devotees, *human ecology* with its origins in developmental anthropology (see Bennett 1993) produced wildly divergent connotations. At one level ecology was merely a synonym for "community" (see Hawley 1950, 1986); at the other extreme, it stood for either fierce environmentalism or crude biological determinism (and all sorts of combinations in between, note Smith 1971; Theobald 1972; Clapham 1981; Drucker 1993). This quest for the ecological underpinning of human systems produced a rich array of studies and spawned a number of unique transdisciplinary hybrids, including cultural geography, tribal studies, quality of life (QOL) research, ecofeminism, and branches within landscape architecture and environmental health.

From this wide range of human ecology offspring, it is perhaps the original work of Amos Hawley (1950, 1986) that most nearly resembles the meaning that this discussion seeks to develop. Moreover, this basic vision of communities (and firms) as primary mechanism of human adaptation and creativity can also be viewed through the lens of management theorist Peter Drucker (1993). Finally, a new ecological vision should also recognize antecedents in the *social ecology* perspectives of Emery and Trist (1973).

Besides developing intricate taxonomies of community interactions, Hawley's aim was to foster a new transdisciplinary field like the one arising between chemistry, biology, and zoology. In the social sciences, this type of intellectual cross-fertilization managed to thrive for a decade or so until it ran into a powerful countervailing emphasis on specialization in academic institutions. Systems of reward (tenure, promotion, etc.) militated against transdisciplinary effort. In a handful of universities autonomous departments evolved, but few survived later retrenchments. Furthermore virtually none of these departments were able to forge a truly new integrated discipline. Given their inherent transdisciplinarity and interest in interactions within "the firm," it may be that management studies will seize the ecology gauntlet. So contends Peter Drucker (1993). Drucker himself draws upon earlier ecological visions, "boasts old and distinguished lineage," and includes such luminary figures as himself, de Tocqueville, de Jourvenel, Toennis, and Simmel, as well as "institutional economists" (442). His life and work, while more practical than scientific, exhibit the essence of an ecological enterprise. Drucker studied the rise of the modern corporation as a social phenomenon and looked at management as a process for harnessing its societal potential (note 1954, 1959, 1971, 1985). He also studied the implications of larger societal changes upon the corporation (see 1993, 1994). He points out that

> there is one continuing theme, from my earliest to my latest book: the freedom, the dignity, the status of the person in modern society, the role and function of organization as instrument of human achievement, human growth and human fulfillment, and the need of the individual for both, society and community. (1993, 450)

Another hallmark of Drucker's "ecological vision" was the notion that the social scientist should strive to shape as well as understand societal change. He explains that

The next thing to say about the work of social ecologist is that he must aim at impact. His goal is not knowledge; it is right action. In that sense social ecology is a practice—as is medicine, or law, or for that matter the ecology of the physical universe. Its aim is to maintain the balance between continuity and conservation on the one hand, and change and innovation on the other. Its aim is to create a society in dynamic disequilibrium. Only such a society has stability and indeed has cohesion. (1993, 454)

Nowhere perhaps are these features better demonstrated than in the work of the late Eric Trist (1910–93). Trist's various writings, and particularly his coauthored book *Toward a Social Ecology* (Emery and Trist 1973), went a long way toward solidifying the elements of an ecological perspective. Trist was clearly a proponent of the "engagement" of social inquiry and society, yet he was no *social engineer*. His work emphasized broad-based participation. That is, he studied the actual involvement of diverse groups at the grassroots level and believed open participation was a vital feature of adaptive societies. From his early work on "self-directed work teams" in the mining industry to his studies of "sociotechnical systems" the emphasis was on the role of individuals in the design of their own systems (Emery and Trist 1973; Trist 1979). Participatory concepts such as "industrial democracy" and "quality of work life" were clarified through this research.

Trist's work was also highly contextual and focused on the necessity of "social networks" and other forms of collaboration (e.g., "interorganizational domains") as mechanisms of individual choice. The *contextual interdependencies* that interact between individuals and their environments combine with other key factors (e.g., "socioecological values") to present a complex *causal texture* (Emery and Trist 1973).

Trist and his colleague Fred Emery constructed a social appraisal that moves from "is" to "ought" by contrasting the "structural presence" with the "cultural absence" (Emery and Trist 1973). They suggest that values are only just beginning to catch up with structural adaptations emerging from "turbulent fields." Thus, assessments are needed

which enhance our capability to cope with the increased levels of complexity, interdependence and uncertainty that characterize the turbulent contemporary environment . . . communal rather than individualistic regarding access to amenities, cooperative rather than competitive regarding the use of scarce resources; yet personal rather than conforming regarding life styles and goals. (Emery and Trist 1973, 172–73)

Eric Trist is also best known, perhaps, for his advocacy of *adaptive planning,* and many misconstrue this to imply some type of centralized authority. Trist explicitly denied the ability of hierarchical or technocratic administrations to pursue the types of long-term learning processes required for resolving complex social dilemmas. He suggested that centralized planning was a product of a dying industrial age; it "represents closed-systems thinking, the machine theory of organizing, the maximization of power—everything which the encounter with higher levels of complexity and uncertainty has shown to be unworkable" (Emery and Trist 1973, 203). In the final analysis, Trist's primary contribution was his view that a true science of the human ecology cannot ignore the values that shape social evolution.

From Organizational to Institutional Ecology

It is worth noting in this historical review that many other scholars have laid claim to an ecological point of view. One particular set of scholars, while diverse, has been identified with a basic approach known as *organizational ecology* (e.g., Aldrich 1979; Hannan and Freeman 1989; Amburgey and Rao 1996). This approach is often interwoven with more general organizational sociology and/or institutional approaches, yet it shares a somewhat narrow view of organization evolution anchored in standard Darwinian ideas (e.g., mutation, selection, retention) and population dynamics. Essentially, the focus of this research is on "organizational foundings" and "mortality." Notions borrowed from population biology (e.g., fitfulness, size, density, resource dependency, etc.) are used to explore how firms and/or industries change over their entire life span (usually several decades). These perspectives are useful and generally speaking constitute a significant alternative to some of the simple economic approaches to organizational studies. However, being essentially taxonomical, it is limited in its understanding of process dynamics (especially of the nonlinear sort). As some might observe, organization ecology, given its glacial evolutionary model, is not really very well tuned to radical change and creativity. Therefore, while several specific studies are rich in insights, they are limited in scope and often tangential to the epistemic perspectives of Drucker and Trist. The basic organizational ecology approach has been substantially augmented by groups of sociologists seeking to blend it with various elements of the *neoinstitutional* approach. While their focus is still pretty much on formal organizations, their concern for environmental and behavioral contingencies and process dynamics is dramatically expanded. The new approach to organizational sociology is well represented, by W. Richard Scott and John Meyer (1994) and their colleagues at Stanford's Center for Organization Research (also see Perrow 1991). Their approach involves both formal theoretical and empirical work, and is generally exemplified by the following types of concerns.

- How the rules and structures "institutionalized" within the wider environment are reflected in the structures and "routines" of organizations.
- The extent to which organizations become dependent on the "patterning" within the wider environment, as opposed to "internal technical and functional logics," and level of "coupling" (à la Weick 1976, 1979).
- Which of these environmental patterns manifest themselves as "hardwired controls" or through "meaning systems"?
- The degree to which environmental patterns can be described as "rationalized" and "rationalizing."
- The level of isomorphism between the organization of society and a society of organizations.

The major contribution of this type of institutional analysis is a much richer picture of organizational rationality. Scott and Meyer explain:

> Our efforts here are to support a vision of cultural rationalization that is far from simply dependent on the interests and power of a few rational actors or groups in an a priori world. . . . [W]e think the most interesting and useful forms of institutional theory depend on showing the collective and cultural character of the development of institutional environments . . . central institutional effects entail not influences on actors but the creation of actors, not changes in incentives but transformations in meaning systems. (4–5)

Given the central role of organizations in societal ecosystems, this work is likely to be highly instrumental in the eventual movement toward a more complete set of ecological understandings. A more far-reaching framework of the ecology of institutions, which includes formal organizations, will probably by necessity involve a number of additional and in some cases alternative concepts and constructs.

Elements of an Institutional Ecology

A science of social systems would have institutions as one of its primary units of analysis. Recall that institutions can be any one of many patterns of human interaction ranging from informal rules to complex multiorganizational arrangements. While institutions are far from static, they are at least somewhat stable. As in quantum physics where relationships define reality, it is these semi-stable process conditions that exude influence over products. In other words, institutions can be assumed to exhibit substantially consistent patterns throughout a particular analysis. As Thorstein Veblen (1934) explains:

> The institutions are, in substance, prevalent habits of thought with respect to particular relations and particular functions of the individual and of the community; and the scheme of life, which is made up of the aggregate of institutions in force at a given time or at a given point in the development of any society, may, on the psychological side, be broadly characterized as a prevalent spiritual attitude or a prevalent theory of life. (190)

More importantly, the focus on institutions stands in stark contrast to the neoclassical emphasis on individuals. Individuals still have relative autonomy, "free will," and so forth, but they cannot be studied in isolation from their cultural settings. Again, Veblen provides a useful characterization of cultural context of behavior in his classic *The Place of Science in Modern Civilization* (1919).

> To any modern scientist interested in economic phenomena, the chain of cause and effect in which any given phase of human culture is involved, as well as the cumulative changes wrought in the fabric of human conduct itself by the habitual activity of mankind, are matters of more engrossing and more abiding interest than the method of inference by which an individual is presumed invariably to balance pleasure and pain under given conditions that are presumed to be normal and variable. (191)

Focusing on institutions brings several rather curious variables to an analysis of human behavior. Essentially, these involve multiple forms of rationality. Given these often deeply embedded informational and preferential parameters, choices are usually systemic. Even when highly hedonistic or atomistic motives are at work, human institutions usually involve collaborative processes. Finally, successful or performance enhancing outcomes are subject to a number of cognitive as well as collective constraints (e.g., ceremonial and/or bureaucratic).

Elements of an Institutional Ecology

Institutional Variables
  Multiple rationalities
  Systemic choices and synergism
  Collaborative processes and interdependence
  Societal dysfunctions and collective constraints

Evolutionary Dynamics
   Self-organizing systems
   Autopoiesis
   Resiliency
   Creative as well as adaptive learning

The ecological portion of an institutional ecology imposes a handful of additional constraints and opportunities. Obviously, the basic resource endowment is a critical variable. However, from this unique analytical perspective, it is not so much the environmental contingencies facing a particular system that are important but rather the processes through which the system faces them. The crux of ecological interaction becomes a set of critical *evolutionary dynamics*. While not identical, these dynamics are similar with those currently emerging from the study of complex nonlinear dynamical systems in the natural sciences. Among other things, these involve perpetual novelty, self-organization, creative as well as adaptive learning, and resiliency.

Institutional Variables

Multiple rationalities provide a useful way of looking at the mixture of motives that makes up individual as well as systemic choices. Perhaps the clearer depiction of the multiple types of rationality emerges from the work of Max Weber (1947). For Weber, rationality took a number of forms: "formal, practical, substantive, and theoretical" (see Kalberg 1980). *Formal rationality* is usually associated with his idealized version of bureaucracy and involves calculated efficiency, order, and regulation. *Practical rationality*, on the other hand, describes self-interested behavior and is most like the version of rationality made popular by neoclassical economic theory. *Substantive rationality* for Weber was a broader form of social rationality. It doesn't necessarily involve the means-ends calculus of either formal or practical rationalities. Rather, it provides a standard for orderly action through the application of value postulates. Kalberg (1980) explains that these value postulates imply "entire clusters of values that vary in comprehensiveness, internal consistency, and content" and they "may *not* be readily identifiable by their participants" (1155). *Theoretical rationality,* by contrast, involves more ethereal constructs that give "meaning to life events" but do *not* necessarily order action. However, when linked to ethical or "substantive rationality," it can influence behavior. In fact, it can be used to frame the various types of rationalities and/or make preconscious elements conscious. Obviously, the four types interact and combine, making any actual behavior a composite, yet for certain types of behaviors different elements will dominate. More importantly, the same behavior by different individuals may involve different combinations. In the context of multiple rationalities, individuals still choose rationally, but they may not necessarily be rational about (or even aware of) their choice of rationalities. Moreover, the presence of multiple and collective rationalities makes most choices more systemic than individualistic.

Systemic choice, as a conceptual foundation, is a natural outgrowth of the problem posed by multiple and composite rationalities. If individual choices are as muddled as a social-ecological perspective maintains, then modeling such choices becomes an intractable mess. However, if as the previous chapter suggested, economists and social scientists generally speaking are most often concerned with what James March labeled "systemic rationality" (1986) and merely assume that "calculated rationality" is the same thing, then one has the starting point for an entirely new set of models. Neoclassical reductionism sees all rationality in terms of Weber's pragmatic category. An ecological perspective on the other hand sees most rationality (even self-interested) as systemic. Recall that for March (149) *systemic rationality* involved "adaptive," "selective," and "posterior" types of reasoning. For purposes of simplification, one might think of these *learned rationalities* as a type of *systemic choice.* That is, they can be viewed as the *decisions that complex systems (of individuals within institutions) arrive at incrementally through adaptive and creative learning, under conditions of synergism.* Learning and adaptation can be both conscious and preconscious and involve all the various forms of Weberian rationality. However, normative simulations of choice would tend to simplify contextual parameters (particularly constraints associated with unrealistic belief systems) and ultimately lead to performance enhancement. Yet, it is entirely possible that certain ritualistic associations would through the course of multiple simulations exhibit robustness in coping with novel environmental conditions, as well.

It is important to reiterate that systemic choices are not necessarily devoid of individual agency and awareness. However, it is possible to imagine informational attractors of such intensity that myriad individual choices still tend to coalesce around a particular set of trajectories. This type of "entrainment" is especially relevant to various market clearing phenomena, identified as the core element in neoclassical economic theory. However, by focusing on the process by which individuals coevolve with their institutions, rather than autonomous, ahistorical decision points, even market dynamics could be better understood. To start, markets require several institutional mechanisms (e.g., the control of monopoly power) in order to work effectively. Furthermore, markets place informational and transactional requirements upon the individual that actually could not be met individually. Only through multiple iterations involving choices about rules and outcomes are information and transaction costs collectively incorporated. Hence, the choices cannot realistically be characterized as individual or even as merely aggregations of individual choices. Systemic choice is needed to conceptualize how individuals actually interact with the real world processes of aggregation. Even if individuals are not completely aware of their roles in collective choices, their free agency is more fully represented within these institutionally bounded forms of rationality than under assumptions of individual utility. For under the latter systems, maximizing behavior dictates a particular outcome. Hence, the agent is not really "free to choose" in the neoclassical model. Systemic choices, in their actual dynamics, range of possible combinations, and unpredictable outcomes, create many more "degrees of freedom" via synergistic interactions.

Synergism is a very simple concept with extremely important epistemological implications. Generally speaking, synergism refers to the process by which complex systems evolve, and the presence of this process makes it virtually impossible to predict the behavior of the system by looking at the parts separately. Synergism explains why certain alloys (e.g., chrome-nickel-steel) are much stronger than their constituent metals. As mentioned in chapter 2, the basic concept of synergism was originally fleshed out by Hermann Haken (founder of the Stuttgart School of Synergistics), for whom it was, among other things, the mechanism by which chaos is retransformed into order (see Haken 1978). The most elaborate conceptual development for social inquiry is Peter Corning's magnum opus, *The Synergism Hypothesis* (1983). For Corning, it represents the nexus of "progressive evolution" and the foundation for his own elaborate ecological approach. He admonishes:

> if we wish to explain an actual case of societal development, we must take the entire structure of human needs into account. A full explanation of how the sequential patterning of human choices, or teleonomic selections, occurs involves an examination of the dynamic interaction among a great many factors: climate, geography, resources, arable land, demography, technology, economic and sociopolitical organization, and, not least, interactions with other human populations. (14)

Here again, Corning's approach seems to bring an unyielding level of complexity to social inquiry. Fortunately, synergism also provides clues to nonreductionist simplification. In a technical sense, the study of synergism draws upon certain recent advances in *combinatorial mathematics*. Stated simply, this burgeoning field describes the dynamics by which each step produces multiple possible successors. Artificial intelligence systems are often expressly designed to avoid "combinatorial explosion," (where the number of possible steps rapidly rises toward infinity). For a number of complex problems, "synergistics" provide a shortcut through the complexity by isolating reordering dynamics. The focal points are those critical junctures where combinations produce *qualitative* as well as quantitative changes.

Collaborative processes and interdependency present a very different focus for social inquiry. Again, neoclassical theory assumes competitiveness between individuals, and even evolutionary alternatives often assume milder versions of social Darwinism (i.e., survival of the fittest). Institutional ecology, on the other hand, is primarily the story of cooperation. As Robert Axelrod (1984) demonstrated, even adversarial games (prisoner's dilemma), if repeated, evolve through reciprocity ("tit for tat") toward cooperation. In a larger context, Karen Monroe (1983) suggests that "altruism" is a type of "evolutionary rationality."

The level of cooperation within and between a given set of institutions evolves through a complex process of "collaboration" and "defection." Scholars who study these processes from a "computational" perspective (e.g., Glance and Huberman 1993) have already isolated "group size," "time and level of membership," and "amount of information" to explain the dynamics of particular "social dilemmas." Moreover, they describe these processes in terms of sudden shifts of alliance, or "outbreaks of cooperation" and "relative stability."

Societal evolution, obviously, involves collaboration at the macrolevel as well as the microlevel. August management scholars, the likes of Edward Deming (1993) and Peter Senge (1990), suggest that cooperative processes both at the level of the work team and between firms within a particular industry explain successful performance (also note Maccoby 1988). Economist Brian Arthur (1990) described the formation of multifirm networks as the basis of "increasing returns." Not only is "no man an island," but no firm can succeed solely because of competitive markets. "Building a better mousetrap" is still a key success factor; however, several individuals usually collaborate in the innovation, and multiple institutions must cooperate in paving and lighting "the path to one's door." Methods that illuminate these complex social interdependencies go well beyond existing organizational and industrial economics, not only because of the collective unit of analysis but because of the focus of synergistic dynamics.

From an ecological perspective, collaborative systems are more likely to emerge within highly *participatory institutional arrangements*. Moreover, in evolutionary terms, active and open participation enhances adaptive capabilities (note Emery and Trist 1973). As Ashby's (1956) famed "law of requisite variety" maintains, regulations and "error control" within complex systems required an equally robust set of channels (204–12). Political scientist Laurent Drobuzinskis (1987) maintains that these imperatives from cybernetics and self-organizing systems can be applied to a variety of sociopolitical situations. Furthermore, his definition of participation includes "markets" and "voluntary associations" and also direct legislative and bureaucratic involvement. For management theorist Ralph Stacey (1992) it is participation that sets up the necessary "dynamic tension" for self-organization within corporate structures. In fact, he maintains that "it is vital to sustain the paradox of simultaneous flexibility and control" (170). As Stacey suggests, currently popular "self-managing teams" are only partially concurrent with "self-organizing processes."

Sociologists who study multifirm alliances and network formation (e.g., Grabher 1993) describe a similar set of participatory tensions and dynamics. Furthermore, they emphasize the learning and adaptive capabilities that these multifirm systems engender. Grabher explains that

> Networks open access to various sources of information and thus offer a considerably broader learning interface than is the case with hierarchical firms. In allowing for ambiguity in the perceptions and orientations of the individual exchange partners, networks are particularly adept at generating new interpretations and innovations. (10)

Of course, networks can also collude to monopolize information and periodically delimit participation.

It is noteworthy that the selfsame processes that generate positive synergy can also exacerbate various *societal dysfunctions* and engender *collective constraints*. Besides the cognitive limitations that can contribute to aggregate suboptimality, various human imperfections can interact to create widespread societal dysfunctions, ranging from environmental maladaptations to bureaucratic pathologies and from monopoly to massive inhumanity (e.g., genocide). The growing emphasis on "neoinstitutionalism" and various *law and economics* studies suggest these possibilities but continue to characterize the processes in individualistic terms. From an institutional ecology perspective, it is the formation of collective constraints that becomes paramount. As Garrett Hardin (1968) observed, the tragedy of commons necessitated "collective coercion, collectively agreed upon." Moreover, while markets are often the answer to excesses of hierarchy (e.g., capricious bureaucracy), these markets, especially when they are reinstated, are the result of collective action and careful institutional maintenance.

Likewise, barriers to market entry are often maintained by institutions ranging from cliques to clubs and cults to cartels. While those economists who study industrial organization have identified some of these tendencies, their models generally neglect the evolutionary processes by which collusion and bureaucratization build up and break down. The rare exception is Mancur Olson's (1982) work on the long-term sociopolitical implications of his "logic of collective action." His sweeping overview speculates about the historical impact of certain "social rigidities" upon general economic well-being. For example, his speculations include, among others, the following.

- There will be no countries that attain symmetrical organization of all groups with a common interest and thereby attain optimal outcomes through comprehensive bargaining.
- Stable societies with unchanged boundaries tend to accumulate more collusion and organizations for collective action over time.
- On balance, special-interest organizations and collusion reduce efficiency and aggregate income in the societies in which they operate and make political life more divisive.
- The accumulation of distributional coalitions increases the complexity of regulation, the role of government, and the complexity of understandings and changes the direction of social evolution. (74)

In a similar fashion, organizational theorists Katz and Kahn (1968) hypothesized how "noncompetitive subsystems" will continue to be sanctioned and/or subsidized by the macrosystem (e.g., the nation) until it is overloaded. A nonlinear, dynamical-systems perspective reduces this "doom and gloom" perspective by adding the possibility for dramatic reversals of social misfortune (note Jantsch 1980, chap. 9).

Evolutionary Dynamics

Self-organizing systems set up powerful dialectical forces within processes of societal entropy, outlined in the previous section. Dissipative structures and self-organizing dynamics appear to operate at levels ranging from the genetic codes (Kauffman 1993) to international trade (Dosi and Soete 1988; Arthur 1990) to the biosphere (Lovelock 1979). In short, self-organization is a ubiquitous feature of evolutionary systems. This constitutes a majestic change in perspective. Prigogine and Allen (1982) maintain that the patterns of "metafluctuations" that arise in self-organizing systems *cut across* the commonly used measurements of change. They contend that, heretofore, change was thought of in one of the following three mutually exclusive fashions.

- The phenomenological approach, in which equations representing the average values of each macroscopic fluctuation are invented.
- The stochastic approach, where evolution is described as the probability of transition at a particular moment.
- The dynamic laws, which describe the microscopic properties of the systems, and where evolution is both deterministic and reversible. (3–5)

For them, the concept of self-organization reconciles these different approaches to change.

In the social sciences all three approaches have been utilized from time to time, and unique blends have even emerged. However, as suggested earlier, evolution in general is usually represented in a narrow Darwinian fashion with some sort of probabilistic potential for mutation. Of late, this simple sociobiological viewpoint has begun to give way to more complex synergistic formulations (e.g., Corning 1983; Rothschild 1990). Yet, not even these modified models of complex adaptation fully appreciate the role of self-organization in evolution. Erich Jantsch (1980) explains:

> Neither the old concept of a teleological (goal-seeking) evolution, nor its contemporary modification in the sense of a teleonomic evolution (goal-seeking via a systemic network of possible processes) corresponds to the new paradigm of self-organization. Evolution is basically open. It determines its own dynamics and direction. This dynamic unfolds in a systemic web which, in particular, is characterized by the co-evolution of macro and microsystems. (184)

While such an intrinsically fluid world may be quite a frightening prospect, it actually frees humans from misperceived inexorable forces. As Prigogine and Allen (1982) point out, Darwinian evolution merely replaces one benevolent impersonal deity with another. They elaborate that

> Darwin's ideas belong to the same phase of nineteenth-century thought as laissez faire economics—the doctrine that in a free-for-all competition the best will always win out anyway [by contrast]. . . . The evolution of complex systems . . . presents real choices and real freedoms. In consequence, we have the responsibility of trying to understand the dynamics of changes in order both to formulate realistic objectives and to discover which actions and decisions should be taken in order to move closer to them. (38)

At the institutional level self-organizing evolution generally manifests itself in *autopoietic processes*. Since equilibrium equates to stagnation and death, healthy and stable systems are not in equilibrium, they are constantly restructuring and renewing themselves. As Jantsch (1980) describes: "Autopoiesis is an expression of the fundamental complementarity of structure and function, that flexibility and plasticity due to dynamic relations, through which self-organization becomes possible" (10). It is autopoietic processes that give institutions a certain level of autonomy within their environments and often exhibit the preservational behaviors once associated with "systems persistence."

Autopoietic structures, even highly persistent ones, are eventually displaced by dissipative processes. Inherent *autocatalytic* dynamics amplify small fluctuations until the system reaches a critical instability threshold (or bifurcation point) and a new structure emerges. This is a *dissipative structure.* As alluded to previously, institutions usually conspire against these breakthrough events, but there inevitably is embedded within the very dynamics that give them the ability to live, grow, and evolve. For human systems, Erich Jantsch (1980) describes this process as follows.

> the principle of creative individuality wins over the collective principle in this innovative phase. The collective will always try to dampen the fluctuation and depending on the coupling of the subsystems, the life of the old structure may therefore be considerably prolonged. (10–11)

From a policy or practical management perspective (to be discussed further in later chapters), it is often this prolongation of structural stability that organizations wish to promote. However, self-organizing systems provide a unique set of perspectives on these preservational tendencies. The lessons are fourfold. *First and foremost,* the tide of change can never be stemmed completely. *Second,* the path of change cannot be predicted precisely, but "autopoietic memory" preserves a map of change amid "macroscopic indeterminacy." *Third,* if organizations really want to manage the change, they must begin to introduce change into the system. Studies on the "control of chaos" illustrate how dampening of a particular oscillation is brought about by introducing a countervailing oscillation. Trying to preserve a limit cycle that is evolving toward chaos cannot be achieved by merely introducing another limit cycle or fixed-point attractor. Moreover, and *fourth,* small changes are a better mechanism for managing change. Ali Çambel (1993) points out

> that in a chaotic system numerous unstable orbits exist, and one can stabilize the one most conducive to achieving a given system stability by imposing only a small stimulus. Nonchaotic systems are not sensitive to low-level stimuli. (216)

Hence, if one can begin to isolate the patterns of oscillation, one can begin to experiment with the design of small systems changes.

This final lesson is quite similar to those gleaned from inquiries into the nature of resilient systems (note Holling 1978). *Resiliency* is essentially the realization of Nietzche's famed dictum: "that which does not kill us makes us stronger." In nature, dynamic stability is maintained through the struggle for survival; if the level of struggle subsides, the system actually becomes less healthy (or "brittle"). Conventional economic "production functions" assume a static equilibrium devoid of these continuous disturbances, an imposition that in reality would mean certain demise to a living system. As C. S. Holling and William Clark (1973) described:

> Few systems have persisted that stay in equilibrium. Ones which are do not last, for all systems experience shocks and traumas over their period of existence. The ones which survive are explicitly those which have been able to absorb these stresses. They exhibit an internal resilience. Resilience in this sense determines how much disturbance—of kind, rate and intensity—a system can absorb before it shifts to a fundamentally different behavior. (247)

Holling and colleagues (1978) studied diverse natural systems including forests and fisheries and concluded that managed systems become increasingly "brittle" (less resilient) as managers strive to reestablish some sort of mythical equilibrium. By contrast, systems that are allowed to experience periodic shocks are likely to evolve into greater stability over time. The fact that these shocks can often exhibit fairly dramatic swings of population within a particular species had already been demonstrated in "predator-prey" studies (e.g., Peschel and Mende, 1986); however, it has only been recently that periodic oscillation has been generally associated with healthy systems. Institutional systems, however, generally conspire to avoid and/or ignore natural oscillations. The heart of any resilient system is what Donald Michael (1973) called *error-embracing* behavior, rather than the typical bureaucratic cover-up. In other words, "learning to plan" for a highly uncertain and turbulent world demands "planning to learn" and ultimately will entail creative as well as mere adaptive learning.

Creative learning is an extremely mysterious concept, despite the fact it is central to those processes that distinguish human systems from the rest of the natural world. Of late, learning has become a integral feature of microeconomic analysis, but this is merely a convenient assumption used to bolster preconceived calculations of strategic equilibrium. In essence, learning is the mechanism by which agents are inspired to choose the strategy that the model says they should. Of course, no real learning goes on since the games are completely predetermined. Research into organizational learning, on the other hand, has not been so matter-of-fact about the mechanism of learning and actually has striven to identify the various constraints and opportunities for collective adaptations. Still, creative learning is more than mere adaptation.

The original emphasis on learning in institutions can be traced back to the early studies of bureaucratic dysfunctions (Merton 1940; Crozier 1964; Meyer et al. 1985), the most damning of these being Crozier's characterization of bureaucracies as organizations that "cannot learn from their own mistakes." Nonetheless, the focus on how firms actually learn began with Cyert and

March's *A Behavioral Theory of the Firm* (1963). As Glynn, Miliken, and Lant (1992) point out, modern approaches to organizational learning can be divided into two distinct camps. The first, which they labeled the *adaptive-learning* approach, is represented by the Cyert and March tradition (1963) and is aimed primarily at adding behavioral richness to the basic neoclassical theory of the firm (see Levitt and March 1988). By contrast, the second school of thought is more of a *knowledge development* approach, aimed at issues of environmental turbulence and change.

The knowledge development approach is anchored in work of Chris Argyris (1976) and Donald Schon (Argyris and Schon 1978). They distinguished "single-loop learning" (simple problem solving) from "double-loop learning" (that which addresses underlying assumptions). They describe the second loop, with which many organizations have problems, as the one that "connects the detection of error not only to strategies and assumptions for effective performance, but the very norms which define effective performance" (22). Recently, Joup Swieringa and Andre Wierdsma (1992) have added a third loop that raises questions about the organization's very being (note 41–42). They also place greater emphasis on the interaction of individual and systemic learning and suggest their "triple loop" is a function of highly turbulent environments.

While the previously mentioned knowledge developers allude to the potential for creative learning, particularly in double and triple loops, it is best highlighted in Peter Senge's *Fifth Discipline* (1990). For Senge, creativity can play a role in all levels of organizational learning but is perhaps most important at the "generative" level, where individuals and organizations must converge upon the structures that simplify complex systems.

Of course, the exact nature of creativity is a matter of considerable debate. One form that these debates take is the human versus artificial intelligence controversy (note, e.g, Churchland 1990 vs. Searle 1992), but this merely distracts attention from the evolutionary significance and institutional implications of creativity. As Joseph Schumpeter (1934) pointed out, human creativity in the forms of innovations and entrepreneurship is the primary engine of capitalist economies. These "heroic individuals" are, in turn, institutionally bounded in such a way that creativity is actually a collective enterprise. Moreover, it is becoming increasingly clear that processes by which innovations emerge and take hold (particularly those of a technological variety) are best understood in terms of self-organizing systems (Dosi et al. 1988). Even the underlying mental processes by individual and collaborative action seem to be governed by similar dynamics (note deBono 1985; Guastello 1993). In sum, any model that characterizes learning as adaptive responses or merely trial-and-error processes ignores a vast reservoir of human potential in the form of breakthrough innovations.

From a purely process perspective, if the potential for innovation is dramatically enhanced through institutional interactions, then human creativity is substantially a matter of collective evolution. MIT's Steven Kim (1990, paraphased from 36) outlines the "factors of creativity" for organizations as follows.

- Critical attributes of a problem are the purposive aspect.
- The diversity factor is the association of previous objects.
- A creative solution might be a similarity or contrast between diverse elements.
- Ideation through imagery is a critical component.
- Externalization of an intermediate result facilitates feedback and incremental arrival at a solution.

While these factors appear here as fairly linear, in characterizing information processing activities, Kim invokes deBono's "lateral thinking" and includes iterative cycles. More importantly perhaps, Kim invokes the likes of Poincaré, Simon, and others to argue that creativity is a long-term evolutionary process, involving literally generations of individuals. In the PBS series on *The Creative Spirit* (Goleman, Kaufman, and Ray 1992), the evolution of creativity is described in self-organizing terminology: they suggest that

> whether creativity happens over millions of years in plants and animals, or whether it happens in a few minutes when a human being solves a problem it follows the same master plan. . . . In the first phase, after exploring all sorts of options, the system essentially invents itself. In the second, the system establishes a formal pattern based on what now works best. In the third phase, the living system has to break the boundaries of this established pattern in order to bring in what is new and continue to grow. (151)

From an ecological perspective, creativity not only thrives near the edge of chaos, it is as much a systemic process as it is a matter of individual genius. As a careful student of scientific creativity, F. David Peat (Bohm and Peat 1987; Briggs and Peat 1989) maintains the potential for novelty is embedded within systemic processes themselves. As he and Briggs explain:

> creativity can be pictured as circling around the problem or creative task, bifurcating to new planes of reference, returning to the old plane, branching to another plane and to planes that lie within planes. This . . . effort engenders a far-from-equilibrium flux that destabilizes the limit cycles of habitual thinking. It also couples and phase locks feedback among several planes of reference and begins to spontaneously product a self-organization. (194)

In order to release this natural wisdom of systemic processes, it might be prudent to periodically suspend a portion of individualized initiative and fuel collective creativity. Facilitating initial perturbations and allowing network incubations may be individual acts, but the processes they unleash are clearly systemic.

Concluding Ecological Observations

Ultimately if institutional ecology is going to become a major approach to applied social inquiry it will have to demonstrate prescriptive as well as descriptive integrity. In applied social research, scientists are constantly being asked to move from description to prescription, especially in the realms of business or public policy. It isn't enough to identify the complex confluence of elements that converges within a particular decision situation; one must identify tools that clarify, if not specify, a particular decision. Unfortunately, nonlinear dynamics do not necessarily yield simple "optimal solutions." Accounting for the complex institutional ecology is not like merely adding a sensitivity or similar analysis (e.g., decision trees, etc.) to a simple linear program (e.g., benefit-cost analysis). However, the normative applications are not hopeless. One can simulate the types of institutional learning and adaptations that emerge from "systemic choice" situations. Admittedly, *process* understandings do not readily yield *product* conclusions. However, computer models that include the decision heuristics associated with a variety of process dynamics could also be used to more readily approximate the range of options likely to emerge from a particular institutional configuration. In a sense this is quite similar to the approach proposed by Brian Arthur (1991) and John Holland (Holland and Miller 1991) to build models that simulate actual behavior "using artificial adaptive agents." These learning agents pursue rational strategies but under differing constraints or contextual parameters; hence, they often "meliorate" rather than optimize. Moreover, these calibrated decisions dynamics often produce "a threshold in discrimination among pay-offs below which humans may lock into sub-optimal choices" (Arthur 1991, 358). The greater the "perceptual difficulty" the less likely that human learning will adapt its way to a "standard economic equilibrium." Now this may seem obvious from a psychological point of view, but it is nonetheless insightful to economists. What makes this approach interesting to the institutional ecologist is that it would be possible to set up the experiment in such a way that the simulated trials serve as a decision aid. It sets up a process for learning about learning. That is, it would allow one to visualize how uncertainty is incrementally reduced, rather than merely being represented by a set of probabilities.

For economists, these adaptive algorithms would provide a much closer approximation of their "stylized" assumptions about learning and thus could be readily plugged back into their models of expected utility. As Holland and Miller (1991) explain, "adaptive agents" give economists an artificial "reality check." They elaborate:

> By executing these models on a computer we gain a double advantage: An experimental format allowing free exploration of system dynamics, with complete control of all conditions; and an opportunity to check the various unfolding behaviors for plausibility. (370)

Shifting environmental contingencies can be imposed on simulations or programmed into the systems of "emergent behaviors" via Holland's (1992) periodic process of "perpetual novelty."

For the institutional ecologist, this approach at least begins to admit that *systemic choices* are not necessarily identical to the strategic choices of individuals. What is missing from this approach, however, are the suboptimal patterns that may emerge from institutionalized rituals and/or the *super-optimal* alternatives that result from collective or individual creativity (e.g., a technological breakthrough). The former might be easily approximated by various bounds or constraints, yet they may exhibit a more profound drag on rationality allowed for in their processes of constant improvement programmed into adaptive algorithms. Meanwhile, the latter elements of creativity and innovation are much more difficult to calibrate. Elaborate "search algorithms" can capture some of the flavor of creativity through multiple trials, in the face of highly novel conditions. Moreover, the ability of these models to partially reinvent some of their own procedures introduces the appearance of "double-loop learning" (à la Argyris 1976). However, true flashes of novelty on the response side may involve "triple-loop learning," (see Swieringa and Wierdsma 1992), and computers may be ill equipped to question their own being. These issues of whether or not computer-generated behavior duplicates true human creativity are, of course, the primary source of disagreements over the nature of artificial intelligence and are unlikely to be resolved soon. Yet, for many an institutionalized decision setting the mere ability to learn from simulated mistakes when, at present, most organizations are unable to learn from real ones would certainly constitute a methodological advance. If breakthrough innovations require real rather than artificial agents, these tools might free them for this pursuit. As an employment advertisement at a large computer firm read: "looking for individuals with the real stuff to work on artificial intelligence." In sum, while these machine models are far from complete, their comparative richness and dynamism may ultimately allow them to spawn a new generation of decision support tools. When compared to existing linear programming (e.g., benefits vs. cost) and static-knowledge "expert systems," models derived from the ecological perspective described herein have much greater heuristic value.

CHAPTER 6

The Nexus of the New Praxis

An ecological perspective, enlivened by the insights of nonlinear science, provides a vital glimpse at the nexus of some of the more successful management innovations of recent years. In general, it explains why some institutions become increasingly brittle in the face of turbulent change and others maintain a level of resiliency. Specifically, it suggests clues regarding the underlying logic of Japanese innovations, such as *total quality management* and *continuous improvement*. Initially, an ecology of institutions illuminates and codifies some of the parochial wisdom of reflective practitioners. For instance, it lends credence to the notion that mastering change, especially of the discontinuous variety, does not entail constant novelty. Rather, it often relies on the processes of accumulation and coordination to create new vectors of opportunity. As Stuart Kauffman (1995, 216) illustrates with his notion of "Red Queen Chaos" (where one must keep running to stay in one place), continuous change is a very unhealthy peak along a "fitness landscape." The secret is to accept that institutions are designed to inherently dampen the forces of change while not ignoring that successful dampening often results in distorting and amplifying those selfsame forces. The poker game of *strategic management* is not merely a matter of knowing "when to hold 'em and when to fold 'em," but in recognizing that both strategies are part of the same process of renewal and evolution. Sometimes one just needs to "stay in the game" long enough for a winning hand to be dealt, and still other times it is necessary, although not sufficient, to speed up the shuffling and dealing. Meanwhile, the game can usually be strengthened by building up the betting (investments in information technology and quality production) and by expanding the number of players (density of networks). Like many games of chance, the randomness is prized yet seldom fully present. Nevertheless, the interplay of randomness and pattern create a world of expected surprises.

Culling Concepts of Change

Nonlinearity not only teaches the expectation of change, it recognizes that change is usually associated with increasing complexity. Thus, usable knowledge or *praxis* (the effective blend of theory and practice) involves not only an awareness of the basic dynamics, but also a catalog of contextual settings. While not always a substitute for personal experience, the observations and speculations embedded within the folklore of a given field are often useful, and this seems the case for management. Many of the lessons of nonlinearity are already intricately interwoven into the existing literature of management, especially some of the more impressionistic tomes. Collectively, these contemporary classics generally involve the anecdotal observations of senior scholars and/or practitioners. These reflective gestalt approaches often avoid myopic perspectives that arise from dogmatic attachment to the prevailing empiricism. In other words, while lacking in rigor, they often escape mortis. This "big picture" approach is a mixed blessing, however. Occasionally, elemental insights are gleaned from the nooks of sweeping generalizations and are reluctantly incorporated into more conventional inquiry. Yet, more often than not, when a set of observations strikes a familiar chord, it is incorporated, whole cloth, into the prevailing folk wisdom. Thus while various tracts such as *In Search of Excellence* (Peters and Waterman 1982), *The Changemasters* (Kanter 1983), *Intrapreneuring* (Pinchot 1985), *The Fifth Discipline* (Senge 1990), and *Total Quality Management* (Ross 1993) are influential in practice, they are rarely fully integrated into the theories that drive managerial research.

The Unconventional Wisdom

Over the last decade or so, a handful of the contemporary classics has engendered a new view of change. Historically, change, to the extent that it was dealt with at all, was generally a product of external forces. Relatively few dealt with change as the nonlinear interaction of internal and external processes. Fewer still realized that the dynamics of these processes are inherently discontinuous. While discontinuities were observed in the environment, this ebb and flow was rarely attributed to the patterns of organizational response. The following review is designed to be representative, not exhaustive, of those scholars who glimpsed this more complex nature of change.

Charles Hampden-Turner's (1990) best-seller is perhaps the most folksy of the prevailing folk wisdom on change. His observations are based upon his own executive level experience and extensive interviews with management personnel from widely diverse firms. The crux of his approach is the notion of "value reconciliation" through the process he calls *cybernetic learning*. Turner recognizes that paying careful attention to "feedback" makes management systems inherently nonlinear. He explains that

> While technical or formal rationality is linear, you reason, you act, you achieve accordingly; encompassing reason is circular and iterative. You probe, discover something interesting, reflect, cogitate, and probe again.

. . . This journey has a direction, toward an ever richer synthesis of values, toward mounting complexity, toward packages of knowledge more intensely and aesthetically organized. . . . (xiii)

In essence, turbulent environments demand a skillful "helmsman," one who can accommodate conflicting values while keeping an eye on the ultimate course. The course is oriented toward evolutionary viability rather than short-term profitability. Moreover, for Turner, true "helmsmanship" recognizes trade-offs between "economies of scale" and "economies of flexibility."

A complementary set of perspectives can be distilled from the much more detailed case analyses of C. R. Hinnings and Royston Greenwood (1990). Drawing upon the organizational design perspective (e.g., Galbraith 1975), they establish "archetypes" consisting of "ideas, beliefs, and values" that constrain change. Since these characterizations greatly enhance the picture of change in "capacities" they could be used to flesh out the notion of core competencies emerging from the "resource dependency" perspective. However, the gem of their conceptual explorations is the realization that "change and stability are two sides of the same coin" (191). Moreover, they conclude that something like an institutional ecology perspective is needed to fully understand organizational change. They indicate that because "the same pressures can produce different consequences," scholars must delve into the following factors.

1. It is the joint and interactive effects of external and internal pressures and the way in which these produce incompatibilities that matter.
2. These joint and interactive effects will differ according to the particular position of an organization at a particular point in time (history and institutional location).
3. Not only is the position of an organization important, but in understanding consequential change it is necessary to know in which direction it is currently moving. (202)

Another prime example of the collective wisdom is Peter Senge's *Fifth Discipline* (1990). Its primary focus is "organizational learning," which goes well beyond traditional characterizations of environmental adaptations and moves toward "generative learning." Senge sees this process as the crux of human creativity, innovation, and long-term evolution. His concept of ubiquitous change and organizational visioning also corresponds to recent developments in the sciences of nonlinear dynamical systems. Essentially, this view maintains that amid complex and often chaotic systems, individuals can still choose their own trajectories and learn how to bring them about. For Senge, the linchpin of this process of cybernetic self-wiring is the integrative capacity of "systems thinking."

Perhaps the most extensive representation of the parochial wisdom is W. Edwards Deming's (1993) collection of observations, published just before his death. Deming, who was originally trained in physics, is, of course, most famous for his work on quality management in Japan during the 1950s. This collection, from a long lifetime of experiences, has the rather ambitious title *The New Economics for Industry, Government, and Education*. The message, however, is quite elemental and eloquent. Essentially, Deming argues for a simple systemic view of the world in which nonhierarchical organizations emphasize greater cooperation and less competition (note particularly chaps. 3 and 4). In addition, he reiterates a number of well-known lessons about the inevitability of "variation." These lessons, which form the basis of his unique technique, tend to contradict various popular "quality-control" methods (e.g., zero defects, six sigma, etc.). What is perhaps more interesting is that Deming's approach can be retrofitted to demonstrate certain applications of "chaos theory" (e.g., Priesmeyer 1992). Stated simply, this approach strives to discover an organization's natural rhythms prior to establishing "upper and lower limits." As more of these simple notions are given theoretical and practical relevance, perhaps W. Edwards Deming's legacy will continue to grow.

The Zen of Japanese Management

A major addendum to Deming's legacy is the mirror that Japanese management philosophy holds up to the antiquated linear thinking of U.S. firms. The Japanese-management style was much admired yet misunderstood during the 1980s. Yet, like most management fads, admiration quickly faded, and during the 1990s it was mistakenly associated with certain failings in the greater Asian macroeconomic model. While obviously interrelated, state-level practices do not always correspond to corporate cultures. While somewhat beyond the scope of this current discussion, it is well to note that had the participatory proclivities of nonlinearity prevailed in both spheres, as well as in global financial networks, much of the economic dislocation accompanying the end of the millenium might have been averted. Moreover, the message regarding the ill-fated blend of near dynastic nepotism and free enterprise should not be lost on the rapidly developing or re-developing (e.g., former Soviet bloc) world alone. Constant vigilance toward the potential for "crony capitalism" is especially needed in the developed world, where corporate and governmental consolidations, amid the pressures of globalization, often breed corruption (see Korten 1995). However, these macro concerns need not divert complete attention from microdynamics. At this level, the operation of Japanese firms and industries are still instructive. They represent the embodiment of dynamical processes and thus hold the key to successfully implementing such techniques as total quality management (TQM). In short, these dynamics are the Zen of these various managerial innovations. Moreover, like the Zen version of Buddhism, this appreciation of internal dynamics is so subtle it is often completely overlooked in explanations of Japanese commercial prowess.

It is, of course, the tremendous postwar recovery of Japan that prompted academics to probe the nature of their business practices in the first place. Since 1955 their economy has led the world with an aggregate growth of ten percent per annum. Scholars who marveled at this miracle have attributed it to many factors, ranging from cultural values to governmental policies (e.g., Johnson 1982; Gresser 1984; Ouchi 1984). During the 1980s, "Japanese management" became the buzzword in corporate circles. William Ouchi (1981) labeled it *Theory Z,* indicating how it fit into neither of McGregor's (1960) famed categories of management styles (i.e., X = mechanical and Y = humanistic). Ouchi (1984) describes how the strong corporate cultures in Japan, with their lifetime employment and emphasis on human capital enhancement, combined with visionary leadership to explain commercial success. "The type Z organization succeeds largely because its culture offers employees a stable social setting in which to get their bearings and draw support to cope with and to build the other parts of their lives" (197). Others focus on the ruthless tactics of modern day samurai, the advantage of integrated banking and trading combines (*keiretsu*), and the central focus on growth and global markets (see Abegglen and Stalk 1985; cf. Imai 1986) to explain Japanese success. Still others focus on the role of MITI (the Ministry of International Trade and Industry) and other governmental institutions (Johnson 1982). However, these various views of Japanese management practices and/or public policies may be missing the real essence of the Japanese experience. Japanese expert Ian McMillan (1985) explains:

> Much of the foreign interpretation of Japanese management is either one sided—with more recent emphasis on success factors—or one dimensional . . . training and employment practices are treated in isolation from the hardware or technology issues. . . . [Also] firm level types of factors—human resource strategies or marketing issues—are isolated from broader industrial goals and public policies. (16–17)

In essence, a gestalt or systemic view of Japanese management gives a much clearer picture of the nature of their successful strategies. Obviously, cultural and political disparities between the United States and Japan make a difference. The fact that the Japanese universities produce approximately ten engineers for every lawyer, and in the United States the ratio is exactly the opposite, probably has an impact. For example the Japanese prowess in process engineering probably results from the synergy of workforce and reward systems. Generally speaking, a comparison of U.S. and Japanese high-tech industries yielded items quite similar to Erich Trist's comparison of old and new sociotechnical paradigms (see Brown and Daneke 1990). That is, Japanese firms exhibit patterns congruent with the normative implications (see table 5) of "sociotechnical systems theory" (SST). In a recent article Charles Manz and Greg Stewart (1997) contend that a blend of perspectives from STS (à la Emery and Trist 1973) and TQM should be highly instrumental in addressing the apparently conflicting demands for "stability and flexibility."

At work in the Japanese firm (or any firm for that matter) are many nonlinear processes, and it is their awareness and nurturing of these processes that explain much of their relative vitality. Most prominent among these are the "experience curve" and "network externalities." U.S. economists and management specialists have been aware of these processes (Hirschman 1984; Katz and Shapiro 1985; Arthur 1983), yet their overall importance has been somewhat overlooked. The *experience or learning curve* describes the simple yet powerful phenomena of performance improvements that accumulate as a result of experience. For example, unit cost reductions take place that are not only the result of increasing labor productivity but occur across all cost categories (e.g., overhead, marketing, etc.). In essence, experience cascades and collides to create learning throughout the organization, and this learning is reflected in real cost reductions over time. Studies of the experience curve have demonstrated 10 to 30 percent cost reductions across a range of industries per experience doublings (Conley 1970,

TABLE 5. Management Styles

United States (Old Paradigm)	Japan (New Paradigm)
Focus on technical efficiency	Focus on sociotechnical joint optimization
People as extensions of machines	People and machines as complementary
People as expendable	People as a resource
Maximum task breakdown, simple narrow skills	Optimum task grouping, multiple broad skills
External controls (supervisors, specialist staff, procedures)	Internal controls (self-regulating subsystems)
Tall organization chart, autocratic style	Flat organization chart, participatory
Competition	Collaboration
Company's purposes only	Employee's and society's purposes
Alienation	Commitment
Low risk-taking	Innovation

Source: Derived from Brown and Daneke 1990.

8). Essentially, the experience curve is a primary example of "increasing returns," a fact that flies in the face of traditional economic theories (i.e., "the law of diminishing returns"). *Network externalities* is the term economists use, which implies that these extramarket phenomena are somehow aberrations. In reality, they are quite ubiquitous (note Maruyama 1982; Arthur 1988; for a nontechnical discourse see Arthur 1990). Feedback within these networks often generates signals that completely contradict the logic of the market. As Brian Arthur (1988) observed, these networks can cause "lock in" and allow an inferior technology to gain a predominant position. As Magorah Maruyama (1982) points out, these processes of "deviation amplifying, mutual causality" are quite common in nature. In the institutional world, these industrial cascades may or may not entail chaotic attractors, yet the dynamics can still be quite dramatic. With or without the exact labels, Japanese managers seem to appreciate these nonlinear processes and network dynamics. Through their *keiretsu* they use integrated networks of banks, suppliers, distributors, and downstream users to dampen shocks and accelerate movement along the experience curve.

Japanese firms also appear to make use of these network dynamics at the internal organizational level. They recognize, along with Ralph Stacey (1992), that "self-organizing networks operate in conflict with and are constrained by hierarchy" (184). They make use of networks within (i.e., self-managing teams) and an emphasis on continuous learning to produce the environment of "Kaizen" or constant improvement. As Masaaki Imai (1986) explains:

> Kaizen strategy is the single most important concept in Japanese manage-
> ment—the key to Japanese competitive success. . . . Both labor and man-
> agement speak of the Kaizen in industrial relations. In business, the concept
> of Kaizen is so deeply ingrained in the minds of both managers and workers
> that they often do not even realize that they are thinking Kaizen. (A10)

By focusing on continuous learning and improvements, Japanese firms embody change. Their acceptance of a Heraclitian world of constant adaptation is manifest in their flexible ("just-in-time") manufacturing. Moreover, their strategic management systems are designed to increase adaptability. They don't try to "outguess" the future, they prepare for change, and in this way they create their own futures. As Ilan Vertinsky (1987) maintains, Japanese strategy exhibits a bias toward "resiliency" (à la Holling 1973), and this, in turn, reflects various cultural values regarding the nature of "uncertainty." He explains that, in Western thought, there is an emphasis on certainty, thus

> there is a tendency to rely on prediction . . . and language habits . . . [that]
> promote confusions between certainty and belief. . . . In contrast, Japan's
> culture emphasizes harmony and tolerance of contradiction. Its language

permits or even encourages ambiguity. Thus the duality of management based on prediction and the quest for resilience may survive the threat of overconfident but uncertain knowledge. (156)

While managers from other cultures, especially the United States, may find it difficult to duplicate the Japanese mind-set, ecological analysis may make their institutions less inscrutable. For example, Ikujiro Nonaka (1988) applies the idea of "self-organization" to explain the strategy choices of Japanese firms. Furthermore, he (Nonaka 1990) invokes notions from earlier cybernetics theory, specifically "requisite variety" (see Ashby 1956), to explain how such firms use "redundancy" as an adaptive strategy. Like the requirement of multiple receptors in order to filter noise from a turbulent signal, reserve resources make required changes less onerous. By often having excess managerial capacity, Japanese firms are much more capable of redirecting activity as novel circumstances arise. However these built-in sources of adaptive capability are usually identified as a potential shortcoming by Western academics and consultants, especially in light of the declining performance of the Japanese economy during the mid-1990s.

While faddish trends such as "reengineering," (Hammer 1990) were sweeping over U.S. boardrooms and classrooms, the apparent sluggishness of Japanese recovery was being blamed on the selfsame factors previously identified as strengths. For example, Jim Champy (Champy and Nohria 1996) contends that Japan is "endangered by the past." In other words, items such as "lifetime employment" and the reluctance of Japanese managers to computerize their own offices are identified as fatal flaws. From an ecological perspective, these rather minor instances of Japanese managerial recalcitrance are unlikely to exact a fatal toll. Japanese reluctance to follow fads may prove a blessing in the long run. Moreover, in broader context, these various short-term profiting schemes popular in the United States may well be a throwback to a bygone era of industrial organization. Economic globalization has actually made the "management model of industrial organization" obsolete (see Hearn 1988). Japan has represented a far more organic organization model. The Japanese system—with its wide-ranging information and learning networks—has weathered numerous evolutionary crises since the turn of the nineteenth century. Blessed neither with natural resources nor success in war, Japan has managed to adapt to continuing global resource and technological crises because it was not wedded to outmoded processes of markets or hierarchies (Aoki and Dore 1994). Only time will tell whether Japan constitutes the industrial organization of the future; however, from an ecological perspective, it already provides valuable lessons regarding the institutional dynamics of change.

Strategic Management Systems

The primary vehicle for coping with change forces at the firm or agency level is *strategic management*. Once called planning or policy, the field of strategic management as an item in business (and recently public) administration curriculum has experienced an unprecedented level of growth and intellectual transformation in recent years. A few decades ago in the era of U.S. market hegemony, *marketing* was all the rage, and the art of packaging and advertising was not limited to products but included political leaders, and so forth. During the era of "junk bonds" and "corporate raiders," *finance* became the reigning subfield, and all the top MBAs wanted to be investment bankers. Similarly, demand for courses in strategy began in an era in which corporate long-range planning was the watchword. Interest was even sustained during an era in which planning was largely discredited. Hence, over the last thirty years, corporate strategy grew from one section in a general management course to a complete course, to a capstone seminar, to multiple courses, to entire academic units. Most business schools still cannot afford the luxury of a separate department of strategic management, but in many places it has at least been added to multipurpose departmental names.

The Evolution in the Field

As a distinct field of inquiry, strategic management has noticeable origins in the systems thinking of the early 1960s. Prior to this it was merely a somewhat specialized corporate activity becoming increasingly important as conventional budgeting and control techniques were expanded beyond the customary single-year format, through the use of five-year projections. In the late 1940s, von Neuman and Morgenstern introduced the idea of strategic "reacting" (see Bracker 1980) to more immediate changes in business conditions. Peter Drucker (1959) introduced the modern version of business planning, distinguishing between forecasting and planning and emphasizing creative dimensions of the latter. In the early 1960s, Alfred D. Chandler (1962), a business historian, developed vital perspectives on the centrality of goal formulation and coined the observation that "structure follows strategy." Ansoff (1979) and Ackoff (1981) combined these observations with those of applied general systems theory to codify what is commonly thought of as the standard normative model of strategic planning.

By the 1980s, increasingly turbulent environments, including accelerating cycles of recession, precipitated a radical reassessment of planning practices, especially those that relied on mathematically sophisticated prognostications.

Business Week (1984) reported that "Clearly, the quantitative, formula-matrix approaches to strategic planning . . . are out of favor" (63). However, by this time strategy development in mature firms had evolved beyond mere strategic planning to strategic management. Hax and Majluf (1984) described the evolution of strategic planning as involving five distinctive epochs: budgeting and financial control, long-range planning, business policy, corporate strategic planning, and strategic management. By strategic management, they implied a more fully integrated rather than isolated activity. Meanwhile, "strategic management" as a distinct field of study began to develop rigorous empirical studies. The development of a large-scale database coincides with this emergence (e.g., PIMS; see Buzzel and Gale 1987). Yet, as with applied social research generally, the pell-mell pursuit of more rigorous methodologies (i.e., quantitative) created curious conceptual deficiencies. Those who were defining the field back in the 1970s decried the lack of conceptual development (note Schendel and Hoffer 1979), and in a more recent reassessment, Schendel and Cool (1988) concluded that "there still is no central organizing paradigm for the field" (27). Therefore, viable theoretical building blocks and important empirical insights often became isolated.

Concern with this malaise of atheoretical empiricism caused a "back to basics" movement of sorts in which scholars focused on midrange theories (note Barney 1989; Burgelman 1988; Mintzberg 1990; Venkatraman 1990), yet these formulations have proved difficult to integrate into an alternative paradigm. In addition, the ever-popular quantitative studies of the often weak relationship between planning and performance continued to cast a practical cloud over the entire enterprise (Christensen and Montgomery 1981; Montgomery and Singh 1984; Reed and Luftman 1986; Laverty 1989; Hart and Banbury 1992). The sheer amount and respectable rigor of this work aside, the cumulative impact has been very disappointing. Daft and Buenger (1990) contend that much of the collective knowledge of strategic management is simply irrelevant (also note Beer 1992). Bettis (1991) invokes Daft and Lewin's (1990) "straitjacket" indictment of organizational science generally to describe the field. That is to say, strategic management became constrained by its own preoccupation with inductive methods.

As in other branches of management, economists rushed in to fill the theoretical void and fashioned a new deductive approach to strategic management in the late 1970s to mid-1980s, Rumelt, Schendel, and Teece (1994) offer the following reasons for the rise of economic approaches.

- The interpretive power of economics with regard to mounting bodies of data;

- The importance of the "experience curve" to increasingly diversified firms;
- The problem of "profit persistence" in increasing competitive global markets;
- The constant conceptual evolution, embracing various neoinstitutional and behavioral elements (e.g., transaction costs, agency, and game theories); and
- The increasingly academic (e.g., disciplinary) atmosphere within business schools. (paraphrased from 527–55)

Nowhere perhaps were these trends more profoundly exhibited than in the overwhelming popularity of Harvard professor Michael Porter's (1980, 1985) so-called competitive advantage approach. He capitalized upon the shifting emphasis within "industrial organization" (IO) economics during the rise of global competitiveness (see Shapiro 1987). IO had previously focused on limiting monopoly, but via Porter and others (e.g., Rumelt 1974; Hatten and Schendel 1977; Spence 1977; Caves 1980), it began to focus on viable firm strategies within oligopoly. Unlike the conventional normative approaches of the time, which emphasized consistency between internal and external forces such as (a) company strengths and weaknesses, (b) implementor values, (c) environmental threats and opportunities, and (d) broader societal expectations, Porter introduced elements of industry structure. Moreover, he emphasized "five forces" of competition within an industry. These include (Porter 1980)

- bargaining power of suppliers;
- barriers to entry;
- threat of substitution;
- bargaining power of buyers; and
- rivalry among existing firms. (4)

Strategies derived from this analysis strived for a "defendable position" against the competitive forces. Generally, this involved either "cost leadership," "differentiation," or "focus."

Porter's initial perspectives were substantially added to by work on "sustainable advantage" (e.g., Ghemawat 1985, 1991) and various efforts to extend the *resource-based* perspective (e.g., Barney 1989; Grant and Boardman 1990; Peteraf 1991), Furthermore, new "transaction cost" and "information-based" theories produced many interesting insights into the nature of strategic choice as well as organizational behavior generally (see Eisenhardt 1989). Meanwhile, the notion of "core competency" was expanded to incorporate these extensions of microeconomic logic (see Prahalad and Hamel 1990). Yet to the extent that the new strategic management remained rooted in the old economics (e.g., neoclassical theory), perspectives were still limited. David Teece (1984) noted fundamental tensions between orthodox economics and the field of strategic management. These included

- "treatment of know-how";
- emphasis on comparative statistics and "focus on equilibrium";
- suppression of entrepreneurship;
- use of stylized markets; and
- assumptions about rational behavior. (80–81)

By the 1990s, continuing concerns regarding the conceptual integrity of various economic approaches set in motion a gradual return to more systemic types of analysis. Initially, this involved attempts to expand the behavioral and institutional elements. For example, Raphael Amit and Paul Shoemaker (1990) began building a new conceptual base drawing upon ingredients from such far-flung corners as traditional institutional economics (e.g., Schumpeter 1934), and "decision theory" (e.g., Kahneman et al. 1982). They recognize that empirical studies of "key success factors" are, at best, "ex post" explanations of a firm's past and perhaps fortuitous (rather than strategic) performance. Meanwhile, "ex ante" models say very little about the "dimensions of competition" that are likely to prevail in the future. The missing links obviously involve "uncertainty," "complexity," and "organizational conflicts," as well as required "competencies." Along similar lines, Jeffrey Williams's (1992) extension of *sustainable advantage* (e.g., Rotemberg and Saloner 1990) represents a significant theoretical departure. He took the conventional *resource-based* and *core capability* notions into fairly uncharted realms by directing attention to various "fast-cycle resource" domains (e.g., high-tech industries) where "intense rivalry" and "Schumpeterian dynamics" require "frame-breaking" strategies (i.e., ones that change the basic rules of the game).

Perhaps the most significant advance in the economics of strategy in recent years has been the rejuvenation of game theory by Adam Brandenburger and Barry Nalebuff (1996). Their contribution, which they label *co-opetition,* applies gaming simulations to illustrate those practical business situations where cooperative discretion is the better part of valor. The actors in the games include customers and competitors in an industrial ecology seeking win/win solutions. As James Moore (1996) suggests in his own bioecological observations on the current business era, the new environment heralds *The Death of Competition.* As noted earlier (see chap. 3), this emphasis on cooperation amid a resurgence of interest in game theory opens the door for nonlinear tools and strategies.

From Old to New Systems Perspectives

Apparently, all during the reign of the economics approaches, various systemic elements were continually creeping in. While many of these elements were derived from earlier mechanical systems formulations, a handful anticipated a more ecological or living systems perspective. In some cases, attempts at retrieving old systems theoretics laid the groundwork for these new systems concepts. For example, concepts such as "purposive design," "adaptive planning," and "strategic innovation" came directly out of the work of earlier systems theorists (see Emery and Trist 1965; Ackoff 1970; Catanese and Steiss 1970). Ashmos and Huber (1987) outlined many misconceptions about the basic research paradigm of general systems and identified "missed opportunities" for enhanced organizational understanding. They also described how systems thinking could be enhanced through recent advances in organization theory. More important, they concluded that such a revised systems paradigm would be especially instrumental in studies of "organizational change" and "strategic choice." A similar conclusion was reached by Igor Ansoff (1987), who alludes to an evolutionary systems paradigm as a means of integrating diverse empirical observations about "strategic behavior."

Since various *advanced systems* concepts (i.e., nonlinear dynamics) have been around for some time, it is not surprising that a few of their elements filtered into management studies even as they were just gradually taking hold in the sciences. These early applications, while incomplete, provide a number of useful insights into the nature of complex strategic change. One early innovator, whom students of management theory would expect to find in the forefront of this as well as other movements, is Gareth Morgan. The crux of Morgan's work in this area is his assertion of a new logic for the evolution of complex systems that he calls *systemic wisdom*. However, this contribution might have been lost in his overall critique of conventional approaches to corporate strategy. He correctly identifies how a couple of the dynamics isolated by modern cyberneticians wreak havoc upon traditional linear planning devices still popular in some corporate circles. Morgan wants students of strategy to take note of Maruyama's (see 1982) speculations about "deviation amplifying mutual causal processes." This positive feedback may, according to Morgan, cause certain strategic adaptations that actually increase the level of turbulence. Interestingly enough, Maruyama's own translation of these notions for corporate strategists (1982) does not lead him to completely despair of the possibility of purposeful policy. Kenyon De Greene's (1982) evocation of C. S. Holling's work on "resiliency" (1978) also supports the prospects of adaptive management. De Greene suggests that it is advisable to design "safe-fail" (rather than fail-safe) systems that build up the firm against large-scale shocks by creating a series of small shocks

(334–35). Gemmill and Smith (1985) also used the logic of "dissipative structures" to illustrate how firms can create new internal configurations in response to environmental turbulence. They argue for processes of adaptive response akin to "symmetry breaking" dynamics exhibited for a vast array of natural and artificial phenomena.

Of late a few scholars have even brought recent advances in nonlinear science to bear in strategic management, albeit in a fairly metaphorical fashion. For example, Ralph Stacey (1995) describes this contribution in the following fashion.

> The two perspectives of strategy process most firmly established in the literature. . . assume the same about system dynamics: negative feedback processes driving successful systems (individual organizations or populations or organizations) towards predictable equilibrium states of adaptation to the environment. This paper proposes a third perspective, that of complex adaptive systems. The framework is provided by the modern science of complexity: the study of nonlinear and network feedback systems, incorporating theories of chaos, artificial life, self-organization and emergent order. Here system dynamics are characterized by positive and negative feedback as systems coevolve far from equilibrium, in a self-organizing manner, toward unpredictable long-term outcomes. (447)

In his earlier work (1992), Stacey describes the critical elements of the strategic thinking required for a nonlinear world. These include

- . . . toward a concern with the effects of the personalities, group dynamics, and learning behaviors of managers in groups;
- . . . toward the creative instability of contention and dialogue. . . ;
- . . . toward examining, understanding, and dealing with organizational defense mechanisms and game playing;
- . . . toward an understanding of group learning as a complex process of continually questioning how people are learning;
- . . . toward the opening up of contentious and ambiguous issues;
- . . . toward developing new mental models to design actions for each new strategic situation. (120–21)

Stacey's more recent work (1996) takes these observations one step further and uses complexity theory to explore the origins of organizational creativity. Collectively, his work provides a provocative guide for future research on the part of strategic management scholars.

Organizing for Self-Organization

Strategizing of the ecological type might be easy for academics armed with hours of adaptive simulations. However, the amount of learning required for the typical firm to master its own unique change dynamics is daunting, to say the least. Organizations, particularly highly bureaucratic ones, are unique in their inability to learn. Nonetheless, learn they must, especially as the pace of change continues to quicken. The study of learning within organizations provides many clues for improved pedagogy, albeit often much more descriptive than prescriptive. If one reviews the literature of learning one would probably be struck by the vast impediments to the processing of collective experience. Fortunately, a better understanding of these basic processes illuminates a number of escapes from cycles of trial and error, as well as error and error. As Peter Senge (1990) maintains, the art and practice of organizational learning are greatly enhanced through the development of a systems perspective. For him, systems thinking is the *Fifth Discipline* of learning, the one that integrates all the other "learning disciplines" (i.e., personal mastery, mental models, shared vision, and team learning).

Learning of the sort envisioned by Senge is only represented in a handful of actual managerial technique or traditions. One in particular that has been an icon in recent years is total quality management (TQM). This is not to say that all examples of TQM involve organizational learning of a systemic variety. It merely implies that organizations that pay more than lip service to the notion of "continuous improvement" also tend to embody learning processes of a more advanced sort. For these relatively rare organizations, TQM represents a minor managerial revolution. In a sense, TQM is a technique ahead of its time. With its emphasis on enhanced information flow and incremental change dynamics, it might be descriptive of the very nonlinear dynamics now found in normative theories of organizational learning.

The Learning Organization

To start with, the basic notion of organizations that learn is somewhat alien to those social scientists who adhere to strict notions of methodological individualism and rational choice (discussed earlier). As anthropologist Mary Douglas maintains (1986), the reductionist view of collective action is very delimiting, especially when learning is the issue. She contends that institutions (including formal organizations) can think and usually in ways that make the whole greater or lesser than the sum of individual thinking. She explains: "For better or worse, individuals really do share their thoughts and they do to some extent harmonize their preferences, and they have no other way to make the decisions except within the scope of institutions they build" (128). While thinking is not necessarily the same as learning, organizations are indeed capable of collective adaptations, and a few may even engage in creative coevolution with their environments.

Once again, studies of organizational learning, while often quite diverse, usually fall within the parameters of either of the two distinct approaches (see table 6). The first approach, derived from *behavioral or neoinstitutional economics,* is concerned primarily with describing how organizations achieve *adaptive responses* (see Levitt and March 1988). The second, with origins in *organizational development,* traces the patterns of *knowledge development,* with an aim toward prescribing cognitive processes (note Argyris and Schon 1978). While clearly unique approaches, the results of these studies are not nearly as mutually exclusive as one might think. Systemic understanding, while not completely reconciling them, can draw insights from both traditions.

Recall that behavioral economics was designed to clarify the various contextual elements that "bound rationality" and buffet the microeconomic theory of the firm (Cyert and March 1963). With specific reference to learning, this approach seeks to understand and capture mathematically the experiential nature of organizations. This approach assumes that the behavior of individuals within organizations is mostly a matter of routine; hence, contrary to much of neoclassical economics, behavior is history dependent and independent of individual memory. Barbara Levitt and James G. March (1988) elaborate: "Routines include forms, procedures, strategies, conventions . . . also the structure of beliefs, frameworks, paradigms, cultures that buttress, elaborate and contradict the formal routines" (320). According to this approach, learning is essentially a matter of "trial and error." Successful behaviors are repeated; unsuccessful ones are avoided. Learning and change both go on incrementally with organizational goals periodically adapted in response to experience. By

TABLE 6. Approaches to Organizational Learning

Theoretical Tradition	Behavioral Economics	Organizational Development
Focus	Changes in organizational routines, goals, and structures	Changes in knowledge structures and causal patterns
Unit of analysis	Collection of individuals with simple goals, search rules, levels of conflicts	Processes of belief systems formation and associated dynamics
Method	Formal models	Case studies
Examples	Herriott, Levinthal and March 1985; Levitt and March 1988	Argyris and Schon 1978; Swieringa and Wierdsma 1992

contrast, organizational norms are not usually the objects of change. Furthermore, the environment is usually portrayed as stable, although experiencing some gradual fluctuation.

By definition, this approach is *not* oriented toward turbulent environments, yet its formalization of various "standard operating procedures" provides contextual richness for the models that eventually will be. Writing for economists, Herriott, Levinthal, and March (1985) describe a world in which learning does *not* always lead to optimal choices, and where "fined tuned allocations" at equilibria are *not* reliably better than "rougher-tuned adjustments" (227). More importantly, they suggest that by introducing "modest learning complexities" to their model, one can begin to visualize the "ways in which learning occurs along several interacting dimensions and within an ecology of learning" (219).

In what might even be perceived as a step in a more normative direction, Cohen and Levinthal (1990) describe the processes that determine an organization's "absorptive capacity." These include the abilities of the groups of individuals who act as communication conduits as well as how the system is structured to transfer knowledge across intraorganizational units. They also allude to enhancements in communication or system structure for knowledge to be more adequately transmitted through the organization.

Given its connections to the field known by the Academy of Management as "organizational development and change," it is not surprising that the second approach to learning would be much more normative in its content. The focus on *knowledge development* has at its core the various conflicts over information, policies, and norms, where both internal and external environments can experience dramatic fluctuations. Moreover, the primary aim of inquiry is *corrective action*. According to the *developmental approach* organizational learning detects and corrects mismatches between expectations and outcomes. Correction involves integrating the divergent actions to be regularized in organizational structures (Argyris and Schon 1978, 20).

As suggested above, Chris Argyris and Donald Schon (1978) provide a basic approach that is probably most famous for its characterization of "single-loop versus double-loop learning." *Single loops* leave organizational assumptions and norms pretty much intact. *Double loops* raise questions about the adequacy of underlying norms and procedures. They describe how this additional feedback loops link the "detection of error" (in both strategies and assumptions) to the "effective performance." Obviously, most organizations need the most help with facilitating double loops.

These notions and the case studies that explore them are relatively simple, yet they may strike an intuitive cord of understanding. Furthermore, from a clinical standpoint, some of the actions taken as a result of this more action reoriented research have been profound improvements. The basic appeal of this approach is in its depiction of nonlinear dynamics harboring the potential for precipitating "symmetry breaking" realignments.

Other linkages between the knowledge development approach and more advanced systems thinking are also possible. The work of Joop Swieringa and Andre Wierdsma (1992) is especially instrumental in this regard. They describe the process for *Becoming a Learning Organization,* such as a strategy of continued development, a structure of organic networks, a task-oriented culture, and supportive information systems. Plus, as described in the previous chapter, they add yet another loop to their learning process, one that questions the very "being" of the organization. "Triple-loop learning" is governed by the types of dynamics that one might associate with strange or chaotic attractors. As their list of ingredients implies, Swieringa and Wierdsma see traditional hierarchical and/or bureaucratized organizations as poor internal environments for learning. When faced with the types of turbulence demanding triple-loop responses such organizations usually experience self-destructive behaviors.

These insights into learning processes, while incomplete from an ecological perspective, provide valuable clues to ecosystem change. Thus, they can be brought to bear in more expansive simulations of learning dynamics. Behavioral elements illuminate contextual properties and process constraints, despite the fact that their somewhat less than fluid notion of institutionalization is delimiting. Furthermore, their use of formal rigor is methodologically inspiring. Meanwhile, the knowledge development approach relies on assumptions that are at least metaphorically compatible with ecological perspectives elluded to above.

Inquiries into the institutional ecology (which include nonlinear simulations) could be used to bridge the intellectual gaps between the two distinct realms of learning research. Beyond the specification of a more powerful and behaviorally rich set of search algorithms, provision could be made for significant rule changes and modifications in search parameters. Rule changes, in turn, could be governed by "fuzzy logic" distributions, in order to approximate self-organizing dynamics. In this way simulations could explore "selection" amid multiequilibria or to test "resiliency." Such systems would not only model truly adaptive learning, they could learn to model adaptively. Meanwhile, informed by these studies, students of organizational development could design appropriate combinations of structural features, communication processes, and rule-making systems that more fully embody the ecological nature of change itself.

TQM as Theoretical as Well as Industrial Revolution

While only a partial approximation of the full spectrum of learning possibilities, one organizational reform that appears to embody some self-organizing properties is TQM. In a curious way, TQM provides a portal from the traditional realms of management science to the new age of nonlinear thinking. In today's environment, where consumers' expectations are ever changing, the static linear models of management spell precipitous decline. TQM may be the first major victory of an alternate paradigm. Beyond being the innovation of choice during the last 1980s, TQM represents a fundamental shift in perspective. At a recent International Conference on Advances in Management, there appeared to be consensus that TQM constitutes an "alterative theory of the firm" (note Christensen 1994; Watson 1994). That is, it flies in the face of the standard microeconomic theory of the firm (e.g., short-term utility maximization, etc.). Moreover, in those instances in which TQM accounted for much of the success of a particular firm or industry, the instrumentalities cannot be explained using the standard logic. In terms of key success factors, they are much more systemic and far less technique driven than one would presuppose. TQM, when it works, literally creates a radically new organization ecosystem (note again Watson 1994).

This is not to say that TQM as technique, rather than basic transformation, is without its faddish elements. Indeed, given corporate preoccupations with quick fixes, TQM is often only skin deep. Superficial or cosmetic TQM is often worse than no TQM. In one of the popular "cookbook" texts on TQM, Capezio and Morehouse (1993) suggest that they are *Taking the Mystery out of TQM;* however, they may also be taking out the magic. Implementing the "letter" without the "spirit" misses the essence that made TQM so successful. Yet getting at the Zen of TQM is no simple matter. Perhaps a bit of history will help.

TQM has its origins in early systems applications. Its earliest blood relative was work that was done in "statistical process control methods" at places such as the Bell Laboratories in the 1920s and 1930s. These and other systems methods proved their mettle during the Second World War. Unfortunately, the postwar boom and hegemony of U.S. industry caused a declining interest in quality control approaches. Of course, this lack of interest was not universal. As mentioned previously, W. Edwards Deming, a student of Bell's Walter Shewhart, found a literally "captive audience" for these ideas in Japan. Deming, and others who had developed statistical devices for the war effort, were asked by Douglas McArthur to aid in rebuilding the Japanese economy.

What began as a set of techniques gradually grew into an integrated theory of management. Moreover, this gradual refinement was aided by a real world laboratory experience. As alluded to earlier, certain unique features of the Japanese culture obviously exuded influence over the character of TQM. Over the years various scholars, interacting with many practitioners, integrated observations into a continuously improved model of *continuous improvement.* For example, a fellow visitor to Japan, Joseph H. Juran (1904–94), actually coined the term *TQM* and added his own unique approach that emphasized the conversion of financial planning and control systems over quality improvement devices (note Juran and Barish 1951). Likewise, General Electric's Armand Feigenbaum developed unique methods for calculating the costs of quality control. His strategy distinguished between prevention, appraisal, and internal and external costs (note Feigenbaum 1961). Over time, TQM has evolved from a collection of flow charts, "Pareto pictures," scatter diagrams, control mechanisms, customer satisfaction questionnaires, and "customer-supplier chains" into a full-blown philosophy of the firm (note Capezio and Morehouse 1993).

The larger implications of TQM were probably best developed in the work of Deming (note 1986, 1993). His famed fourteen-point perspective is summarized as follows.

1. Create an overall commitment to excellence;
2. Deemphasize oversight and increase inspiration;
3. Move away from inspection of defects to process improvements;
4. Shift from lowest price to highest quality suppliers;
5. Develop "continuous improvement" systems;
6. Implement career enhancement training as well as training in TQM;
7. Reward individual initiative as well as teamwork;
8. Diffuse expertise in the basic tools;
9. Avoid penalty systems and enhance systems of "mutual respect";
10. Reemphasize interdepartmental communication;
11. Continually inspire team spirit;
12. Empower individual employees as well as teams;
13. Eliminate quotas, replace them with "baseline measures"; and
14. Engage all aspects of the organization in the transformation to TQM.

In other words, unlike its implementation in many U.S. firms, agencies, and universities, TQM is not a minor tune-up or even a major overhaul; it is more like trading in one's motorbike for a Maserati.

By adding their own unique Zen features to TQM, the Japanese did not merely refine it, they transformed it. In their hands, the underlying philosophy of TQM was fully realized. In keeping with the notion of constant improvement, they continually developed novel elements of implementation. For example, Ishikawa (1984) added the famed ingredient of "quality circles." These mechanisms of participatory improvements and team building have become a mainstay, even among firms who don't practice all the other aspects of TQM. Yet it is probably two other scholar/practitioners who did the most to advance the art of TQM. Their innovations are the "Shingo system" and the "Taguchi method."

The Shingo system. Shigeo Shingo is known as "Mr. Improvement." He codeveloped Toyota's famous version of "just-in-time" manufacturing and is best known for his "poka-yoke system" of "zero defects" (see Shingo 1986). He contends that statistical quality control (SQC) is useless unless a conscientious system of corrective feedback is built in. Shingo was very skeptical of the use of SQC and once asked a plant quality officer (who was proudly displaying his two hundred control charts), "if he had a control chart of his control charts." The Shingo system focuses on individual worker initiative and "self-checks," which integrate everyone in the plant into the inspection processes. Shingo also emphasized the integration of numerous electronic signaling devices to aid worker vigilance.

The Taguchi method. This is the product of another near legendary figure in the Japanese quality movement, Genichi Taguchi (1987). His approach shifted attention away from a constant focus on minute improvements to the production line to continuous product design enhancements. The aim of these design changes was not just to build a higher quality device but to realize production efficiencies. The goal is a product with such robust design that it offsets any fluctuations in production quality. The Taguchi method's integration of process and product design uses statistical tests in an experimental fashion. Various combinations of production and product factors are compared to project an optimal mix of cost and uniformity conditions. These tests can often be burdensome, since possible combinations can quickly balloon into the thousands. However, Taguchi invented a way of sorting combinations into a smaller set representing the range of possible outcomes. He also developed an assessment that relates the cost of quality to variations in process. This notion, known as the *quality loss function,* captures additional incremental costs of a product being "out-of-spec" (missing a specification). Taguchi's method has caught on in several U.S. companies (e.g., IBM, ITT, and Ford) and has saved millions in manufacturing costs while raising the ultimate level of product quality.

Keys to the Kingdom of Quality

In those places outside of Japan where TQM is working, it usually represents just such a corporate epiphany. Consider the example of Selectronics, a small but growing San Francisco Bay area firm. The CEO of Selectronics, Walt Wilson, had learned about TQM while, as an IBM employee, he spent time in one of their Japanese operations. He also witnessed firsthand how IBM was failing to compete in the new world of accelerating product life cycles. Even after Selectronics won a Malcolm Baldridge Award for quality, he kept pushing major cultural changes within the firm. He did away with symbols of rank, broke down hierarchies, and empowered employees to step into the process of meeting and anticipating customer demands. Teams (and individuals for that matter) can even stop the production line to make necessary modifications. The firm engages in extensive training and has truly embodied the notion of "continuous improvement." Yet more importantly, it appears to have figured out the ultimate dilemma of TQM, that being how to reward individual initiative as well as teamwork.

This latter issue is worth addressing at a bit more length. Obviously the U.S. ethos of "rugged individualism," combined with the real need for a certain level of entrepreneurship, mediates against the type of team mentality prevalent in the Japanese firm and society at large. Yet, the need for developing interacting systems in which individuals complement and support one another remains paramount. In his book *The Force of Ones* (1994), Stanley Herman described and resolved the dilemma of cooperation in very interesting ways. Herman begins by assuming that the role of the individual has been largely neglected in recent years, despite the general societal atomization. Next, he points out that individual creativity is an organization's best hope of adapting to highly turbulent environments. During incremental change periods concern for "group think" can be minimized, but, when the going gets tough, managers need mavericks (venturesome risk takers) to get going. Beyond these points, Herman also adds some insights into career coping strategies and politics versus power in the workplace. However, the point he only partially makes is perhaps the most important for the purpose of this discussion. Stated directly, individuality is not at odds with, but rather is essential to, authentic TQM. If participatory management and team building are to work, then self-confident and competent individuals are essential. Empowerment without enlightenment is futile. This is why training and career enhancement are so critical. As Ruth Crowley (1993) points out, a truly TQM environment demands that employees do the following:

- contribute their intelligence and effort to exceed customer expectations;
- have a voice in their own professional development;
- experience a match between responsibility and authority;
- be aligned with the unit or organizational goals; and
- participate as valuable members of teams. (1–2)

Balancing of organizational and individual motivations has always been a vital managerial activity; however, TQM transforms them into cannons. Through this transformation old forms of cajoling and/or manipulating individuals must be abandoned for the sake of greater mutuality. As Thomas Patten (1992) suggests, TQM requires a new, nonbureaucratic "politics of managing." Learning these new systems of interaction requires recognition of the emerging "new work order." As Charles Handy explains, in his recent epic *The Age of Paradox* (1994), the current epoch has literally shifted the ownership of the "means of production from the capitalists to the workers." Knowledge workers, by definition, embody the means of production. At firms like Microsoft what individuals carry around in their heads is more vital than all the plant, equipment, and rolling stock. Even in firms that are not necessarily knowledge intensive, it is the "human capital" that is becoming increasingly important to long-term survival of the enterprise. So maintains Jeffrey Pfeffer (1994), who sees people as the ultimate source of "competitive advantage." In the current era of global interdependency in which firms share technologies and markets, the people power (i.e., how much a firm has invested in its employees) will be what separates the winners from the losers. Pfeffer's (1994) review of a handful of successful companies echoes the concern of Deming. Accordingly, highly effective firms emphasize the following: "employment security, recruiting selectivity . . . high wages, incentive pay, employee ownership, information sharing, self-management, teamwork, skill development, cross-training, symbolic egalitarianism, wage compression, promotion within the business, long-term perspective on employees, behavior measurement and feedback, and a coherent management philosophy." While these items seem burdensome, it is Pfeffer's conviction that they lead to the long-term viability of the firm. These speculations also find an additional measure of empirical confirmation in the study of Baldridge Award winners by Richard Blackburn and Benson Rosen (1993). While the results are somewhat tautological, they found that "best practice" human resource experiments with quality initiatives demanded revolutionary changes in the way organizations train, empower, evaluate, and reward individuals and teams (49). From an ecological point of view, it is the diversely skilled and adaptive set of employees that provides the "requisite variety" required to face the challenges of turbulent change. The employees are, in short, more resilient. One cannot necessarily reengineer the future, but it is possible to design a firm that capitalizes on change.

Beyond TQM

Given that TQM is basically a product of an earlier systems epoch, it is only partially representative of recent advances in nonlinear thinking. Of course, as alluded to earlier, the actual practice of TQM is very different from the early systems theory. In essence, it is only marginally dependent upon statistical control methods and/or other remnants of early management science. Moreover, where it has been most successful it exhibits an uncanny similarity to basic ecological principles. Nevertheless, if TQM were reconceptualized in terms of more current adaptive system theoretics, it might be easier to design supportive institutions. Dooley and Bush (1994) describe TQM as a "stepping-stone" between the "Newtonian paradigm" and the "complexity paradigm." While this is probably true, few if any of its adherents are even remotely aware of this paradigmatic purgatory. However, the more thoughtful are most likely aware that TQM doesn't fit existing models of management. Thus, some may be inspired to push on to a new paradigm of managerial process. Initially, the ideas derived from nonlinear systems provide vital insights into the forces currently at work in transformational workplaces. Ralph Stacey (1992) contends that the dynamics of self-organization occupy a precarious "middle ground" between traditional hierarchy and structural empowerment (169–73). In this way, they explain the apparent paradoxes alluded to earlier (e.g., innovation vs. shared culture and flexibility vs. control). Moreover, Stacey maintains that the "creative tensions" required for adaptive responses demand a set of apparently "contradictory structures." These structures are especially alien to current linear views of TQM. It is not a mere semantic distinction that he differentiates "self-organizing networks" from the currently popular self-managing teams. To paraphrase Stacey (184), the essential differences include the following.

- Self-organization is fluid, with informal, temporary teams forming spontaneously. By contrast self-managing teams are permanent and formally established parts of a reporting structure.
- Top managers cannot control self-organizing networks; they merely impact boundary conditions. They can, however, control structure of self-managing teams.
- Participants determine self-organizing networks, while top managers usually set the conditions and boundaries for self-managing teams.
- Self-organizing networks involve conflict and are constrained by the hierarchy, but self-managing teams replace the hierarchy.
- Self-organizing networks are energized through conflict, while dispersed power in self-managing teams is supposed to lead to consensus.
- Self-organizing networks empower themselves, yet self-managing teams still acquire power from top management.
- Self-organization grows out of cultural differences; self-management is based on strongly shared culture.

It is noteworthy that given various contextual sensitivities, Stacey's distinctions may rarely be so mutually exclusive. Actual processes will be shaped through the institutional interaction. Few managerial activities are ever completely spontaneous in the fashion Stacey implies. Nevertheless, the crux of his distinction remains germane, especially the portion that describes the tensions that arise in systems of unequal power and how self-organization tends to work against hierarchy. These elements may go a long way toward explaining the conflicts present in partial or incomplete transformations.

The more interesting issue by far is that even *when self-organizing networks dominate a system, anarchy does not reign. Patterns of order emerge from the decentralization chaos.* As Mitchel Resnick (1994) points out with his analogy to bird flocks, amazing synchronicity arises in decentralized networks through adherence to a handful of rules of interaction. Birds do not follow a leader; they follow simple rules. The monolithic flowing and jamming of traffic on a crowded highway provides a similar example. Patterns of interaction, *not* centralized control mechanisms, dictate the progress of the whole. Managers do not as much manage as they orchestrate these types of interactions. Obviously, one can aid in the clarification of the rules and/or institutional designs that govern interaction. However, an appreciation of a particular firm's institutional ecology is a prerequisite for experimentation, and such experimentation involve much less hubris than the term *TQM* normally connotes.

From an ecological perspective, the tools and institutions of TQM are themselves subject to continuous improvement. The most fundamental tool of TQM has been, of course, the *statistical process analysis.* This well-established innovation shifted focus from simple product inspections to process assessment. Advanced systems applications could further shift the focus to changes within the processes of control. For example, a traditional control chart plots significant variations in product quality so as to establish the upper and lower limits or the *confidence band,* but nonlinear charts would plot the operation of the confidence band itself. That is, they would measure the responses to variation and the efforts at constant improvement over time in order to assess the quality of quality adjustments. By plotting these incremental changes on a *phase plane chart,* oscillatory behavior can be studied, and *patterns in the rate of change* that do not appear in conventional analyses can be identified (see Priesmeyer 1992, 141–47). This discussion will have more to say about this technique later as it is similar to other patterns of change calculations. For now, suffice it to say that as applied to statistical control methods, it not only provides a buffer against overadjustments, it accelerates the buildup of knowledge within the learning process.

Ultimately, this double variation approach, which is made possible through the use of nonlinear calculations, addresses the major weakness of the "operational benchmarking" made popular in conjunction with the Malcolm Baldridge Award. Originally designed to facilitate the transfer of "best practices" between organizations, it is being combined with competitive analysis to identify performance niches as well as quality gaps (Richardson and Taylor 1994). In the words of Peter Senge (1990), none of these various "snapshots" and their associated "tools" deals with the dynamic complexity very well at all (267). While phase planes are merely another snapshot, so to speak, they are a nearer approximation of the dynamism. Moreover, by literally embodying the adaptations within the production process (including innovation) they may provide a more tangible spur to further creativity than the vague rhetoric of "reengineering."

Another subtle yet significant factor that nonlinear logic contributes to TQM is in making error less onerous. TQM, in general, and statistical control, in particular, allow margins of error to become matters of standardized probability and hence accepted as the norm. *Chaos theory teaches one that much of the cumulative error results from minor variations rather than major mistakes.* While not necessarily generating the Japanese model of blamelessness, nonlinearity at least facilitates a more ready embracing of error. And, embracing error is at the heart of organizational learning, especially creative adaptations. Individuals are unlikely to experiment in a system that punishes error. What has always been so paradoxical about hierarchy is that it attempts to fix individual blame for collective errors. Using Csikszentmihalyi's (1993) notion of complexity, such a system has reversed the balance of "autonomy and integration." In order to inspire individuals to prize their part in the whole, they can't be held responsible for interactive errors. Competency grows when one learns to interact so as to reduce errors, without the fear that his or her personal head will roll if the team or product or plant fails. The idea of the healthy family may be instructive since it provides a safe environment for learning. Individuals need to be safe in their failures for complexity to foster adaptability (Csikszentmihalyi 1993). Integration cannot be based on shared visions alone; it must include shared responsibility. Those systems that are designed to accept failure will be more resilient in the long run.

Conclusions

In sum, TQM and similar reforms tend to recognize the internal brilliance of these less organized forms of organization. The synergism possible through allowing inherent nonlinearities to follow their unique geometries can make the whole much more powerful in pursuit of quality. When it hosted the World Cup in 1994, the United States not only learned something about the grace and beauty of soccer, it learned about cumulative effects of complex geometries. As one commentator observed, when played at this level, victory is made possible through "the democracy of imagination." Set plays don't work very well in soccer. Scoring opportunities are the culmination of complex interacting vectors, which cascade toward an explosion of focused energy. Creativity reaches its crescendo through the blend of teamwork and individual athleticism. Therefore, world-class soccer is a wonderful metaphor for management innovation, particularly its more nonlinear elements.

In the final analysis, if TQM or the next generation of managerial reforms is comprised of fundamentally accurate depictions of healthy organizational forms, then they will thrive, assuming they don't run afoul of some type of macroeconomic catastrophe far beyond their adaptive capabilities. Apparently the basic logic of TQM is held to be sufficiently important to prompt the Directorate for Social, Behavioral and Economic Sciences of the National Science Foundation to commit an entire program to the study of "Transformations to Quality Organizations" (NSF 1995). Interestingly enough such "transformations" to various elements of TQM (i.e., employee participation) appear to follow a pattern of nonlinear learning, at least at first blush. James Dean and Paul Goodman (1994) contend that integration of total quality (of the sort that assures "sustainability") follows a model of "dynamical learning." In other words, implementing TQM involves learning how to learn. Moreover, to the extent that these devices allow organizations to learn about the nonlinear nature of change, particularly the complex participatory character of adaptive responses, then choices will truly become more strategic.

CHAPTER 7

A Range of Practical Management Applications

Beyond their obvious applications in the realms of traditional quality control, nonlinear concepts and methods have several additional practical applications. In fact, it is probably these various tricks and gadgets that will catch on well before the theoretical understandings sketched out in the preceding. Just as the "quick fix" mentality engendered use of TQM without full appreciation of either its prerequisites or implications, chaos and complexity tools may be prone to misapplication. However, widespread use may inspire the quest for further conceptual integration. Hopefully, misplaced pragmatism and/or mere popularity will not perpetuate the growing gulf between theory and practice. Since the worship of technique is likely to continue apace, a review of some of the less graven images may be appropriate.

The primary function of nonlinear applications is to describe the processes through which order dissipates, yet from a management perspective, attention is usually focused on how order emerges. Viewed comprehensively, each living organization has its own unique set of metabolic processes that must be monitored to discover its general state of health. From this basic perspective the potential for growth and adaptation can be given preliminary appraisal, and this appraisal can be incorporated into decisions ranging from marketing to finance. Furthermore, these key incremental decisions, when viewed in the context of long-term systemic choices, can be seen as symbiotic or synergistic considerations. Even if one's vision is a bit more myopic, the value of using tools geared to a much more fluid reality should become readily apparent.

Where the Churning Rubber Meets the Rising Road

A tire advertisement became an all-purpose euphemism for the heart of practicality in the late twentieth century. "Where the rubber meets the road" came to signify the point at which a promising perspective is forced to deliver on its promise. A more appropriate analogy might be James Bond landing a sports car on the roof of a speeding bullet train. A perspective on the nature of chaotic reality is itself in flux, and existing managerial reality while antiquated is nevertheless a moving target. A moderately modified perspective, even if incomplete, might still provide potential performance payoffs of a relatively immediate variety. Generally speaking, most of the current performance measures invoke a rather static picture of past practices. They tell management how well they did but not how they and the firm are doing. Particularly, measures indicate existing problems but often fail to signal future difficulties. Sometimes, poor signaling combines with institutional pathologies to create a type of bureaucratic obliviousness. Consider how Chrysler Motor Corporation paid huge bonuses to midlevel management (based on positive quarterly reports) just months before it was required to seek the largest government "bailout" in the history of the United States in order to avoid bankruptcy. Tools derived from nonlinear dynamics cannot necessarily pinpoint exactly when significant turbulence will overtake a firm, but they can illustrate how a firm is likely to deal with turbulence and thus signal needed design changes.

Phase Planes for Fun and Profit

Except for some of the TQM efforts mentioned earlier, many if not most firms measure performance in standard terms such as profit margins, return on equity, market share, and so on. While reported on a quarterly basis, and used to construct trend assessments, these indicators rarely portray a truly dynamic picture. However, these same data can be reconstructed in a way that provides much more telling pieces of information, and this information can be used to foster more effective organizational designs. This can be accomplished by using the simple technology of "phase plane diagrams." H. Richard Priesmeyer (1992) was the first to apply this technology to practical management problems. He elaborates on the implications of phase plane analysis as follows.

> When we quote a total sales figure for the period we throw away all the intricate, dynamic information that describes the trajectory from zero to that total. . . . If we expect to manage sales, we must manage the trajectory. We don't go to the moon by noting its location and shooting at it. We go to the moon by first understanding the complex forces which determine our trajectory, and then managing the changes in that trajectory to arrive at the moon. (19)

He proceeds to explain that business involves managing " evolving patterns of performance," using tools that focus on the changing trajectories of complex systems. The *phase plane* is the primary device for depicting the interaction within nonlinear systems. Essentially, it is a graphic (two-dimensional) display of what physicists and mathematicians refer to as the "phase space," which is the road map of a given oscillating phenomenon. The phase plane attempts to capture the accumulation changes associated with a particular trajectory. The data points plotted on perpendicular axes represent evolutionary behavior of a system, rather than merely output indicators. While not assuming direct causality, the variable that appears the most independent goes on the horizontal axis (see fig. 8).

For instance, an assessment of market share could compare changes in a firm's measurements vis-à-vis its major competitor. Rather than merely giving a set of sales figures, this analysis tells the manager what trajectory (the path from the center point of 0) they are on. In this way he or she can focus on the complex set of contextual features that governs the behavior of particular trajectories and thus impact the evolution of performance over time. More importantly, by picturing *trajectories* and conducting various dimensional analyses, one can seek to discover the exact type of dynamics at work (e.g., the location or "basin" and type of "attractor"). This discovery may, in turn, suggest any number of unique interventions. For instance, generally speaking, the more chaotic and/or "strange" an attractor, the more subject it will be to small countervailing oscillations. High sensitivity to initial conditions can be seen in marginal changes that cause the cycle to swiftly diverge to an erratic pattern (e.g., period doubling). This also means that a relatively tiny nudge will return the behavior to a tighter orbit. In highly turbulent situations, sophisticated models may be needed to test for exactly how many drops of oil will calm the troubled waters. Yet in many instances, a simple overlay of marginal change data will also provide a picture of the organization's natural rhythms. Sometimes, periodic swings are completely natural, and thus what may appear to be chaotic is actually part of the system's long-term limit cycles. It is well to keep in mind that healthy systems experience periodic oscillations. Recall that fixed point and/or extremely tight limit cycles while creating the illusion of stability also signal dead or dying systems. Hence from time to time, skillful managers may even wish to artificially introduce shocks into the system to maintain a certain level of organizational "resiliency" as well as growth and development. Honda Motor Company was extremely successful through creating this type of dynamic tension that Richard Pascale (1990, chap. 1) labeled the "paradox of fit versus split"!

Nearer to the mark, in terms of practicality, phase plane diagrams have many concrete applications beyond generic strategizing (for more elaborate examples see Priesmeyer 1992). As mentioned previously, they can be used to convert static statistical control mechanisms into vivid dynamic pictures and thus energize the organizational learning implied by TQM. Inventory analysis and production management are obvious areas of application. By mastering the "ebb and flow" of vital production elements, devices such as "just in time" can be more readily employed. Furthermore, custom designs are more easily added to these adaptive manufacturing procedures.

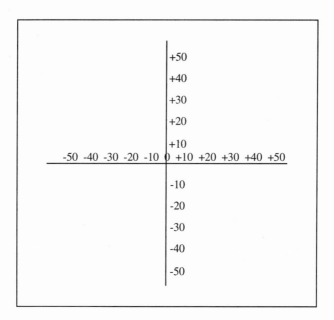

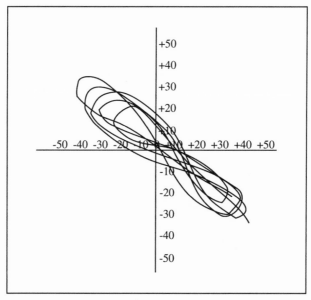

Typical Oscillation

Fig. 8. The Phase Plane

Operations researchers, especially of the European variety, have a well-established tradition of addressing nonlinearities. Therefore it is not surprising that chaos/complexity applications are more substantially developed in realms readily amenable to engineering applications. Yet, success in these relatively mechanical activities has also produced a narrow view of applicability. Since its inception during the Second World War, operations research (OR) has blended engineering and social inquiry methods but still carries the stigma of being much more about things than people. Obviously conventional linear programming techniques were much more isomorphic with and thus successful in manipulating physical systems. However, as nonlinear logic would predict, nothing fails like too much initial success. As Pierre Hanson (1989) observed, the economic turbulence, which began with the first oil shock, caused a crisis in operations research. Or, it failed to keep pace with increasingly complex and diverse managerial demands. Yet, out of this "crisis" has come a good deal of methodological introspection and innovation. OR is now beginning to be a much less physically oriented discipline and is again mirroring its sociotechnical origins. With the decline in manufacturing in the West, actual use of OR teams within corporations may remain sparse, however. This provides all the more reason for research findings of operations researchers to be incorporated into service and/or generic management tools. For instance, the "complex method" applied to *nonlinear goal programming* and resource constraints has found applications in multi-item inventory systems (see Padmanabham 1990). Moreover as mentioned earlier, the development of various parallel processing and genetic algorithm approaches opens many avenues for representing complexity and learning within all sorts of production processes (note Kumar and Narendran 1991; Tsujimura 1992; Venugopal and Narendran 1992).

While machines usually behave in predictable ways, occasionally they do not; and as production becomes more a matter of information and/or service delivery, the probability of complex dynamics increases. Moreover, as a production process learns and pursues constant quality improvement, the dynamics of change become ubiquitous. For any number of unique and interacting factors of production (e.g., changes in supply, work process, finished goods, etc.), the construction of phase plane analysis provides useful insights into these dynamics. Obviously, the core motivation in plotting the ebb and flow of these dynamics is to control the inefficiencies of excess and/or insufficient capacity. In the past, firms tended to err on the side of excess, assuming that warehousing was a way of life. The modern or postmodern firm does not want expensive inventory to pile up and/or inhibit flexibility. Moreover, once it has invested in a knowledgeable labor force it does not want to lay them off and/or have them merely standing around. Many of these concerns can be addressed through conventional network or queuing analysis; but the interplay of rates of changes involves inherent nonlinearities and sensitivities. The simple technique of overlaying these various patterns of change or trajectories provides a powerful new management tool (see fig. 9).

This reconceptualization of supply and demand in terms of multiple factors not only reduces reliance on excess inventory, it represents the inefficiencies that result from systemic lags in response to change. Here, any shift away from optimality (45 percent of the axis point) constitutes accumulating inefficiency. Even if one assumes a traditional input/output or "black box" approach, phase plane calculations can offer increased precision with regard to sources of instability and/or successful interventions. If one tweaks the system in one way or another, the result in overall performance is readily apparent. Moreover, by locating the exact basin of attraction along the production axis, one can unlock the set of structural features requiring attention (e.g., product design, materials specification, inspection procedure, consumer monitoring, etc.). Most importantly, the interaction of cost and quality can be highlighted.

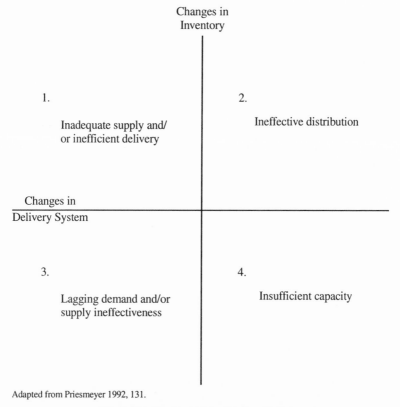

Adapted from Priesmeyer 1992, 131.

Fig. 9. The Nonlinear Production System

As mentioned earlier, phase planes can also be used to augment conventional quality-control charts. In this context, control of quality moves well beyond establishment of allowable limits to the analysis of factors affecting quality, not the least of which relates to the state of employee involvement and knowledge. In short, phase planes can blend efficiency and effectiveness.

Beyond Marketing and Market Share

A systemic and/or ecological approach to performance appraisal also dramatically alters the role of marketing within the production process. Over the years, marketing as a field of study has discovered numerous aberrations in conventional supply/demand or market signaling patterns. As alluded to earlier, these might be thought of as "lock in" (Arthur 1990) or network externalities (see Katz and Shapiro 1985). In essence, market share is often a product of mutually amplified distortions in the marketing system. Other factors such as "brand recognition," "niche formation," fad behavior, and so on, can easily create situations where the price and the demand go up simultaneously. In nonlinear dynamical terms, the price and quantity attractor is a function of diverse structural factors, only a few of which have anything to do with markets in the conventional sense. One need not necessarily know exactly what these factors are to discover how a particular trajectory is likely to work. Here again, phase planes provide a useful device for isolating trajectories that run contrary to traditional curves. Yet beyond these simple applications, ecological factors could be combined with various macroeconomic factors to provide a new era in market research.

The institutional changes associated with the increased use of chaos/complexity techniques are likely to accelerate the onset of the so-called virtual marketplace. Systems that recognize the role of consumers in product design are likely to amplify these trends. Early in the next century, 75 to 80 percent of all households in the United States will have either access to a computer network and/or cable TV, and these systems will be used to interact more directly with the marketing process. Systems are already in place in which individuals can select their own advertisements, get more detailed information, and even place orders over "the Internet." Glitzy ads will soon have to be augmented with serious information, and as consumers become better informed they will have a larger role in product development. The "focus group" may eventually give way to electronic communication. Information is not necessarily the primary commodity of the emerging era, yet it is the process through which this commodity will take shape. Bart Nooteboom (1992) argues that the world described by "postmodernist philosophy" is the key to the development of market strategy. According to Nooteboom, the world is becoming one of mutual "interplay of

firms and their environments." It is also a world market by "dynamism, disequilibrium," "learning by doing," and "Schumpeterian" economics (70–76).

Marketing, with its origins in psychology and sociology and its accounts of
evolving technological demands, is clearly a realm for complex ecological
perspectives. Marketing researcher Frank Cespedes (1990) takes just such a
perspective in his analysis of "bottlenecks of attention." He describes how firms
can use existing structures and still maintain information flexibility, if they are
willing to use "customer channels" as "incubators" for new product-market
development. These trends do not necessarily spell the demise of Madison
Avenue's slick campaigns; however, an increased emphasis on substance over
pure style is an inevitable result of increased information processes and more
active (and interactive) consumers.

The data available by refocusing on two-way information flows can be
subjected to nonlinear analysis. The goal in this case is to stabilize the distribution system, and this can be accomplished by expediting the feedback of
information collected down the channels back toward the producers. As nonlinear systems, distribution channels often exhibit efficiency through cycles, and
plotting these cycles is a much better indication of stabilization potentialities
than conventional sales data. Moreover as alluded to previously, as consumers
begin to respond in ways other than merely voting with the dollars, the sensitivity
of these systems will increase geometrically.

Nonlinear tools can also be used to test strategic assumptions in the field of
marketing, and this role is likely to be a point of early inroads. Increased
consumer sovereignty is likely to exacerbate already accelerating "product life
cycles." The ability to more nearly approximate these dynamics is obviously an
attribute to be prized. The life-cycle notion generally identifies distinct phases
in the life span of a given product (e.g., growth, maturity, decline, etc.) (see fig.
10). Prior to and during each stage a particular set of marketing strategies comes
into play. For example, as a product is newly introduced and just before what
will hopefully be the growth stage, marketers must alert consumers to its
potential advantages. If the product is truly new and has clear advantages, it will
experience rapid growth early on in its entry to the market. Other firms witnessing this growth will enter with similar products, and competition should cause
growth to moderate as the product moves toward the mature stage. "Shakeout"
occurs at this stage, and marketers employ differentiation strategies in order to
cull out market share. As the market becomes saturated and begins to decline,
other firms exit as "shakeout" continues. During this late mature stage, competition can become fierce, with "price wars," and so on, and only those firms with
"comparative advantage" will remain in a particular product market. Decline
gradually accelerates as major players exit. Usually a couple of firms gain the
dominant share, yet new upstarts will usually enter and carve out niches.

Eventually a totally new product will topple the market into a new cycle. Historically, the total life cycle could take several years, yet in recent years products like personal computers have reduced the cycle to several months.

The key to understanding these accelerated evolutionary dynamics is projecting from the trajectories generated around the industry attractor. This involves expanding the focus of the analysis a bit to look at the total cycle with monthly data dating back to the initial introduction stage (for slower cycles quarterly data is probably sufficient). Rates of change in key variables (sales and profitability) are plotted on the phase plane to illustrate the configuration and velocity of the cycle.

While it is difficult to predict the pattern exactly, one can anticipate transitions by watching the interaction of variables. If a trajectory begins to return to the horizontal axis, a precipitous drop in the growth rate of profits may be signaled, and if it drops below the axis then one can anticipate the onset of

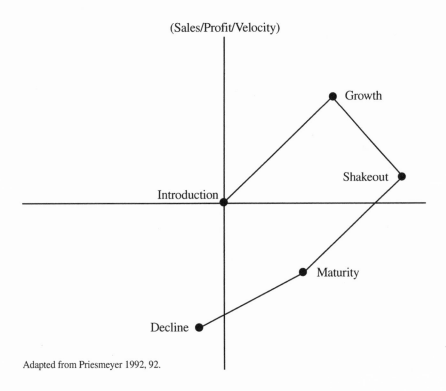

Adapted from Priesmeyer 1992, 92.

Fig. 10. From Limit Cycle to Life Cycle

maturity. When it moves back and crosses the vertical axis, the product is entering the decline stage.

As one begins to focus on changes in conventional indices and cross-index-ing, the implications for more strategic assessments should become obvious. By integrating the types of strategic management practices noted in chapter 6 with simple phase plane analyses, it is possible to dramatically revise traditional portfolio assessments (see fig. 11). Designations such as "stars," "dog," "cash cow," and so forth, are not only misleading, if a firm stops to milk, in today's turbulent environment, the dogs quickly overtake it.

When compared with conventional linear strategic assessments, the strate-gies suggested by this nonlinear dynamical approach may be somewhat coun-terintuitive. With specific regard to growth rate and market share, conventional

Adapted from Priesmeyer 1992, 96–98.

Fig. 11. Nonlinear Portfolio Appraisal

assessments provide a rather static view of these vital elements. They provide a snapshot of where one is but not where one is going. Changes in the vital indicators are what are crucial, and by combining these indices along a common axis, a motion picture of the transitional forces is provided. Plus, even generic knowledge of what quadrant a particular product is entering provides vital clues to appropriate strategies (e.g., increasing the promotional budget, paying bonuses, retraining or firing managers, and redesigning or repositioning). For instance, if a product is in the quadrant where market share is increasing but growth rate is declining, the ability of the product to survive the shakeout may be in question, even though it has a substantial niche of the market. With the overall pie declining, the slice may be insufficient, depending on the performance of other products. Since the era of the cash cow is virtually over, decisions to refocus or sell off may depend on how rapidly it is moving toward the quadrant where market share and growth are both declining. Conversely, if market share is decreasing while the market is rapidly expanding, it is probably time to reposition and/or differentiate. Conventional measures may support the same conclusions, but the information may be too late in arriving. Keying on transformational dynamics is even more critical if one is involved in a highly volatile, innovation-driven industry. As Silicon Graphics' Ed McCracken (see Prokesch 1993) observed: "The key to achieving competitive advantage is not reacting to chaos in the marketplace, but in producing that chaos" (178).

The New Financial Management

Nowhere, perhaps, is the impact of nonlinear thinking more apparent than in the realms of accounting, budgeting, and financial management generally. In the annals of managerial reform, meaningful innovations usually involved substantial alterations of the budgeting process. Particularly in the public sector, major epochs of reform are associated with a particular budgetary strategy (e.g., PPBS, zero-base, and so on). The reasons for this overemphasis on the budget per se should be obvious. If one could redirect the principal conduit of resources toward rational (goal maximization) analysis, then all else good and just would follow. Unfortunately, this "switching station" model of the budget was rarely congruent with reality, and in government management, politics usually introduced its own brand of suboptimality. More importantly, for the purposes of this discussion, budgeting and finance introduce many nonlinear elements into these systems of linear goal programming.

As Robert Finney (1993) observes, budgeting often involves planning for "the unknown." He maintains that the two most important problems facing would-be systematic budgeteers are "uncertainty of the future" and "uncontrollability" of external factors (20). Despite the great deal of attention given to problems of uncertainty in capital markets, return appraisals, and performance assessments (note Vertinsky et al. 1990; Mukherjee 1991; Plath et al. 1992), the tools of financial management remain quite antiquated, to say the least. Nevertheless, the budgetary process remains the nexus of control. Accountant Robert Eiler (1990) points out that financial management systems are regarded as the logical embodiment of processes for reducing the overall complexity of the competitive environment (45). These responsibilities have generated subtle forms of technocratic collusion but few financial forecasts that accurately represent "societal complexity" (Gauci and Baumgartner 1989, 154). Besides a handful of applications to the stock market (see Barnett et al. 1987; Burr 1989; Boldrin 1990; Vaga 1994) chaos and complexity theories have made few inroads in microlevel financial management arenas. Therefore, the potential for a major methodological contribution is substantial.

The Ecology of Budgets

Initially, nonlinear assessments could be integrated with basic production analysis. Generally speaking, the production process is evaluated by aggregate cost measures, and this unit cost data is fed back into periodic pricing decisions. Here again, these assessments usually fail to account for the pattern of changes in critical cost factors over time. Variability in unit costs is rarely traced directly to specific production processes. Yet, it's simple enough to construct multiple phase plane diagrams that compare integral ingredients (e.g., raw materials, labor, capital equipment, quality assurance, etc.) to overall cost. In this case the trajectories represent the sensitivity to changes in constituent cost elements. Moreover, it is possible to test assumptions about specific investments and potential impacts on costs and quality.

Budgets are often allocated on a project by project basis. In this case, the budget itself establishes the parameters of the limit cycle. However, actual performance requirements may demand a diversion from this attractor basin. Conversely, the trajectory of a particular project may quickly exceed its budgetary boundaries, irrespective of ultimate performance. It usually goes without saying that uncertainty and uncontrollables undermine "the best-laid plans of mice and men." Cyclical patterns in these larger phenomena can be addressed at the macromanagement level; however, it is also possible to use nonlinear assessments to track divergence from a particular budgetary path early enough in the life of a project to make strategic determinations. A diagram that illustrates how changes in the level of expenditure align with the projected budgetary orbit provides an early warning system. Moreover, by overlaying performance projections, prognostications regarding project outcomes can be placed within budgetary perspective, thus bringing about the return of effectiveness measures.

This not only gives greater immediate control over expenditures, it allows projects that are over budget at one point in the cycle, but on or below target in others, to be continued without undue stress.

These simple applications to budgeting, of course, quickly bring nonlinear calculators into near proximity to the roaring vortex of modern management, for example, corporate finance. Financial management is rife with possibilities and pitfalls. As alluded to earlier, it may be a clear condemnation of the current status of corporate enterprise and/or the entire economic system to suggest that finance has become more important than, say, manufacturing know-how. The era in which the typical manager could generate greater return by trading paper than by building an innovative design is, hopefully, over. Finance, however, is still vital, and issues such as funding and cash flow are paramount. Navigating the typical balance sheet has obviously become more complicated, with comparative figures such as ROA ("return on assets"), not to mention the converging pressures of leveraging, mergers and acquisitions, and so on. From the institutional ecology perspective, the various measures and concepts of financial management can be reduced to a handful of straightforward composite indicators, which tell the financial story in terms of evolving interrelationship.

The Art of ROA

Phase planes can be constructed to combine diverse information (e.g., income statements, the balance sheet, and cash flow reports) in new and interesting ways. For example, the traditional income statements can be converted into a map of the *net profit trajectory* and the balance sheets into a picture of the *debt to equity transformation*. Furthermore, these can be integrated with other ratio and change-over-time data to produce a chart of the *returns and turnover*. For example, a phase plane that looks at changes in profit by changes in assets (see fig. 12) would provide a more meaningful assessment than conventional ROA statements. Standard reports can tell managers where the firm ended up during any particular quarter. But, an oscillation between declines and increases in profits might be common, especially in periods of "downsizing." Moreover, when combined with more generic portfolio style analyses, an ROA phase plane might indicate situations where "downsizing" will not sustain the presupposed performance improvements. Recent studies suggest that the economic and/or manageability benefits of downsizing may be short lived. In his review of a range of findings, Wayne Cascio (1993) contends that unless a firm is also willing to redesign its basic management philosophy (away from command, control, and compartmentalization and toward "continuous improvement"), then neither the economic payoffs (i.e., "lower expense ratios, higher profits, increased return-on-investment, and boosted stock prices") nor the organizational benefits (e.g., "smoother communication" and "greater entrepreneurship") are likely to emerge. Nonlinear analysis may suggest whether or not a firm is even in a position to embark on this thoroughgoing redesign.

At a more macrolevel, nonlinear financial management will aid in this long-term transition. It is not too difficult to imagine that the generic managerial reorientations are greatly delimited by traditional financing theories and methods. Corporate finance has not experienced theoretical innovation since the consolidation of concepts during the 1950s by Franco Modigliani and Merton Miller (see Dornbusch et al. 1987), and these were substantially wedded to traditional equilibrium notions. Nancy Nichols (1993), in her review piece in the *Harvard Business Review,* observed that chief financial officers (CFOs) make decisions based on sorely antiquated theories, theories that have failed to

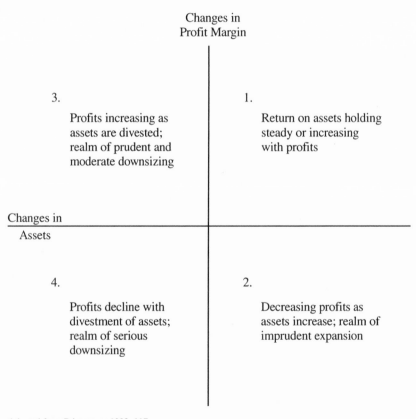

Changes in
Profit Margin

3.

Profits increasing as
assets are divested;
realm of prudent and
moderate downsizing

1.

Return on assets holding
steady or increasing
with profits

Changes in
    Assets

4.

Profits decline with
divestment of assets;
realm of serious
downsizing

2.

Decreasing profits as
assets increase; realm of
imprudent expansion

Adapted from Priesmeyer 1992, 117.

Fig. 12. Nonlinear Assessment

keep pace with the "globalization of markets" and "increased technological firepower." In essence, the basic "capital asset pricing model (CAPM)" is subject to serious criticism (59–60). Unfortunately, while pointing to a few nonlinear type innovations, she doesn't really develop an alternative theory. Knut Aase (1993) demonstrates mathematically that the CAPM fails to account for various "jumps" in the aggregate consumption process. Moreover, he argues for the use of an ancillary theory of "diffusion" to account for gradual adaptations to equilibrium. Similarly, Gregory Huffman (1992) illustrates the need for models that address information asymmetries inherent in actual capital markets. Eventually, however, these patchwork approaches to finance theory will give way to a more viable assessment of the institutional ecology of corporate and global finance. In the meantime, CFOs can use a few simple phase plane diagrams to augment their outmoded methods.

This is particularly cogent if one compares a nonlinear analysis with the standard *asset ratios assessment.* For example, the turnover rate might remain relatively constant from reporting period to reporting period, while small yet dramatic change forces are at work. Moreover, even if the CFO or his or her staff notices subtle changes, they do not immediately know exactly where the changes are coming from unless they check the rate against a number of indicators (e.g., sales, inventory, productivity, etc.). In essence, the ratio is both an oversimplification and, yet, a more complex way of doing things. By shifting the focus to the interrelationships between changes in assets, one has a composite and fluid picture without sacrificing vital information.

Even when standard analyses, such as *cash flow statements,* give a glimpse of the magnitude of change, this remains merely one point along a trajectory; thus, it does not capture the patterns of systemic changes. A cash flow phase plane would incorporate systemic behavior patterns over time (e.g., seasonal cycles). The institutional information embedded in these patterns becomes more transparent and thus manageable. While the CFO is probably aware of patterns, he or she may not understand them well enough to anticipate their onset and/or engage in delicate redesigns. Depending on in which quadrant one finds oneself, a different set of measures for balancing sources and uses is readily suggested. Opportunities for novel interventions can also be explored (e.g., new stock issues, etc.). Moreover, subtleties that arise out of differing financing vehicles can be tested along with traditional leverage (i.e., debt vs. equity) considerations. These types of subtleties are extremely important to new ventures.

Last but not least, financial phase planes illustrate patterns that harbor the potential for amplifying tiny instabilities into major catastrophes. As mentioned earlier, the key to understanding the full implications of chaos theory is that both limit cycles and chaotic attractors share roughly the same internal propensities (albeit dramatically divergent sensitivities). While most of the data subject to the purview of a given CFO will quickly collapse toward a particular limit cycle, the possibility, albeit remote, for period doubling or other chaotic behavior is ever present in most nonlinear systems. Hence, models that comprehend the full range of systemic interactions are much more likely to display the true risks associated with a particular set of financial trajectories. In the past, these risks and/or uncertainties were accounted for in terms of probabilities. While non-linear models do not escape this probabilistic world, they embody it in such a way that transitions are more readily managed. Like the world of quantum physics, exact points become probabilistic, while relationships become determi-nistic. Where dollars and cents are concerned, this handle on an uncertain world is a distinct improvement, even if it is not a panacea.

What should be increasingly apparent, whether one embraces nonlinear methods or not, is that the financial dimensions of the firm are far too important to be left to traditionally equipped economists, which include those trained in the subfield of finance. The microeconomic theory of firm is not only ill suited to the complex contextual ecology of corporate finance, it is out of step with macroeconomic realities. Charles Ellis (1992) describes a paradigmatic revolu-tion in the field of financial analysis that provides a useful analogy to financial management in general. Essentially, he claims that the "dominant paradigm" of investment is fashioned around the single product/market scenario. Moreover it ignores long-term evolutionary dynamics such as those manifest in the shift from product-driven to client-driven economies. Ellis seems astonished that major macroeconomic trends have not engendered a more ecological approach to corporate finance. Perhaps they eventually will.

The Requisite Disorganization

Recognizing these types of lacunae between theory and practice reminds one how tools often have a life of their own. Thus it now seems an appropriate time to note that phase planes, or whatever nonlinear tricks of the trade eventually arrive into the lexicon of postmodern management, no matter how plentiful they become, do not guarantee corporate success. While necessary, the use of nonlinear tools is not a sufficient condition. As with TQM, it is possible to have all the trapping of practice with virtually none of the philosophical under-standing. Moreover, in the particular case of phase planes, it might be more advantageous for corporate leaders to understand the underlying ecology than to have results of the analysis. Information about trajectories is impor-tant, but it does not automatically produce the types of understandings required for effective intervention. The corporate "Zen," as it were, involves not merely recognizing nonlinearity, it entails being nonlinear. If TQM demands decentralization, then the true corporate embodiment of chaos and complexity requires disorganization.

In absolute terms, TQM has meant not only a development of other essential indicators of a firm's metabolism (namely, quality) but also a focus on radically different types of corporate relationships; in essence, an emphasis on suppliers, customers, and employees as integral members of the firm's family. As alluded to previously, the feedback and feedforward that define these relationships are by definition nonlinear parameters. They are vital elements of the firm's ecosystem linking internal and external environments. TQM as a managerial tool focuses attention on the new communication channels, but additional nonlinear thinking is needed to clarify, filter, amplify, and/or dampen the signals in such a way as to enhance the overall viability of the firm. Initially, firms can develop a number of useful tools and concepts to aid in this process, but ultimately (as with TQM) these tools must be replaced with a transformation of individual and institutional attitudes. In other words, a bag of tricks must evolve into a change in the *mental habits of management* for a reform to become fully operationalized. Corporate creativity and commitment cannot merely be programmed into even the most sophisticated simulations of nonlinear learning.

In an almost religious sense, nonlinear learning systems involve a certain level of believing before the seeing. If corporate executives are merely faking it, or attempting to manipulate employees, customers, and so forth, the strategy usually backfires. Thus, creating a nonlinear corporate culture will, in the long run, be more important than the use of any particular tools and concepts. Nevertheless as scholars of policy and management begin to explore these concepts in their research, as well as train a new generation of managers with their teaching, both the spirit and the letter of nonlinear management should be instilled. Not only will a more "user-friendly" set of concepts be engendered, but the general philosophy of adaptive systems will become more widespread.

Tools for the Twenty-first Century

Practical applications of various advanced systems and/or ecological concepts will eventually go far beyond the handful of techniques and strategies currently associated with the total quality movement. As suggested previously, what made TQM such a powerful set of tools is its somewhat accidental ability to tap into certain inborn tendencies within the ecology of complex organizations. As management scientists come to better understand these ecological elements, a vast panoply of new tools will emerge, and thus, the current gulf between theory and practice will be dramatically reduced. As one of the more imaginative management theorists, Gareth Morgan (1993), explains:

> We are leaving the age of organized organizations and moving into an era
> where the ability to understand, facilitate, and encourage processes of
> self-organization will become a key competence. (xxii)

At present, however, there is but a small and fairly arcane set of tools for
exploring the self-organizing dimensions of human systems. Since the word
organization is derived from the Greek phrase *orgon,* which means *tool,* the
notion of tools of self-organization may be an oxymoron or at the very least
redundant. Be that as it may, studies of complex self-organizing systems do
suggest a few practical applications of methods as well as concepts.

As mentioned previously, John Holland's (1992) work in *adaptive algo-*
rithms, for one, appears to be an immediate source of useful applications.
Characterizing a firm as a set of "adaptive agents" operating within an established set of rules (both internal and external) not only allows one to operationalize various behavioral understandings (à la March and Simon 1958) but also
to simulate any number of alternative arrangements and thereby test their impact
upon the processes of self-organization. Simulation is a widely used tool in
engineering and its allied sciences but has tended to fall into disfavor among
management scholars who preferred empirical inquiry and/or the formal logic
of economics. Mechanical or analog simulation devices are widely used in
training for any number of professions; thus, it seems somewhat strange that
managers should not use this technique to test out assumptions and behaviors
prior to the implementation of a given policy change. Such testing of adaptive
assumptions would be especially useful in conjunction with the newly emerging
applications of *game theory* to corporate strategy (see Brandenburger and
Nalebuff 1996 and chaps. 3 and 6 of the present work).

The key to self-organizing simulations is the opportunities to grow novel
responses. Like genetic systems that encode learning and adaptation over
numerous generations, simulations model the processes of learning by depicting
rules that over time begin to rewrite themselves. In essence, they serve as a
surrogate for "ontogenetic learning" (à la Wiener 1948). Thus, learning, which
is often merely assumed in various "game-theoretic" approaches to strategic
analysis, is made much more explicit. As suggested in the preceding such
simulations provide an instrument for learning about learning. Skillful managers
will sit down at a computer screen and introduce alternative assumptions or
protocols into a set of search and learning algorithms derived from their firm's
ongoing behavior. They will be looking to see how these changes affect the
firm's learning capabilities. If the firm is sufficiently adaptive, these simulations
will be "full of surprises," and feeding these novel results back into the system
should accelerate the processes of adaptation or destruction.

In contrast to the somewhat homeostatic analogy of metabolism, these
simulations map the metametabolism of the firm. The level of *brittleness* versus

resiliency is displayed. In essence, the potential for the firm to self-organize given certain levels of environmental turbulence and internal learning capabilities can be assessed. If the firm is extremely bureaucratized and brittle, then management strategies from downsizing to the introduction of small amounts of turbulence are suggested. It is well to note that downsizing in itself will not necessarily increase adaptability and given the threat to individual agents may even inhibit learning. Simulations that include information about internal psychological states can be used to identify trade-offs between disorganization and demoralization. By including these types of concerns adaptive algorithms themselves begin to evolve from their origins in the biological metaphors toward the emerging era of the brain metaphors. Here the analogies such as *synaptic strength* and *associative memory* begin to suggest new managerial response models.

As this era begins to fully unfold tools derived from the new cybernetics may become managerial mainstays. As alluded to earlier, concepts ranging from *parallel processing* to *fuzzy sets* are beginning to filter into the managerial nomenclature and will eventually develop their own associated methods. Initially, many of the tools will be fashioned from the format of *cellular automata,* given its power for simple graphic visualization. However, as the field of cognitive science races ahead, many more powerful mechanisms of mental representation will suggest useful managerial applications.

Mental Habits of the New Managers

Advances in the cognitive sciences and neurosciences may aid in the discovery of the final piece of the managerial puzzle, that is, the emergence of new mental habits. Again, merely focusing on tools will not guarantee that transition to third-millennium management. Moreover, while the cognitive sciences are likely to provide insights into processes of *intuition and creativity,* these will probably remain resistant to fixed formulas. Thus, the ability of individual managers to inspire their own nonlinear inspirations is all the more crucial. This is real "self"-organization. It is at this point of attitudinal transformation that a viable theoretical foundation takes on added practical value. Just as some self-help psychologists have found a cornucopia of useful concepts in the theories of cybernetics and self-organizing systems (e.g., Maltz 1960), these notions can be useful to spur evolution at the level of the individual as well as the firm.

If the tools of nonlinear management are to avoid becoming merely the second coming of Frederick Taylor, the distinction between old and new systems theory is one that managers must live as well as learn. In his sweeping review, *The Evolution of Management Theory: Past, Present, and Future,* William Roth

(1993) describes the revival of systems theory in terms of a key distinction in the way personnel are represented.

> In the "business world," there is a better "fit" when one recognizes that "workers" are purposeful rather than purposive systems like machines. . . . [Workers, obviously have different needs] . . . periodic training in new technologies, periodic evaluations, word processing skills. . . . [Also] private needs which were far more complex, and [involve] not only the immediate work environment, but also the home and community. (125)

He adds the following distinctions regarding the *sociotechnical systems* movement (à la Emery and Trist), suggesting that it grew from the realization that due to the increasing degree of turbulence found in the environment, the increasing difficulty in generating projections that remained accurate for the necessary length of time, organizations had to be restructured so that they were capable of learning from their environment on a continual basis and of adapting rapidly to what they learned. In order to "plan" effectively in this manner, therefore, management systems had to be structured in that way that took the greatest advantage of the eyes, ears, and expertise of all employees on all levels. More open communication channels had to be developed. Increased access to information had to be allowed. Problem-solving and decision-making procedures had to be modified (126–27).

Ultimately, open systems thinking not only defines the tools, it is the key to the mental habits of the new management. In his pop-management blockbuster, *The Fifth Discipline,* Peter Senge elaborates on the importance of systems theory. He maintains that "systems thinking" is the fifth discipline and that it integrates all the other disciplines, prevents gimmickry, and blends theory and practice. Moreover:

> Without a systemic orientation, there is no motivation to look at how the disciplines interrelate . . . it continually reminds us that the whole can exceed the sum of its parts. . . . For example, vision without systems thinking ends up painting lovely pictures of the future with no deep understanding of the forces that must be mastered to move from here to there. (12)

In the final analysis, the search for praxis, while difficult, is not fruitless. Without clearer epistemology the methodology is unlikely truly internalized. Hopefully, this review of some of the more ready-made applications of nonlinear thinking will convince the reader to engage in a bit of nonlinear behavior by going back to the earlier chapters and reexploring the theory with renewed enthusiasm.

CHAPTER 8

Macrodynamics and Transformational Forces

Much of the discussion thus far has revolved around how complex nonlinear dynamics engender certain macrostructures and how those macrostructures might influence microbehaviors. Obviously, the behavior of individuals and institutions at the microlevel also exudes a powerful impact upon the patterns that form at the macrolevel. These patterns are not only provide "rules of thumb" for strategic choices, they are often amplified in such a way as to constitute full-blown transformation forces that overwhelm strategic assessments entirely. That is to say, even those planners and policymakers who appreciate the dynamics of macrostructures, and the bounds of institutional learning capabilities, can still be dumbfounded by the generic transformations they themselves are helping to shape. However, as social scientists in general and management scholars in particular gain greater experience with the larger and larger gestalt of their enterprise, perhaps even these epic transformations will seem not nearly so inexplicable. The beauty and wonder, as well as potential terror, that await social scientists at the level of macrodynamics may ultimately lead to the design of more resilient and creatively adaptive institutions and, in turn, influence the emergence of unique macropatterns.

The emergence of macrostructures, while governed by simple rules, results from a myriad of microinteractions, including the influence of those at the level of emergent structures themselves. In the economic sphere, these various patterning processes can self-organize into simple short-term cycles or accumulate in "long waves," potentially producing massive economic dislocations. Massive shifts from the typical ebb and flow of human activity often result from, as well as result in, major cultural and political upheavals (wars, plagues, famine). Both at the macro- and the microlevel the processes of technological change provide a paradigm case of nonlinear dynamics. As such, this domain is often the point of introduction for many an otherwise orthodox economist or management scientist.

This curiosity regarding the processes of nonlinearity is likely to become even more compelling as industrialized nations struggle to adapt to the most monumental technological transformation in human history—the information revolution. Technologies ranging from cellular phones to communication satellites and computer networks are not only allowing information to become a commodity, they are unlocking the genetic structure of society itself. Thus, this current wave of innovation may be the most pivotal in human history.

Focusing on these societal level or macrodynamical systems often generates a sort of ecological farsightedness. The discovery of certain underlying rhythms can create the illusion of a deus ex machina, when, in fact, macrodynamics are mutually causal with microbehaviors. Irrespective of their global scope, these major change dynamics both shape and are shaped by individual and microsystem behaviors. For example, the prime mover in Joseph Schumpeter's (1942) macroeconomic worldview is the heroic entrepreneurial individual and the associated industrial environment. Without the individual's and the system's transrational choices, the macrodynamics of "creative destruction" would *not* exist. However, once they do exist, they exude tremendous influence over the behavior of individuals and systems. In a similar fashion the synergistic and symbiotic interplay of macro- and microdynamics of all sorts forms a seamless web of iterative cause and effect. When macrolevel forces are discussed in isolation, as they often were in the past, one may have the mistaken impression that one is dealing with inexorable forces. For instance, "long waves" (the recurring cycles of economic boom and bust) often appear to have lives all their own, especially when cycles exhibit relatively uniform periodicity (every fifty years or so). Once set in motion they do seem to run true to form. But, in reality, the unfolding of any given economic cycle is the actual result of myriad systemic interactions between multiple actors and institutions. While readily discernable patterns may be present, the exact impact of transformational forces might be greatly extended or dramatically diminished in any given period. Furthermore, once freed from the grip of fate, policy designers might be swiftly cast into the gaping jaws of equally indifferent institutional inertia. In the final analysis, few can hope to actually divert or even harness transformational forces, but they can at least attempt to ride the waves of change rather than be crushed by them.

The Rhythms of Commerce

Above and beyond the nonlinearities manifest in the complex interaction of individuals and institutions, and even between firms and industries, are a number of curious clusters of mutual causality. These dynamics often emerge as patterns much like the chaotic rhythms of a healthy heart. *Commerce* is by definition a complex process through which goods and services are exchanged. Economists have long recognized that these processes are periodically buffeted by larger patterns (such as the *business cycle*), but they rarely fully explicate why, let alone how, these macroprocesses work (see Lorenz 1987). Some may realize that these cycles emerge from the combination of microbehaviors and macrodynamics, yet the unique synergism that amplifies small market forces is usually an exogenous concern. Nevertheless, at least their presence is widely appreciated. Much more problematic in appreciation are those cycles that occur over much longer periods of time yet often involve major economic downturns or *depressions.* These longer/deeper cycles named for the Russian economist Nicolai Kondratieff had until very recently been regarded as tantamount to mysticism by mainstream economics. These "Kondratieffs" or *long waves,* extend (fifty years or more) into cycles of boom and bust and are thought to correspond to major technological epochs (see Mensch 1979; also note Freeman 1982).

Numerous other cycles, consisting of patterns and nonlinear dynamics, tend to impinge upon the processes of regional economic development. At this level of economic geography, growth and prosperity are not merely a function of resource endowments and/or proximity to transportation corridors; rather they also include the nonlinear dynamics of industrial location. The firms often distribute themselves in a similar fashion to the flocking of birds or clumping of traffic. In this way, certain *regional attractors* are added to the ecological mix and may serve to catalyze conventional factors such as labor and capital mobility.

From Business Cycles to Long Waves

A certain measure of natural ebb and flow is a fairly well-accepted phenomenon for any given market oriented economy. As statistician Albert Sommers (1985) notes, a glance at economic data "reveals a persistent tendency toward alternating periods of expansion and contraction" (75). He explains that, in the aggregate, economies "shot through with feedbacks from one part of the system to another" will experience cyclical tides of change (shifting from expansion to recession). He contends that these are "familiar to . . . virtually all businessmen, who sense it in their own operations as the conditions confronting them go from strong uptrend, to uncertainty, to strong downtrend; and then on into renewed uncertainty, and then improvement. . . . A change in demand, for whatever reason, is not an event but an alteration of a rhythm—a shock wave that travels down a long and sensitive line of sub-demands (76–77).

These slowdowns and delays in speedup can be likened to the line of cars at a stoplight. The switching of the light can, in turn, be attributed to the same types of lags in supply and demand (involving inventory controls, and so on). But, of course, the processes are a good deal more complex, given feedback and imperfect market signaling, synergistic effects, and so on. Again statisticians (e.g., Sommers 1985) posit the presence of "powerful positive feedbacks," as well as "multipliers and accelerators" (79). These processes are straightforward, but the accumulation of cycles into larger patterns and the role of these patterns in the resulting behavior of industries and firms still seem to elude many an economist.

As Jaap van Duijn (1983) chronicles, industrialized economies are made up of a variety of interrelated cycles, including but not limited to the

- the inventory cycle;
- the fixed-investment cycle;
- the Kuznets cycle; and
- the Kondratieff cycle.

The first two of these cycles are mostly exhibited in the basic business cycle. Thus, it is the latter two that generate the greatest interest in the context of the present discussion.

The *Kuznets cycle,* discovered by American economist Simon Smith Kuznets (1930), is primarily a building and construction model, which fluctuates along an approximately fifteen-year cycle. Essentially, it models the interaction between economic and demographic variables. In the United States, where home building is such a critical industry, these cycles can take on major policy significance. By contrast, the study of *long waves* (or Kondratieff cycles) is, in the words of van Duijn (1983), "a European affair" and generally involves cycles that accumulate in major transformational forces (also see Berry 1991).

Another way to think of these various cycles is to compare them with the various types of attractors. The conventional business cycle is probably much like a limit cycle or perhaps a toris attractor. A Kuznets phenomenon might correspond to more radical oscillations such as a strange attractor. Long waves, to the extent that they exhibit sensitivity in initial conditions, may be the paradigm case of cumulative effects of chaotic attractors and the associated period-doubling cascades (e.g., butterfly effects).

The key point to keep in mind is that these types of cycles are not necessarily regularized patterns. Van Duijn (1983) explains the term *cyclical fluctuations* by saying that the word *cycle* implies regularity ("a self-repeating type of fluctuation of fixed length and amplitude"). In reality:

> no cycle in economic life will have such features. The lengths of cycles vary considerably and so does their severity. Yet they are self-repeating, and theoretical models have been built to explain why this is so. In fact, the essence of every cyclical fluctuation model is the explanation of the turning-points: why does an expansion turn into a contraction, and why does the economy get out of a trough again? (3)

Why indeed? Many a causal explanation has been rendered in the hope of exposing this backdrop of macroeconomic order. However, what is often ignored is that it might merely be the simple churning of the economic ecosystem itself that causes the various cycles to collide, combine, and eventually collapse the wave of prosperity. In fact, Kondratieff himself offered little explanation for the existence of long waves.

Nikolai Dimitriyevich Kondratieff (1892–1932), a brilliant young agricultural economist developed his long wave hypothesis in the early 1920s. He might have gone on to more fully develop his theory had he not been put to death by Stalin in the early 1930s. His view that capitalism would rebound obviously did not coincide with orthodox Marxism. Focusing primarily on the nineteenth century, he (Kondratieff 1935, 111) used somewhat spotty time series and historical observations to define the following benchmarks of long-term cyclical fluctuations.

1. During the rise of the long waves, years of prosperity are more numerous.
2. The agriculture sector is especially depressed during the downswing.
3. Technological innovations (techniques of production and communication) emerge during the downswing, but widespread adoptions await the next long upswing.
4. At the beginning of a long upswing, gold production increases, and the world market is enlarged by the assimilation of new countries, especially the former colonies.
5. It is during the rise of the long wave that the most disastrous and extensive wars and revolutions occur.

Essentially, Kondratieff posited a solid relationship between price movement and generic economic development. The long wave itself was believed to be an inherent element of capitalism, involving endogenous cyclical processes. He suspected that technological change was a key feature among these endogenous forces, yet his untimely death left it for others to more fully develop this theme.

Schumpeterian Dynamics and Technological Change

It was the Austrian economists who did the most to both clarify the various unintended consequences of cyclical fluctuations and identify innovation as the primary engine of capitalism. One in particular, Joseph Alois Schumpeter (1883–1950), has recently been rediscovered. Schumpeter (1934) consolidated the views of Kondratieff and earlier wave theorists into an integrated ecology of economic development. Schumpeter visualized the heroic entrepreneur as the linchpin of cyclical fluctuations. These innovators and their innovations initiate the processes of "creative destruction." Since like Kondratieff, Schumpeter perceived these processes as contingent to economic conditions, innovations played a mutually causal role in economic evolution.

According to Schumpeter (1934) "spontaneous and discontinuous changes" result from "new combinations" of materials and production forces. These combinations arise in innovative activities ranging from the introduction of new goods to the reorganization of industry. In addition to understanding these complex interactions, Schumpeter also appreciated that innovations tend to come in "swarms." Moreover, he associated these swarms of innovations with the onset of the prosperity portion of long waves. Applying these notions, Schumpeter developed the following basic chronology (see table 7).

Great debates have occurred over whether Schumpeter had his years absolutely correct, which seems to miss the point that these cycles need not be exact to tell a very interesting story about the true nature of macroeconomics. Specifically, "periodicity" is pretty much irrelevant, since institutional interventions will elongate or truncate a particular oscillation. Brian Berry (1994) observes that

> institutional changes since the Great Depression have reduced the limits within which prices and growth oscillate, forcing attractor basins towards limit cycles [, yet] long-wave movements [still] . . . display unpredictable dynamic system order, or deterministic chaos, the rhythms of which are controlled by the diffusion and ultimate market saturation of major technoeconomic paradigms. (8)

As Berry implies, institutional constraints have tended to be the focal point among the current generation of economists who still adhere to the long-wave perspective. Gerhard Mensch (1979) speaks of the "stalemate in technology," and Christopher Freeman (1982) illustrates how it is the resistance to technical change that sets in motion economic downturns.

TABLE 7. Schumpeter's Technological Waves

	Prosperity	Recession	Depression	Recovery
Industrial Revolution Kondratieff: Textiles	1787–1800	1801–1813	1814–1827	1828–1842
Bourgeois Kondratieff: Railroads	1843–1857	1858–1869	1870–1884/5	1886–1897
Neo-Mercantilist Kondratieff: Electricity	1898–1911	1912–1924/5	1925/6–1939	1886–1897

Source: Adapted from Kuznets 1953, 109.

Many other scholars have more or less rejected Schumpeter's concern with macrolevel transformations, especially in light of his forecasts regarding the demise of capitalism (1942). However, his observations regarding the microdynamics of technological change and the importance of entrepreneurial systems have been more or less confirmed over the years. Furthermore, the more closely one studies these critical internal elements of innovation, the more one begins to witness the germinal fluctuations that culminate in macrocycles.

The Rise of Technoeconomics

For most of the modern history of economics, "capital accumulation" was the raison d'être at the macrolevel, and technological innovations and entrepreneurship were considered tangential, at best. From time to time concepts of technical change have been reintroduced to economic theory but generally as an afterthought. Attempts were made by the likes of Robert Solow (1957) and others (e.g., Schmookler 1966) to alert their neoclassical colleagues to the centrality of technology. Furthermore, the role of technology within the confines of the conventional theory of the firm and the marketplace was studied extensively (e.g., Jewkes, Sawers, and Stillerman 1969; Mansfield 1968). While quite diverse, orthodox scholars have tended to focus on the following types of specific issues.

- Does the level of research and development (R & D) affect growth and competitive position?
- Does the size and/or level of diversification of the firm affect the level of innovation?
- What factors impact upon the rate of diffusion?
- Does science push or does the market pull innovations into existence?
- Does the structure of an industry (i.e., oligopology) promote increased R & D?

From these basic musings, a number of empirical findings and conceptual advances have gradually modified mainstream thinking about technology. One important departure was Paul David's (1975, 1985) extension of Arrow's "learning by doing" model, which opened the door for further developments in evolutionary explanation. David's illustrations of "path dependency" can now be seen as potential butterfly effects in which small historical events produce dramatic technological trajectories. Another significant advance was Mowery and Rosenberg's (1982) debunking of the "market pull" assumption. As they explain, "the production of new knowledge that underlies and shapes the innovation process is, itself, very inadequately served by market forces and the incentives of the market place" (236). Eric von Hippel's (1988) work on the "functional sources of innovation," "user-driven" and "supplier-driven" innovation, has also made a contribution.

Beyond recognizing the importance of technology, a handful of scholars has sought also to rejuvenate Schumpeter's concern for evolutionary systems. The crux of much of the nonorthodox work has been the characterization of dynamic processes that defy the conventional "production function." A primary contribution to this movement has been the work of Richard Nelson and Sidney Winter (1973, 1977, 1982). They rebuild *search* and *selection* models of the firm from the wreckage of *rationality, maximization,* and *equilibrium* concepts. Their models attempt to address items such as

- the rate of technical change;
- market structure as an endogenous variable; and
- innovation versus imitation within the competitive processes of technical change.

Under the Hood of Capitalism

These and similar conceptual challenges have provided the basis for a new generation of empirical inquiries, ones that actually try to get "under the hood" to see how the engine of advanced capitalism works. For instance, the work of William Abernathy and James Utterback (1978) demonstrates how the occurrence of "dominant product designs" radically alters the processes of evolution within an industry. Essentially, when designs are able to exude influence over standardization, competition shifts to issues of cost and scale and product performance. Recent extensions of this work (see Utterback and Suárez 1990) illustrate how processes, innovation, and integration give significant economic advantages to firms with "highly developed internal technical and engineering skills" and how these processes correspond to "ecological" models. A further refinement along these lines by Rebecca Henderson and Kim Clark (1990) suggests that innovation processes are not merely radical or incremental; rather, certain innovations (they call them "architectural") alter the fundamental "information processing procedures of established firms." They contend that such innovations are "difficult to recognize and hard to correct." Therefore, these concepts may explain both suboptimal investments and patterns of surprise within institutional evolution.

More interesting yet, a small group of technical change theorists (primarily European) relies directly upon the emerging methods and concepts of nonlinear dynamical systems (Dosi et al. 1988). As Dosi and Orsenigo (1988) suggest, these perspectives provide a new orientation toward processes of "coordination and transformation" and the general dynamics of technical change. They point out that standard models of coordination (among plans and actions of individual agents) depend upon the interplay of simple behavioral assumptions (e.g. maximization) By way of contrast, the "core heuristics" of their approach

> depends on the interaction between exploitable opportunities, present in nonstationary environments, which are too complex and too volatile to be fully mastered or understood by individual agents, and institutions which, to different degrees, simplify and govern behavior and interactions. (25)

Moreover, they picture "order in change" resulting from combinations of "(a) learning, (b) selection mechanisms, and (c) institutional structures."

Another perspective upon these nonlinear process of technological evolution is provided by Brian Arthur (1983, 1988, also found in an excellent nontechnical version in *Scientific American* 1990). His focus is dynamics, which, on the one hand, often "lock in" (1983) entire industries into inferior technologies and, on the other hand, generate "increasing returns to adoption" (1988). As mentioned previously, these feedback systems for innovations are similar to what Maruyuma (1982) described as "deviation amplifying mutual causal processes" and also correspond to the emerging emphases among industrial organization economists called "network externalities" (see Katz and Shapiro 1985). Arthur (1988) explains the implications of his work as follows.

> In this new literature, two or more superior technologies compete with each other, possibly to replace an outmoded one. Competition assumes a stronger theory of nonconvex allocation. There are multiple equilibria— multiple possible long-run adoption-share outcomes. The cumulation of small "random" events drives the adoption process into the domain of one of these outcomes, not necessarily the most desirable one. (604)

At a more generic level, Gerald Silverberg (1984, 1988) demonstrates how various nonlinear concepts, particularly those embedded in "selection models," are useful in exploring Schumpeter's processes of "creative destruction." His work (1988) also reconceptualizes how these revolutionary forces impact standard investment procedures. Standard approaches assume that technological frontiers move at an exogenously given and pretty much anticipated rate of growth. "The task becomes considerably more difficult when this rate is made partly endogenous, and when switch points arise between technological trajectories" (544). He proceeds to explain:

> The approach adopted by neoclassical theory—optimal innovation as a problem of maximization or a two-period game—is certainly very much at

odds with the perspective inherent in the evolutionary framework, which, as we shall see, hinges in an essential way on the stochastic nature of search processes, the problem of decision making under irreducible uncertainty, and collective effects. (p. 544)

Recognition of these curious dynamics has caused some scholars to return to Schumpeterian notions and focus primarily upon the peculiar behavior of entrepreneurs (see Bygrave 1989a, 1989b; Smilor and Feeser 1991). Raymond Smilor and Henry Feeser describe the implications of chaos theory to the study of entrepreneurial process as follows.

First, it helps explain the nature of risk in entrepreneurial ventures, especially in terms of the high-equity demands of venture capital organizations. Second, [it explains why] . . . public policy that seeks to target selected companies . . . is doomed to failure. Third, [why] . . . incomplete specification of variables . . . produce[s] intractable results. . . . Finally, [it] . . . provides direction for further research and analysis. (171)

In other words, whether or not scholars and policy practitioners accept large-scale cyclical fluctuations, microlevel phenomena exhibit sufficient nonlinearity to warrant a serious reappraisal of conventional economic practice as well as theory. The new praxis not only recognizes a richer contextual ecology of capitalism but the wondrous patterns and potential policy points that arise from the constant collision of synergistic recombination of these diverse elements.

Regional Attractors and Growing Silicon Valleys

While economic development for "developing nations" is obviously an important domain, regional economic policy in the United States presents an interesting test case of the importance of certain nonlinear dynamics. Not only do "swarms" of innovations occur within a given industry, swarms of innovators also arise within particular geographic regions (note Saxenian 1994). Recognition of this phenomenon, without much appreciation of the underlying processes, caused a deluge of dysfunctional development policies (see Daneke 1989). As Everett Rogers and Judith Larsen (1984) observed, nearly every state and local government across the United States was caught up in a frenzy of "Silicon Valley fever." That is, they believed they could somehow replicate the experience of Santa Clara County, California, and/or Route 128 around Boston. Unfortunately, the issue of exactly how one goes about "growing" a hotbed of technological entrepreneurship was rarely fully addressed.

Amid declining smokestack regions, "economic restructuring," and an increased awareness regarding the importance of technological innovation to the global competitiveness of U.S. industry, state and local governments began to pursue strategies of technological development in the 1980s. Initially this involved attempts to merely attract technology oriented manufacturing, but gradually policies designed to foster homegrown high-tech enterprises began to emerge. While logically linked to factors such as job generation, these initiatives were often ill conceived. They included the following ingredients:

- creating "incubators" (office and lab space and support systems) for research oriented firms;
- developing networks of venture capitalists, innovators, and community leaders;
- providing public research funding and/or insuring small business access to existing R & D dollars;
- setting up seed and venture capital pools, using vehicles such as pension funds;
- establishing additional tax and/or other incentive systems; and
- setting aside research park or similar facilities adjacent to universities.

While these activities were a significant departure from conventional economic development strategies, more often than not they were merely grafted onto traditional approaches. The bulk of the resources still went to incentives to lure new plants to a region. For most, "smokestack chasing" was merely replaced with "chip chasing" (see OTA 1984).

Economic development strategies, usually funded by the states, continue to emphasize tax subsidies and service breaks, along with extolling the virtues of access to transportation systems, markets, raw materials, and cheap labor, despite the fact that these factors are not nearly so important to the formation of high-tech industries. By contrast they require scientific infrastructure (e.g., research universities), a skilled and mobile labor force, a new ventures environment, and amenities associated with a high quality of life. Moreover, the U.S. Congress Office of Technology Assessment identifies additional elements of community culture (OTA 1984, 8).

1. An organizational culture that promotes a common civic perspective and a positive attitude about the region's attributes and prospects;
2. An environment that nurtures leaders, both public and private, who combine an established track record for innovation with a broad view of their community's resources and promise; and

3. A network of business/civic advocacy organizations that attracts the membership of top officers of major companies and receives from them the commitment of time and effort to work on issues of mutual concern, including cooperation with the public sector.

Yet, even if all these elements are present, the "network dynamics" of existing high-tech regions will still exhibit a sort of regional attractor for new start-ups as well as existing firms. As Annalee Saxenian (1994) suggests, after the initial stimulus of large scale defense related research expenditures, high-tech firms tended to cluster within regions where the synergism of university and entrepreneurial energy actively combined. Beginning, as it were, in a pattern of "requisite variety," entrepreneurial deviations are quickly amplified in such settings. "Creative destruction" itself becomes an industry. Eventually, the system evolves from a breakthrough system to a relatively stable production economy. In both cases, the desire of innovators to start up or relocate in a region of critical mass (in terms of venture capital, knowledge workers, and so on) generates the flocking behavior familiar in traffic studies.

This pattern of innovation clustering might cause many local economic planners to despair, observing that "those that already have, get more." While this basically is true, some of the same forces that attract may eventually repel. As life quality amenities diminish, housing costs soar, and competition for highly skilled labor becomes too intense, potential innovators may migrate to other regions. As alluded to earlier, these defections for cooperation also follow nonlinear dynamics (Glance and Huberman 1994). The diaspora from Silicon Valley to places in Utah, Oregon, and Arizona may be a case in point. While some of these regions merely captured assembly plants rather than the research shops associated with a spinoff economy, some of the larger high-tech firms gradually dispersed elements of their research at the hustings as well. Places like Austin, Texas, which built up their basic scientific infrastructure early, capitalized substantially on this secondary research dispersion.

Essentially, the message for would-be high-tech centers is that growing a Silicon Valley is extremely difficult, yet a community can work with various self-organizing processes instead of against them. Some of these processes were recognized several years ago by Jane Jacobs (1969, 1984). In fact in her opus *Cities and the Wealth of Nations* (1984), she sees a definite role for nonlinear mathematics in exploring the intricacies of regional economics. In essence, regions that maintain diversity can quickly reemerge. As she (1984) elaborates:

> regions in economic decline . . . can be rescued by an abrupt, explosive episode of import-replacing that not only disposes of the accumulating stresses and instabilities but also puts the city on a different and better footing for generating further export work. When surface traffic in a city

becomes insupportable and is relieved by a subway, the city has had recourse to discontinuity. (208)

Jacobs was perhaps the first scholar of urban change to realize the nonlinear dynamical character of these processes and thus anticipated recent applications in economic geography. She describes these prospects as follows.

> Mathematicians grappling with the difficult and mathematically controversial subject of discontinuities call the type I am dwelling on "bifurcations." What all bifurcations have in common is that they are not first causes, but responses to prior accruing instabilities and stresses; they "fork off," are discontinuous with what has gone immediately before; and they leave things radically changed. (208)

Like their corporate counterparts, those regional policymakers who learn to expect discontinuities could foster economic development out of the ruble of past economic epochs. When it comes to creating scientifically intensive industries, new ingredients must be added to the mix, but flux is the prime resource, in and of itself.

The Great Information Transformation

As the global economy, manifest most profoundly by the industrialized nations, enters into the fifth Kondratieff, one might be witnessing a transformation unparalleled in human history. Its revolutionary elements are just beginning to be felt, despite the fact that it is obviously well under way. It is not even clear, as of yet, how far along are those nations that are leading the charge. Recall that Brian Berry (1994) believes that institutional changes can prolong a given transformation; they can also forestall and thereby exacerbate economic dislocations. Whether the U.S. economy is now cycling in or cycling out is difficult to say at this point. However, what is relatively clear is that the transformation to an information society is not nearly complete.

In futuristic books such as Toffler's *Third Wave* (1980), the ongoing transformation from an industrial to an information society is heralded as being potentially more catastrophic than the previous transformation from agriculture to industry. Toffler contends that

> humanity faces a quantum leap forward. It faces the deepest social upheaval and creative restructuring of all time. Without clearly recognizing it, we are engaged in building a remarkable new civilization from the ground up. . . . Tearing our families apart, rocking our economy, paralyzing our political systems, shattering our values, the Third Wave affects everyone.

> . . . Much in this emerging civilization contradicts the old traditional
> industrial civilization. It is, at once and the same time, highly technological
> and anti-industrial. (4)

It is worth noting that in any given epoch, all the elements of previous eras are
still present. The United States is still an agricultural (albeit heavily mechanized)
and also an industrial nation. These omnipresent elements from previous eras
might constrain, but also conflict with, the emerging era. Toffler points out that

> the collision of wave fronts creates a raging ocean, full of clashing currents,
> eddies, and maelstroms which conceal the deeper, more important historic
> tides. . . . [T]he collision of Second and Third Waves creates social ten-
> sions, dangerous conflicts and strange new political wave fronts that cut
> across the usual divisions of class, race, sex, or party. This collision makes
> a shambles of traditional political vocabularies and makes it very difficult
> to separate the progressives from the reactionaries, friends from enemies.
> (9)

What is perhaps most interesting from the perspective of the more general
purpose of this book are Toffler's predictions that the third wave will also have
"its own distinctive world outlook, its own ways of dealing with time, space,
logic and causality" (5).

Irrespective of the exact mix of technologies as well as ideologies, the
current transformation will be "grand" to say the least. The exact level of
disruption will depend on the tenacity of existing institutions and the extent to
which they can be made more adaptive through the power of the very ideas to
which Toffler alludes. The tremendous tumult is a source of both institutional
and technological innovation. Moreover, the fact that information (both digital
and chemical) and communications fuel this transformation suggests that the
prospect for significant strides in social/cultural networking is enormous. Some
even see in global communication networks the potential for new forms of
collective consciousness, and the basis for more productive collective action
(Mayer-Kress 1994).

Revolution versus Evolution

While the fits and starts exhibited in the fossil record bear witness to the fact
that evolution is not a smooth continuous process, residuals of Darwinian theory
give the term *evolution* a certain sense of gradualism. The evolution of complex
societies, even if gradual, is so painful that the term *revolution* often seems
more appropriate. Given correct signals and learning opportunities, humans are
among the most adaptive creatures. Unfortunately, institutions usually conspire

to blur the necessity of change and rarely give way without dramatic events akin to "bloody revolution." The economic downturns associated with each new epoch bespeak these revolutionary tendencies. In the past terms like *crises* and *panic* gradually gave way to the less pejorative *depression* and now *recession*. Less onerous phraseology notwithstanding, current national economic planners may be no better equipped to avert an economic crisis than those of generations long past. Megacontrols (ranging from interest rates to built-in breaks on electronic trading) may actually create a false sense of security. In highly turbulent times, thousands of tiny factors, very far removed from the macro-policy levels, can send the entire economy swirling into deepening recessionary cycles. Moreover, at the level of individual households, which neoclassical models extol but largely ignore in the aggregate, "megatrends" can create crises from which only the most creative recover. Retraining displaced workers is much more difficult than it appears, and the processes further strain families that are already assailed on all sides.

As James Beniger (1986) contends, economic revolutions, while driven by technological change, are really about the overthrow and restoration of viable "control mechanisms" (via cybernetic theory). First, Beniger reminds one that the idea of revolution, borrowed from astronomy, was originally applied during the 1600s to movements aimed at restoring a previous form of government or leader, yet with the French Revolution during the eighteenth century, it took on its modern meaning of "abrupt and violent change" (7). Beniger evokes both of these contradictory connotations in his depiction of the "control revolution." It is the lag in the effective management of and restoration of order within technoeconomic changes that generates societal displacements. In essence, it is a "crisis in control."

For Beniger the ongoing information revolution, driven by knowledge industries and advances in "compunications" (the convergence of computers and communications technologies), presents a control crisis of monumental propor-tions. Since control itself is the commodity, it is unprecedented in human history. Beniger (1986) explains:

> digitalization promises to transform currently diverse forms of information into a generalized medium for processing and exchange by the social system, much as, centuries ago, the institution of common currencies and exchange rates began to transform local markets into a single world economy. We might therefore expect the implications of digitalization to be as profound for macrosociology as the institution of money was for macroeconomics. (25–26)

Resistance to this "brave new" digitized world is both very subtle and extremely profound. Beyond the basic dehumanization and alienation of the individual, institutions will become more brittle in their defense of a bygone era. This *brittleness*, in turn, greatly exacerbates the negative consequences of transformation both individually and societally.

In sketching out the fifth Kondratieff, Freeman and Perez (1988) describe several industry level limitations imposed by the previous "technoeconomic paradigm." These include the following.

- Diseconomies of scale and inflexibility of dedicated assembly line and process plant partly overcome by flexible manufacturing systems, networking, and economies of scope.
- Limitations of energy intensity and materials intensity partly overcome by electronic control systems and components.
- Limitations of hierarchical departmentalization overcome by "systemation," "networking" and integration of design, production, and marketing. (56)

As networks of small agile firms cooperate to create the software as well as hardware of new communication systems or the processes and products of bioengineering, dinosaur firms will engage in destructive downsizing, roboticizing, and outsourcing and/or undertake megamergers in order to stem the tide of declining revenues. They will also lobby in Washington, D.C., for protection from competition both foreign and domestic. As the general economy declines, government funding for scientific infrastructure, retraining, and so on, will be rechanneled to provide relief for these dinosaur industries and their investors. These measures will, of course, just prolong the agony.

Eventually, however, the vast potential of new investments and emerging industries will rekindle the prospects of sustainable prosperity, at least for those who can make the leap to the ranks of the "knowledge workers." As self-proclaimed social ecologist Peter Drucker (1994) points out, the era of a "blue collar" middle class, during which formal education was superfluous, was a brief and basically aberrant episode. Individual prosperity, in the information era, will not be easily obtained without a sizable investment in education and/or training.

One additional realm where microinnovations might produce a catastrophic macroeconomic effect is that of the financial institutions themselves. As Franklin Edwards (1996) points out, if inventions such as "derivative markets" and "global hedge funds" remain unregulated, then the potential for a global financial crisis looms large. Interestingly enough, it is the employment of mathematicians and physicists by the economic elite that fostered this potential butterfly effect (note Mulvey and Ziemba 1998). Apparently these so-called "financial engineers" ignore the fact that they may actually be creating the chaos that their sophisticated stochastic programming models are designed to detect well in advance. Both they and government officials who seek to police them would greatly profit from the types of ecological understandings alluded to previously. However, such understandings, at the level of global capital flows, will, in the face of unbridled greed, continue to harbor dangers.

Networks and the Global Brain

For those who make the leap to cyberspace, and even for those left behind, the world will be a dramatically different place. For one thing, the notion of place will be greatly expanded. Initially, one must recognize that advanced communications technologies create a global "common market." Gradually, economic relationships may even evolve to broaden social and cultural exchanges, as society begins to mirror notions such as "the global village." Whether sovereignty will ever be reduced is indeed problematic. For every example, such as the European Union, there are myriad cases of nationalism and even neotribalism, and, of course, religious divisions are still a source of considerable hostility. Nonetheless, expanding networks will introduce the possibility of addressing certain global issues at a new scale and scope. Furthermore, the possibility of massive parallel processing with literally millions of individual inputs portends a level of creative intelligence commensurate with the human brain.

James Beniger (1986) observed that global systematization is a direct result of the information transformation. That is, digitalization, information processing, and networking inevitably engender a worldwide economy with global production and consumption. As Beniger maintains, the perspective of "living systems" can now be applied to the study of multinational interactions.

Computer and complexity scientist Gottfried Mayer-Kress (1994) argues that the Internet is both a product and process of globalization. As such, it is itself governed by nonlinear dynamics and can be used to both simulate and stimulate adaptive learning on a global scale. He suggests that

> we know from the theory of complex neural systems (both artificial and natural) that the connectivity between the individual information processing units is essential for solving large, global tasks. For that reason we think that the conditions for the emergence of a *Global Brain* will become a reality in the near future. (2)

This *global brain* paradigm shifts the focus to three ingredients of a new modeling approach based on the following: (1) distributed, associative information servers; (2) global computer communication systems and their role as empirical research tool; and (3) distributed simulation servers as they develop into complex, adaptive systems in their own right. Unlike a mammoth computer (processing mountains of data and spilling out answers to the human condition) the global brain is like an immense "bulletin board" where ideas interact, collide, and conflict and synergistic solutions emerge. Simulation models used to augment information and test critical assumptions would also be modeled after the behavior of adaptive agents, with these results filtering back through participatory networks. Hence, the global brain is not some type of gigantic guru; rather, it is a forum for collective problem solving. In the following chapter a more detailed assessment of this type of problem processing will be provided. For now, suffice it to say that provision of such a system, in a world where the vast majority of the population is still locked into a mixture of agricultural and industrial epochs, may unleash a new wave of crisis and evolution.

The Mixed Blessing of Biological Information

Since the early 1970s the promise of an even more profound information revolution has been unfolding, that being the genetic revolution. The development of gene splicing and the ability to recombine DNA, when coupled with the complete sequencing and mapping of the human genome, portend a new era of genetic manipulation. The implications for a "master race" or similar hubris aside, the dangers of these information breakthroughs may be as abundant as the benefits. Discovering the "genetic markers" for a particular disease may be of little use and much abuse (e.g., excluding individuals from health insurance plans, and so on). Moreover, in the context of a new era of systems research, these windows into the interworkings of plant, animal, and human genes may be a mixed blessing indeed. As Frijof Capra (1996, 77) points out, advances in molecular biology only served to make it more reductionistic and, thereby, isolate it from systems developments in the larger discipline (especially population biology). He elaborates that

> the "cracking of the genetic code" . . . [had] made us think of the strands of genes in the DNA as some kind of biochemical computer. . . . However, recent research has increasingly shown that this way of thinking is quite erroneous . . . the so called genome forms a vast interconnected network, rich in feedback loops, in which genes directly and indirectly regulate each other's activities. (204)

As Stuart Kauffman (1993) maintains, molecular biology, without an understanding of self-organizing systems, is misguided at best. With specific reference to "cell differentiation," it is not the genetic information that matters as much as the patterns of gene activity (described as state cycles in a binary network; see 479). Thus, ecological understandings are as vital at the microlevel of microbiology as they are at the level of institutions that will govern this new information revolution.

At the level of institutions, many of those individuals chosen to study the ethical and social implications of the human genome map have already been co-opted. In essence, setting aside funding for a small group of social researchers, the sponsors of the Human Genome Project have greatly delimited the discussion of potential problems (see Moore 1997). Scenarios from the realm of science fiction, yielding cloned cadres of genetically perfected beings, need not concern future generations as much as overlooking a variety of institutional shortcomings. Ecological approaches to institutional design could explore a wide variety of scenarios well in advance of adverse consequences. Nowhere perhaps is the exploration of industrial and associated societal trajectories more important than in this emerging technological realm in which life itself is the subject matter.

Conclusions

Irrespective of the exact character of future transformations, better understandings of the dynamic forces at work within and between industries and institutions are crucial. The preceding speculations aside, nonlinear processes at work from the level of the cell to the earth's atmosphere are becoming increasingly undeniable. With specific reference to intermediate cycles at the level of the economy, awareness is becoming more widespread. If potentially chaotic dynamics are at work in these cycles, then the exact configuration of accumulated cycles is indeed crucial. The relative proportions of crisis or cornucopia are virtually impossible to pinpoint. However, if economic policymakers understood these ingredients as well as the interactions that comprise these cycles, inventions might be a great deal more effective. Given the dispersed and decentralized nature of these interactions, interventions would be a good deal less bureaucratic and generally more infrastructural in orientation. Moreover, in keeping with the spirit of learning and adaptation, they would be designed to foster experimentation. The presence of long waves does not imply the future is fixed; it only becomes so if policymakers fail to engage themselves in the learning processes, or lack thereof, that limit oscillation. In the words of Alvin Toffler (1980) "with intelligence and a modicum of luck, the emergent civilization can be made more sane, sensible, and sustainable, more decent and more democratic than any we have ever known" (xxi).

CHAPTER 9

Expanding Systemic Choices

In the final analysis whether a vastly different approach to social inquiry and/or practical management takes hold and prospers depends to a large extent upon its overall utility. The standard test of theory in the so-called hard sciences—does it explain all that the existing theories explain, plus a bit more?—has already been met. Yet, without standardized methods of proof and procedures for replication, social inquiry often relies primarily upon what works. But do these approaches really work? Are claims to parsimonious explanation, actually valid? At this point in the book, the answer to these somewhat rhetorical questions should be obvious. Hopefully, a few additional examples will make it more so. Still, even with its provision for complex interactions and the patterns they produce, one must ask whether an ecological approach is really worth all the effort. It may be that a major factor slowing the progress of adaptive-agents research in economics is that often the simulation results do not differ all that much from simple formal explanations. Even if these economic explanations often involve an elaborate list of "priors" (institutional preconditions), and merely assume learning and adaptation, they are certainly more elegant. However, these solutions rarely emerge so simply in the real world; moreover, when they do, they are seldom very durable. The nonlinear dynamics present in all living systems, including human institutions, have a way of obliterating equilibrium of all sorts, even strategic (or Nash) equilibrium.

If, as Paul Diesing (1982) suggests, social science paradigms tend to evolve in response to major societal problems (e.g., poverty, environmental degradation, etc.), then real progress is certainly possible. The crashing of the third wave (postindustrial epoch) amid mounting global environmental concerns provides ample rationale for unraveling complex forces of natural and social transformation. Moreover, it seems extremely likely that once these forces are better understood the temptation for intervention will be overwhelming.

In recent years, leading textbooks on issues related to the natural environment (especially sustainable development) uniformly allude to a more ecological approach to environmental policy making, and a handful explicitly discusses the role of nonlinear dynamics in the development of these approaches (see Peet 1992; Hawken 1993; Wells 1996). Donald Wells's (1996) book, *Environmental*

Policy, actually has a chapter entitled "Fractals, Butterflies, and an Ethic for Global Ecosystem" (185–98). Yet, what is usually lacking from these discussions of nonlinearities in the ecosystem is the consideration of similar dynamics in the institutional ecology that directly impacts that system. New Zealander John Peet (1992) perhaps comes the nearest to fully integrating the logic of living systems into both realms. Yet, beyond recognizing that human systems are at once "metastable" and "dynamically unstable" (81), he does not really explore the constraints and opportunities imposed by institutional dynamics. Such explorations may in fact be extremely vital to the design of more effective environmental policies, especially given the ongoing global concern with *sustainable development.*

Toward an Institutional Ecology of Ecological Institutions

Recent years have witnessed a significant reconceptualization of the perennial problem of environment versus economics, known as "sustainable development" (SD). While this basic conceptualization has generated much governmental enthusiasm, extensive corporate support (especially in Europe and Canada), and a good deal of intellectual activity, it remains more a vague agenda than a set of policy mechanisms and/or "institutional designs." It might be more useful for sustainability to be explored as an issue of *strategic choice.* As alluded to earlier, the state of the art for such explorations, both at the level of the firm and the level of the state, has been various game-theoretic approaches. In fact, the study of resource economics is increasingly viewed through this lens and associated *public choice* ideas. While extremely enlightening, these approaches, anchored in neoclassical economic theory, do not adequately address the concerns of sustainability. In particular, they seldom address intergenerational and interregional equity issues. *More important, they do not fully comprehend the complexity of institutional change.*

Sustainable Development as Strategy

Environmental policy analysts from the European Community describe "sustainable development" as "a policy and strategy for continued economic and social development without detriment to the environment" (EC 1992, 3). Or, in the words of the *Brundtland Report* (1987), it is "development which meets the needs of the present without compromising the ability of future generations to meet their needs." Despite these types of pronouncements and a measure of academic exploration (e.g., Clark and Munn 1986; Milbraith 1989; Costanza 1991), sustainability remains a vague, "catchall" concept. As such, it has taken on that peculiar political status through which one can demonstrate rhetorical support without necessarily committing to particular policy requirements. Environmental editor for the *Economist* Francis Cairncross observes, "Every environmentally aware politician is in favor of it, a sure sign that they do not understand what it means" (1991, 26). As corporate advisor Stephen Schmidheiny (1992) contends, this rhetorical value is often evoked as a smoke screen for inactivity. Moreover, he points out that

> This is the crux of the problem of sustainable development, and perhaps the main reason why there has been great acceptance of it in principle, but less concrete actions to put it into practice: many of those with the power to effect the necessary changes have the least motivation to alter the status quo that gave them that power. (11)

Nonetheless "sustainable development" (SD) represents a powerful new set of concepts. Reasons for this are manifold but generally relate to the *unique blend of economic and environmental integrity*. The key to SD is that it does *not* separate environmental consequences from social and economic ones. As one corporate executive suggests, "Sustainability should be related to the role of market within the process of development itself." In other words, pricing mechanisms might be sufficiently adjusted so as to allow markets to use resources in a sustainable fashion. While resource and environmental economists have recognized this need and developed specific mechanisms (e.g., marketable emissions permits), a comprehensive reorientation of the market system is a fairly revolutionary idea. It is even more revolutionary when one considers that SD demands that critical resources will not be diminished. Of course, allowances might be made for technological advances to extend resource stocks.

This maintenance of the basic resource endowment is anchored in sound ecological and financial logic. Yet, it often flies in the face of existing institutional arrangements that encourage the *mining* (a term that implies utilization at nonsustainable levels) of natural resources. Subsidies for the extraction of virgin resources often place recycled materials at an extreme disadvantage. In short, institutional evolution is often at odds with the long-term viability of resource systems.

Despite these and various other institutional distractions, numerous firms have sought to become less of a burden on the global ecosystem. While it is often very difficult to distinguish between authentic and merely cosmetic *corporate greening,* in a nonlinear world even small cosmetic changes can be amplified into dramatic global effects.

As often happens with grandiose schemes, "sustainable development" is easier to visualize when applied to the global scale, especially in the context of developing regions. As the *Brundtland Report* (1987) suggests, the primary objectives of SD are as follows:

- reviving growth;
- changing the quality of growth;
- meeting essential needs for jobs, food, energy, water, and sanitation;
- ensuring a sustainable level of population;
- conserving and enhancing the resource base;
- reorienting technology and managing risk; and
- merging environment and economics in decision making. (49)

It is compelling to believe that this model of resource husbandry can be applied in countries that have not yet moved very far along the profligate path of the major industrialized nations. Unfortunately, wise use of resources appears even more difficult for people operating at a subsistence level. As famous naturalist Richard Leakey once observed, "To care about the environment requires at least one square meal a day." Herein lies a double meaning for the term *development.* This type of development will require more than just population controls; it will demand a significant redistribution of resources (and/or financing) to developing countries.

While requiring global thinking, "sustainable development" relies substantially upon local action, especially at the level of the individual firms and states. The link to concepts outlined in the preceding is often quite laborious; however, a vast array of corporate and/or government programs has been undertaken in the name of sustainability. Aside from international agreements (e.g., the Montreal Protocol on Green House Releases) there is a patchwork of programs, mostly initiated by industry, designed either to promote a public image or to achieve immediate production efficiencies. Examples of these activities include the following:

- green marketing;
- ecolabeling;
- environmental auditing; and
- life-cycle costing.

These initiatives are largely individual and primarily unilateral. However, occasionally consumer response is so intense that a new industry-wide standard is established (e.g., "dolphin safe" tuna). Other measures that are clearly cost effective, such as energy-saving devices, are likely to inspire widespread adoption, assuming the initial capital requirements are modest. When large-scale investments are needed, payoffs are remote and/or intangible, and levels of performance are difficult to monitor, corporate greening is likely to be more gradual and/or isolated. In such situations, calls for governmental intervention are usually intensified.

Given past antagonisms, the tools and strategies of governmental intervention are not particularly well suited to the task of engendering increased corporate greening. Thus, in those countries where major sustainability initiatives have emerged, they contradict as much as complement private-sector activities. Examples of such initiatives include the following:

- emission targets;
- fuel efficiency standards;
- national resource accounts; and
- general pollution laws, and so on.

Except for the final category, where specific guidelines for the handling and disposal of a given pollutant are concerned, most of these activities merely serve to underwrite some of the information or transaction costs of industry. Generally speaking, regulatory regimes involve more sticks than carrots (especially in the United States). More useful approaches might begin with more systematic assessments of the *industrial metabolism* (see Clark 1988; also note Ayres et al. 1989).

William Stigliani and his colleagues in the Project on Regional Materials Balance Approaches to Long-Term Environment Policy Planning at IIASA (the International Institute for Applied Systems Analysis) see *industrial metabolism* as a primary mechanism for augmenting various emerging tendencies toward corporate greening. Essentially the concept is an extension of an earlier movement known as *material balance*, which implied that any given industrial process can be redesigned to limit the overall "throughput" (loss of resources and/or return of wastes to the environment). Basically, industrial metabolism traces the path of a given chemical or material through the entire economy, exhibiting the transportation and transformation of the chemical or material, as well as its absorption processes. It is in the vernacular an approach to allow "cradle to grave" analysis. These elaborate assessments bring engineers and economists into the field previously reserved for various environmental scientists. These multidisciplinary teams not only broaden the scope of analysis, they convert it into far more useful information. Moreover, this broadened focus often picks up concerns critical to effective policy choices. As Stigliani and Jaffee (1994) explain, the goal of these studies is to more clearly understand and reduce exposure to toxic chemicals in a cost-effective way. Industrial metabolism

attempts to account for, and distinguish between, the various physical and chemical states of [environmental] toxic materials . . . as a basis for assessing their overall potential for mobilization. However, since such an accounting process is often ignored, the policies and standards set . . . do not, in general, reflect their true hazard potential. A chemical may be very toxic, but whether it poses a problem . . . depends on exposure, and exposure depends on the chemical's mobility and bio-availability. (vii–viii)

This type of modeling effort is expensive and might require agencies with taxing authority, and so on. Moreover, it might demand that firms divulge "proprietary information" about new industrial processes. Nevertheless, it is certainly an attempt to augment environmental awareness with more systemic thinking.

From Resource Economics to an Ecology of Resources

To more fully understand and nurture this emerging corporate environmentalism, it would be extremely useful to know more about the conditions (especially institutional settings) under which organizations choose sustainable paths. Historically speaking, the imprudent uses of natural resources were viewed as "failures" in private markets, thus automatically demanding government intervention. This intervention, in the form of a regulatory apparatus, has grown dramatically in the last few decades, yet resource problems remain unresolved. This and other lacunae have generated a gradual shift in focus from "market failures" to "government failures." Failures of both types are increasingly studied from the perspective of "public choice" theories (which see government agents as "rent seeking" and thus tend to argue for "market mechanisms" where possible).

By contrast an ecological perspective would view market and government failures as elements within a resource system in which a particular institutional mix broke down. Such a perspective would allow for the simultaneous representation of a vast array of individual and institutional choices and their synergistic interactions. Moreover, it would encompass multiple perspectives on institutional designs ranging from simple efficiency and "transaction cost" analyses to complex "resiliency" and "coevolutionary" explanations. Daniel Bromley (1989) describes public policy choices as involving many choice sets (defined by extant rules and conventions) that operate within the context of "institutional arrangements" and "transactions" and at least "four distinct types of institutional change." These changes impact (1) "net social dividend," (2) "distribution of income," (3) "allocation of economic opportunity," and (4) "distribution of advantage" (1989, 47–77). With specific reference to "sustainable development," one might add *intergeneration equity and long-term ecological viability,* as well as the problems of *corporate coordination* across vastly disparate industrial categories.

An extremely instructive example of the public choice perspective is provided by political scientist Elinor Ostrom (1990; also note Ostrom et al. 1994). Considering a range of resource cases, she and her students use a game-theory approach to illustrate how voluntary associations provide the optimal institutional arrangement for averting the famed *tragedy of commons* problem. This concept was coined by University of California–Santa Barbara biologist Garret Hardin (1968). He describes an open pasture, available to everyone in a given village. There are two types of herders, the one who overgrazes and the individual whose herd consumes only its share of the pasture. In this situation, the overgrazer benefits the most, and the fair share grazer is penalized. Meanwhile, the entire pasture gradually deteriorates. Paul Hawken (1993) contends that this concept has widespread applications. Moreover, he points out that the problem

> is not technically about a commons, but an "open access" system where anyone is free to take as much as they want. Commons have historically been extremely well controlled and regulated by the communities to which they belonged; not until colonization and industrialization have they been widely degraded and destroyed. (191–92)

It is noteworthy that in the cases Ostrom analyzes, she does not make this distinction; however, one can readily observe that those cases that involve small community situations were more successful in avoiding a resource crisis. Moreover, those that were successful were not necessarily managing the resource in a sustainable fashion. Even short-run success required an elaborate set of "priors" or preconditions. Among others, these included the following

1. relatively accurate information about the structure and flow characteristics of the resource;
2. absence of extreme conflicts of interests among appropriators;
3. ability of appropriators to communicate with one another and establish trust and shared norms;
4. relatively low transformation costs as compared to potential benefits;
5. knowledge of the effects of diverse rules on behavior and outcome; and
6. availability of entrepreneurship either within the set of appropriators or in the surrounding governance structures. (205–11)

If government is not needed to underwrite these huge informational and transactional prerequisites, then it still must sanction the resulting organizations. Even if so-called special-district governments evolve, their taxing authority and/or police powers derive from the state. At the very least, one ends up back at Hardin's solution of "mutual coercion, mutually agreed upon" (1968, 1247).

Ostrom's analysis is illuminating, but it would greatly benefit from explorations of the nonlinear dynamics of this mutuality. As Laurent Dobuzinskis (1987) explains, a market economy is usually an efficient self-regulating system, more so than administered economies. However,

> it is *not* a self-organizing system. That is, a market economy is reproduced by the polity as a whole. The norms that regulate exchanges of goods and services on national and international markets are often authoritatively determined by political means, or evolved through customs, religious practices, etc. They are *not* spontaneously generated by the economic institutions in isolation from the other societal institutions. (172)

With specific reference to "tragedy of the commons" type situations, if one applies Glance and Huberman's (1994) nonlinear perspective, self-regulation becomes far less sustainable. As they elaborate these

> perturbations are caused by the uncertainty that individuals have about the behaviors of others. If an individual misperceives the level of cooperation in the group, she may erroneously defect and thereby briefly move the system away from equilibrium. The more uncertainty there is in the system, the more likely there will be fluctuations. (1994, 79)

Institutions designed for this more fluid world might seek to dampen inherent oscillations through increased information and/or open participation. Hackett et al. (1994), experimenting with "incomplete information," determined that resolving common property dilemmas requires open communication and accommodation between appropriators. They conclude that

> it is the result from our more complex, incomplete information design which points most directly to why one may observe institutions in the field which combine communication with . . . the sanctioning of nonconforming behavior. Face-to-face communication is a powerful tool. It is handicapped significantly, however, in situations in which group members are unable to develop or sustain the social capital necessary for enduring commitments. (123)

The social capital required to sustain accommodation might come from a "requisite variety" of participants, or it might come from external regulators. The default from voluntary associations to larger regulatory regimes probably involves the system reordering to a higher level of complexity. However, in either case the nonlinear behavior of appropriators as well as external regulators (even if the domain is going to be left to self-regulate) cannot be ignored.

An ecological perspective of actual institutions engaged in resource management cannot begin by assuming away existing institutions, particularly external regulators. Even if one is bent on deregulating and/or having regulators use reinstated market mechanisms (e.g., effluent fees, tradable emissions permits, etc.), the regulators are still present. In the real world, existing institutions are part of the game. Ian Ayres and John Braithwaite (1992) not only built the strategic behavior of regulators into their games, they illustrated a solution pattern that they call *responsive regulation.* They argue that a broadly participatory form of "co-regulation" is superior to traditional notions of "enforced self-regulation," from a practical as well as a game-theoretic perspective. Jenny Steward (1993) further enhances this perspective with her "complementary model," one that allows for variable policy responses (e.g., capacity building, persuasion, or learning). A conceptualization that overlays these types of analysis with that of Ostrom (1990) would greatly enrich the picture of how institutions (both public and private) actually evolve in response to resource problems.

Examples of Ecological Self-Organization

Examples of these curious dynamics can be seen at both the levels of the firm and the nation state. Firm level tendencies are exhibited in trends such as the burgeoning "green marketing" movement. Plus, awareness of international dynamics can be seen in potential approaches to "global warming." From the perspective of institutional ecology, both of these highly diverse domains entail systemic choices. Moreover, as David Cooperrider and William Pasmore (1991) contend, these types of issues also exhibit an emerging "global social consciousness." To the extent that these issues indicate both market failures and government failures, a perspective that illustrates coevolutionary processes should not only provide better social inquiry, it should be useful in the redesign of institutions.

The Greening of the Marketplace

While extremely subtle in terms of their impact on global sustainability, efforts at "green marketing" and "ecolabeling" provide an interesting institutional case. They represent a complex coordination problem where corporate leadership, consumer awareness, and regulatory responsibility have been renegotiated through coevolving institutions. The advent of ecolabels makes significant use of market-like processes, yet it also guards against exploitation of environmentally aware consumers by providing a high-bred system of signal authentication. Moreover, it establishes a vehicle through which consumer awareness can be enhanced by further amplifying the signals.

Whether the results of interest group pressures or more direct market motives, "green marketing" became a watchword in corporate boardrooms by the late 1980s, especially in Canada and Europe (see Westley and Vredenburg 1991; Lampe and Gazda 1992). Meanwhile, leading U.S. business schools have been developing environmental curricula (NWF 1989, 1990; MEB 1993), but corporate America still lags behind the rest of the world. However, as evidence continues to mount regarding the economic returns from "greenness" (see Post 1992; Russo and Fouts 1993) and markets for green products grow, corporate environmentalism is likely to become a universal ethos.

On the other hand, some unscrupulous or merely ignorant firms may continue to "free ride" on this rising tide of added value. If this is the case, it becomes an "appropriability" problem where authentically green corporations are unable to benefit commensurately with their efforts. Defections from cooperation could quickly snowball into institutional failure. For example, just as the label *lite* was shown to be inaccurate in many cases, "green" could become meaningless. Standard regulatory procedures for policing of false claims are probably insufficient to detect abuses in the field of green marketing. Technical expertise and added information gathering are likely to prove too expensive for most already overburdened regulatory agencies.

Ecolabeling evolved not only as a response to the potential for false environmental advertising but also as a device for focusing consumer pressure. It also provided a broad range of firms to engage in the development of "green products." While demanding a certain level of institutional rearrangement, firms voluntarily seek a label, and, of course, consumers voluntarily purchase the products. In the United States, the labeling agencies are even voluntary associations, that is, nongovernmental and generally nonprofit. The Green Seal is the outgrowth of the efforts of Denis Hayes, a longtime environmental organizer (father of Earth Day) and former director of the Solar Energy Research Center in Colorado. The Green Cross and the Good Earthkeeping (a product of *Good Housekeeping*) labels are independent yet industry sanctioned. This multiplicity of labels, coupled with the lack of uniform standards, provides a fertile field for "free riders" or merely consumer confusion.

By direct contrast in Europe, there are multiple country labels, but they have clearer meaning. Germany's *Blue Angel* and the Nordic countries' *White Swan* are perhaps the best known, and both are government sanctioned. The European Community (EC) is also implementing a coordinated program under their *Starred Flower* seal (see EC 1992). Eventually, it will replace individual member labels and provide uniform standards.

In general, ecolabeling programs specify the materials, preparation, and guidelines for disposal of products. These criteria usually consider the complete "life cycle" of a particular product "from cradle to grave." The overall impact is assessed relative to similar products. As with the designation "low-fat," ecolabels do not necessarily suggest that the impact is zero. They merely indicate that several steps are being taken to minimize the environmental consequences, such as using recycled materials and/or pricing in such a way as to finance mitigation. For example, the Nordic program spells out the following objectives (NCM 1991):

1. provide consumers with guidance in order to choose products *least hazardous* to the environment;
2. encourage product development that takes into account environmental aspects in addition to economic and customary quality considerations; and
3. deliberate use of marketing forces as a complement to environmental legislation.

An extremely modest bureaucracy employing a few technical experts conducts assessments to assure that firms have earned a *White Swan.*

Ultimately, programs such as these find greater viability in a mixture of market and governmental arrangements, where strategic choices are clearly of the systemic variety. The mixed motives of short-term profits, midrange goodwill, and long-term environmental integrity suggest a coevolving institutional mix, with only partial stability. Gradually self-organizing dynamics will combine multiple ad hoc arrangements into formal and semiformal institutions that may or may not involve self-regulation. For example, in places like Canada where mutual trust prevails, environmental groups and corporations were able to develop informational stability at the level of voluntary associations. This process, which Frances Westley and Harrie Vredenburg (1991) labeled *strategic bridging,* may become so pronounced at the grassroots level as to render national labeling (the doves in a maple leaf) superfluous. Meanwhile, in the United States, the same dynamics may, given the lack of mutuality, require governmental monitoring (e.g., EPA) even if the instrument of implementation is some type of independent laboratory (like the Underwriters Laboratory, which guarantees uniformity in electrical fixtures). Again, sensitivity to initial conditions brings about differing cooperative outcomes from similar institutional processes.

Warming of the Global Commons

At the other end of the spectrum, so to speak, the warming of the earth's atmosphere presents itself as a truly global challenge. Acid rain, seabed dumping, and so on are commons' problems, but global warming is unprecedented in terms of scope and scale. The sheer size and uncertainty of the problem, combined with highly parochial methods of strategic assessment, have tended to paralyze institutional learning processes. Therefore, conceptual innovations have very real normative implications. Basically, the so-called greenhouse effect involves the buildup of various atmospheric gases (GHGs) in such a way as to dramatically raise the temperatures on earth in a relatively short and historically unprecedented period of time. While there is a good deal of scientific debate regarding the time frame and levels of change, there is a general consensus that a failure to meliorate this process will lead to cataclysmic consequences (Jones and Wigley 1990; Bernard 1993; UN IPCC 1995). Using newly calibrated models, which include a wider range of interactive effects, the UN sponsored an International Panel on Climate Change (UN IPCC 1995) made up of more than fifteen hundred leading climate experts. Their recent report concludes that under the worst case scenarios: (a) sea levels might rise up to three feet, (b) periodic heat waves could become more frequent, (c) hurricanes could intensify, and (d) temperatures and rainfall patterns could shift more radically. In other words, weather could become more chaotic and plant, animal, and human adaptations much more tenuous. How institutions evolve to address this problem will have serious impacts on resource and technological development strategies worldwide and vice versa.

The free use of the earth's atmosphere as a dumping ground is a classic "tragedy of the commons" problem, albeit more complex and convoluted than any explored in the literature. Unlike the cases considered by Ostrom (1990), the costs and benefits of appropriating the earth's atmosphere are *not* very evenly distributed. Owners of a coal-fired power plant in Ohio do not necessarily have to worry about rising oceans in Brazil or dying coral reefs in Australia. Obviously, global warming will eventually threaten the agricultural and coastal regions of the United States, yet these costs may be small in comparison with the benefits that accrue to inequitable use of the lion's share of the world's atmosphere. Despite these difficulties, learned economists, such as William Nordhaus (1990, 1991), have analyzed the warming issues in conventional cost-benefit calculus. Nordhaus calls the *greenhouse* problem the *granddaddy of public goods,* yet he conducts a simplified assessment of the damage function over the abatement costs, with a significant discount applied to future benefits. Irrespective of the fact that current patterns will greatly limit future choices, and that choices by developed nations greatly constrain economic prosperity for the developing regions of the world, current strategists seem to be willing to trust in the adaptability of future generations to resolve the problem and resolve it equitably. Critical assessments of this limited yet policy dominant view have begun to emerge (e.g., Morgenstein 1991; Cline 1992). For example, EPA economist Richard Morgenstein (1991) points out that there are many complex economic as well as scientific issues involved in the problems associated with climate change. Figuring out the costs and benefits of policy strategies depends on four main factors:

1. the breadth of quantifiable damages considered;
2. the number of GHGs for which practical control options are devised (and ancillary net benefits included);
3. the consideration of base case growth, technological damage, capital malleability, and related factors; and
4. the extent to which other policies (i.e., tax recycling/shifting) can be used to offset the macroeconomic effects of GHG policies. (145)

Not surprisingly, he concluded that the situation called for a great deal more research, especially a look at the international context and its impact upon the relative costs and benefits.

Concerns such as these have spawned earnest attempts at more comprehensive analyses (see Sinyak and Nagano 1992; Nakicenovic et al. 1993). Unfortunately, to the extent that such assessments are utilized, it is usually in an auxiliary role to the basic cost-benefit calculus. Likewise, scholars that highlight interregional (Young 1990) and intergenerational equity (Norgaard and Howarth 1991) equity issues have yet to make a major methodological impact. This curious and incoherent conversion of complex (including nonlinear) and uncertain elements of choice to single attribute (monetized), present value (discounted), linear optimization is a prime example of institutionally embedded myopia. If for no other reason than adequate explanation, these issues demand a more ecologically oriented appraisal.

Meanwhile from a normative yet highly practical perspective, if current calculations include assumptions about institutional adaptability, then why not put them to the test? Again, models of systemic choice, patterned after recent advances in artificial systems, could be used to clarify the plausibility of various levels of redesign and thus approximate the institutional sensitivity of strategic choices. For example, the currently popular and primarily passive (business as usual) scenario emerging from cost-benefit perspectives provides an interesting case in point. This scenario, which is mislabeled *no regrets* and prescribes little direct action on behalf of warming alone, nonetheless assumes the potential for rather dramatic institutional changes. As Yuri Sinyak and Koji Nagano (1992) illustrate, "no regrets" requires significant investments in energy efficiency and massive "technology transfers" to the third world. In other words, even if there are "no surprises" appreciable levels of adaptation are still needed but unaccounted for.

Developing actual indices of adaptability takes on added urgency if one assumes that surprises (at the levels of both environmental and institutional change) are more the norm than the exception. With specific reference to global warming, Thomas Schelling (1992) contends that the "reassuring gradualness" that characterizes current strategic assessments is probably "an artifact of the methodology" (3). Global climate will obviously involve high levels of uncertainty, in terms of "values" as well as "outcomes" (see Hammitt 1992). Thus, an emphasis should be placed on *resiliency* (systems that can survive as well as learn from their mistakes) explored through an ecological perspective. Such a perspective is likely to play a crucial role as the synergistic effects accelerate global environmental change in unpredictable ways. Given what is already known about atmospheric and other ecological dynamics (e.g., Lorenz 1984; Holling 1986), unpredictability (of the chaotic variety) is highly predictable.

An institutional ecology perspective, faced with enhancing systemic choices in the midst of great uncertainty, would opt for a type of purposeful policy experimentation at the levels of the firm, the industry, and the region. Presented with such a normative challenge, models of systemic choice can be used to accelerate adaptive learning and even inspire creativity. Initially, policy alternatives can be analyzed in terms of short-term versus long-term costs and benefits, yet in addition, an institutional or "transaction" value can be awarded to choices that expand rather than collapse future choices. Learning can be structured into the design of institutional experiments. To encourage resiliency, experiments might introduce a series of smaller shocks. Pricing mechanisms are obviously predicated upon these notions and tantamount to the testing of adaptability, but markets are rarely viewed as institutional experiments. Yet, if one could structure effluent fees on a graduated learning system, it would be much easier to ascertain the level of adaptability that reinstated markets could actually generate.

This experimentalism is particularly well suited to the global warming problem (note Jankowski 1990). Climatologists Jones and Wigley (1990) admonish policy making to resist the inevitable inertia of uncertainty as follows.

> uncertainties must not be used as excuses to delay formulating and implementing policies to reduce temperature increases caused by greenhouse gases. The longer the world waits to act, the greater will be the climate change that future generations will have to endure. (191)

The first of many viable policy initiatives would be process rather than product oriented. This does not imply a continuation of mere information gathering. Rather, it suggests the establishment of learning mechanisms within the design of alternative institutions. From a very pragmatic standpoint, it may be much easier to get firms and countries to accept a set of learning and experimenting procedures as opposed to a certain number of treaty targets or permits to pollute. Sometimes, resiliency and efficiency will dictate protection of rain forests; at other times they will illustrate investments in alternate coal technologies. A carbon tax may be the approach under certain circumstances, while retiring debt in exchange for lower forest depletion may prove useful in others. In essence, transforming existing energy industries will require an array of policy instruments (including taxes, incentives, and so on; see Steen 1994). Fashioning these effectively will demand a highly interactive and flexible set of regulatory regimes. In this regard the current experience with chloroflurocarbons (CFCs) may be instructive. It already appears that fixed standards and selective enforcement are producing a very lucrative "black market" for R12 (Freon gas). Allowing developing countries additional years to meet the global standard is also allowing them to produce R12 for illegal shipments to countries where the impending ban is already driving up the price of domestic supplies. Similarly, if a coal tax in Germany merely causes plants to relocate to Poland, then the purpose will have been defeated. In other words, the ability for novel adaptations (using a mixture of instruments) during implementation of international agreements needs to be built into the pattern of strategic responses.

Enhancing Global Adaptiveness

When it comes to global issues, perhaps the best that one can hope for is to build institutions that enhance learning and increase resiliency. Networks that form the "global brain" (see chap. 8) can be used to increase the scope and scale of participatory problem solving, but relatively few "tragedies" will actually be averted. Paths for escaping the full brunt of impacts, however, will more quickly present themselves from purposive experimentation (both actual and simulated). Furthermore, many potentially conflicted situations might be ameliorated. With the end of the ideologically based "cold war," scholars have begun to suggest that the conflicts of the future will be "culturally based" (note Barber 1995). While economic consolidation (NAFTA, European Union, etc.) has reduced traditional political boundaries, cultural identity and nationalism (e.g., Bosnia, Quebec, and so on) have been re-creating them. However, existing studies of geopolitics do not include an understanding of cultural clashes short of warfare. Confrontational dynamics that produce a sort of cultural annealing are especially ill understood. Here is a clear place where ecological approaches could have far-reaching policy implications. Cultural anthropologists who have studied how cultures blend into one another could identify threshold points for game theorists and conflict resolution scholars. In this way, rules of interaction could be directed toward facilitating creative responses. Historically, cultural diversity has often yielded hybrid patterns. Consider how elements of the Christian holiday of Christmas actually represent a blending of pagan rituals. Increasingly integrated global communications networks, including economic systems, are likely to accelerate the homogenization of cultural systems, and methods of accommodation that prevent political exploitation and polarization should be prized.

In general, whether at the level of the firm or the international organization, policy making for a nonlinear world is a tenuous undertaking. Hopefully most of the hubris of earlier incarnations of systems thinking has been dramatically diminished during the ensuing era. Often, the most durable solutions to pressing problems are the ones that systems themselves will engender through successive iterations of learning and adaptation. Learning, however, often requires a facilitator. In some other instances, learning demands a demolition specialist who can introduce a sufficient amount of internal (or let in enough external) turbulence to break down the recalcitrance of existing institutions. This brink-manship, of course, requires not only a detailed understanding of the institutional ecology (with its unique arcs of oscillation) but nerves of steel. For many a would-be "philosopher-king" (or mere CEO or world leader) the role of mentor is sufficiently harrowing. It is taxing enough to be expected to interject a modicum of creativity into the loops of organizational learning.

The challenge of being a nonlinear leader is a complex dynamic process by itself. However, several of the basic skills and/or mental habits can be developed, and the emerging sciences of nonlinear social inquiry (including but not limited to psychology) provide vital clues to training regimens. Many of the much admired yet heretofore somewhat mystical tools of creative management may become commonsensical via the logic of nonlinear systems. Responses that enhance the adaptive capabilities of already volatile systems will appear almost magical, and those who are bold or foolhardy enough to wade into the chaos of organizational or cultural change will appear quite heroic. Yet, as awareness grows regarding the living systems character of human institutions, the life expectancy of meddling mentors should be greatly expanded, along with the parameters of systemic choices.

The Care and Feeding of Nonlinear Thinkers

The argument is often made in pages of leading business magazines and even in some scholarly journals that corporate and community leaders are born rather than made. The outlandish compensation packages, "golden parachutes" and so on, may actually be prime examples of amplified distortions in executive labor markets more than an indication of the scarcity of critical skills. Nevertheless, the argument persists. This argument for unique abilities is probably best exemplified in the work of Elliot Jacques (1989). Jacques, a Harvard-trained psychologist (who has consulted with organizations ranging from the U.S. Army and Honeywell, Inc., to a huge Australian mining company), believes that CEOs posses a certain set of cognitive powers that allows them to act in the present while maintaining a fifty-year time horizon. Conversely, folks on the shop floor live one day at a time. Thus, his notion is labeled *stratified systems theory.* According to Jacques, cognitive power is "distributed in discrete population groups," and therefore someone either is or is not a "big-picture" person.

In contrast to this somewhat elitist position, most professional schools tend to believe that, given a certain level of native intelligence, a much larger segment of the population can be taught to be creative managers, public administrators, medical doctors, and so forth. This popular belief is supported by MIT artificial intelligence researcher Marvin Minsky (1985), who takes the antielitist position to an opposite extreme. For Minsky, increasing developments in artificial intelligence will free individuals to explore their creative potential and thereby greatly reduce the current gap between the Einsteins and the "also rans." Based on the assumption that actual intelligence is itself the result of a variety of nonlinear dynamics and that adaptive creatures can even arrange to augment their own creativity, it would seem that nonlinear thinking processes associated with the average executive acumen can certainly be transferred to a significant degree. This latter "care and feeding" model is not only congruent with nonlinear participatory dynamics (see Stacey 1996, 137–64) but coincides with a number of actual cases of corporate creativity (note Robinson and Stern 1997).

In addition to the rudimentary elements of creativity alluded to earlier, some very real patterns emerge within the processes of nonlinear thinking. Creativity educator Edward de Bono (1971) has labeled these patterns *lateral thinking* (i.e., getting off the linear track). Moreover, he maintains that nearly anyone can literally "learn" to think laterally. de Bono points out that his approach to thinking is modeled after "self-organizing information systems." The general ideas that guide his model include the following.

- The mind acts to create patterns, to recognize patterns, and to use patterns but not to change them.
- Sheer continuity is responsible for most ideas rather than a repeated assessment of their value.
- We have developed tools for establishing ideas and developing them but not for changing them.
- An idea *cannot* make the best use of available information; an idea arises from the nature of a sequential patterning system.
- No way of looking at things can be the best possible one.
- Thinking is not only a matter of using concepts but also of being able to change them.
- It is possible to change ideas by developing them, but it may also be necessary to change them by restructuring them.

- The patterning system of the mind needs the introduction of discontinuity to make the best use of available information. (47–48)

In other words, the creative mind must jog itself periodically by exploring discontinuities, and the concepts of nonlinear dynamical systems may be a necessary if not totally sufficient condition for such explorations.

By direct extrapolation, a creatively learning organization needs several creative minds, especially when it is confronted with an increasingly complex and confusing environment. As Ashby's (1956) "law of requisite variety" (see earlier discussion) suggests, a single CEO, no matter how powerful and gifted, is unlikely to generate sufficient novelty to successfully process the onslaught of information bombarding organizations. The fact that organizations need lots of nonlinear thinkers does not necessarily mean that they will always be appreciated and/or well rewarded (except for top management, of course). In his elaborate study of organizational learning, sponsored by the University of Michigan's Center for Research on the Utilization of Scientific Knowledge (CRUSK), Donald Michael (1973) contends that facilitators of "future responsive social learning" must themselves learn to do the following.

1. Live with and acknowledge great uncertainty.
2. Embrace error.
3. Seek and accept the ethical responsibility and the conflict-laden interpersonal circumstances that attend goal setting.
4. Evaluate the present in the light of anticipated futures and commit themselves to actions in the present intended to meet such long-range anticipations.
5. Live with role stress and forgo the satisfactions of stable, on-the-job, social group relationships.
6. Be open to changes in commitments and direction, as suggested by changes in the conjectural pictures of the future and evaluations of ongoing activities. (281–82)

While tools such as *simulated annealing* can illustrate how errors are melded into more strategic solutions, "embracing error" will remain a highly hazardous organizational activity. Most pursue the "cat box strategy" of covering up errors as quickly as possible. Again, the Japanese cultural approach of diverting blame while accepting and correcting mistakes is quite instructive. Obviously, Western organizations will have to find new ways to nurture their nonlinear thinkers if they are to increase their general resiliency, and tendencies toward scapegoating must be replaced with a "safe-fail" mentality. In-service training, in addition to professional programs, not only should begin to introduce the concepts and methods of nonlinear thinking but should also strive to inspire greater tolerance for the culture of creativity. Often this culture involves a great deal more *playfulness* than staid managers appreciate. Yet, a spirit of playfulness is often a prerequisite to successful error embracing.

Rules of Thumb for Developing Rules of Thumb

In organizations where creative learning becomes more or less routinized, the processes of nonlinear patterning become like rules of thumb for addressing a turbulent world. In essence, they develop rules of thumb for developing rules of thumb. With specific reference to the types of global policy problems alluded to in this chapter, the following basic rules might emerge from the processes of thinking about them in a nonlinear fashion.

Rules of Thumb
1. Appreciation of the larger patterns is usually more useful than detailed understanding of the smaller causal underpinnings.
2. When larger scale forces are clouded with high levels of uncertainty, it is better to err on the side of activity.
3. It is usually better to trade long-term resiliency for short-term performance.
4. In complex and chaotic settings small changes may be all that are required to bring wild oscillations back into a stable pattern.
5. It is far simpler and potentially more productive to work with a system's processes of self-organization than against them.

The first rule recognizes that in the grand chess game of macropolicy, discovering the patterns of past victories is superior to a single optimal move. Generic "rules of thumb" in general are usually much more useful than mountains of empirical evidence about rather minor temporal relationships. Rules 3 and 4 are closely related and basically address the tendency of institutions to await the arrival of crisis in order to build consensus for activity. (Global warming is a paradigm case.) Acting incrementally, especially when activities increase capabilities for managing future shocks upon the system, is always superior to the "watch and wait" strategy that prevails in the face of impending global crises. In all of these situations, the sensitivity to initial conditions (especially chaotic attractors) dictates that relatively minor adjustments are often sufficient to dampen a potentially catastrophic process. The final rule of working with self-organization is so simple, it should probably go without saying. However, the years spent covering over or completely denying the efficiency of "markets" (for example) are not merely a burgeoning source of political debate, they are a mounting concern of institutional ecologists. Markets are a powerful policy instrument, and when they "fail" (which usually means they didn't exist to begin with) they ought to be fixed, if they can be. The "public choice" approach discussed previously often fails to appreciate that markets are institutionally determined and that accurate pricing of various "unpriced values" requires some type of authority apparatus. "School vouchers," for instance, are just a distribution mechanism for the "public good" of educational funding, funding that would have been insufficient if left to the larger market. Moreover, "transaction" and "information" costs incurred in choosing a school (not to mention transportation costs) are not equitably distributed. Yet, assuming that these costs can be underwritten by public agencies, school vouchers may be just the device needed to shock the public schools out of lethargy and rekindle learning about learning. In any case, markets often provide their own powerful pedagogy of social learning. While markets are only a pale approximation of self-organizing systems in general, working with them, rather than against them, is usually more efficacious.

Final Thoughts

Practitioners, consultants, and self-help gurus will develop, and already have developed, more elaborate lessons from the theme of nonlinear dynamics. It was not the purpose of this book to necessarily join them in marketing the concept as a "New Age" form of managerial magic. The various practical examples throughout were merely to demonstrate that these ideas are not nearly so arcane as they might appear at first blush. This exercise might even be considered redundant by already successful managers and officials, since even the hard science observations tend to strike a familiar chord with many of them. The purpose of this book was to set forth a challenge to social scientists to flesh out these feelings of familiarity and to get them to add the rigor of their individual disciplines toward converting these managerial intuitions into a more readily transferable form of knowledge. Many of the tools and concepts already used to explore these notions in the physical sciences (where they are already much more than speculative intuitions) are appropriate to the social sciences. Some are not very helpful, however. Sorting through them, as well as developing concepts more ideally suited to particular societal processes, is what this book is all about.

In the purer social sciences better explanation is usually sufficient grounds for theoretical explorations. It is interesting to note that nonlinear dynamical systems theory has already made substantial inroads in disciplines such as anthropology (see Carneiro 1982), where the motive is merely better understanding. In applied realms (the primary focus of this book) where better policy, or improving the human condition, should be the motive (along with more profits, perhaps), the progress remains gradual, at best. Hopefully, this discussion will inspire a few more applied theorists to at least begin to entertain nonlinear systems of thinking (i.e., creative) about nonlinear systems.

Glossary

Adaptation

An entity's ability to reproduce and survive, despite changes in the environment, by changing its structure and/or function.

Algorithm

A formal (mathematical) representation of a series of clear, efficient, and logical steps used to perform tasks or solve problems in a predictable and reliable manner. Algorithms facilitate human capacity for addressing complexities in the environment.

Algorithmic complexity

The level of complexity within a particular computational problem as measured by the smallest number of steps required to adequately describe the system.

Artificial intelligence

The branch of computer science that strives to replicate human intelligence, learning, and creativity.

Artificial life

The field that explores the essential features of "life" itself and simulates the patterns of interaction using computers.

Artificial neural networks

Computer models patterned after neurons in the human brain. Generally speaking they involve interconnected processing units that send signals to one another and turn on or off depending on the sum of their incoming signals.

Associative memory

A mechanism that expands search capabilities by using a variety of conceptualizations or characteristics of the item rather than the specified name of the item.

Attractor

An indicator that describes the particular state of systemic behavior: fixed-point attractor describes a period of steady state equilibrium; limit-cycle attractor describes periodic states of movement around equilibrium; and strange attractor describes a chaotic state with no apparent periods of equilibrium.

Austrian economics

Largely associated with a small group who came to the United States during the 1940s (particularly Schumpeter and von Hayek). While vaguely similar to neoclassism in basic approach, the Austrian school maintains a much more ecological orientation. It is also generally less wedded to marginalism.

Automata theory
The theoretical study of machines and their capabilities for performing tasks and solving problems by algorithms.

Automaton
A theoretical construct describing a machine that operates in an automatic fashion guided by a set of algorithms.

Autopoiesis
The property of a living system that perpetuates itself through self-regeneration.

Bifurcation
A vital element of self-organization, it involves the appearance of an additional pattern of behavior or sequence of states for a system when it passes a critical level of turbulence. Successive bifurcations generally double the value of a given parameter at each fork.

Calculus
Method of analysis and calculation developed by Newton that uses symbolic notation. Commonly associated with differential equations.

Catastrophe theory
A topological theory that describes a system's structure along a continuous evolutionary path, especially when discontinuities occur.

Causality
A relationship between events or activities by which they are assumed to impact one another. Traditionally thought of as entailing spatial proximity and directionality (where one event is a cause and the other is an effect), it can now include "remote" and "mutual" as well as extremely "weak" (as in "pink noise") versions.

Cellular automaton
A computer program or piece of hardware consisting of a web of cells or a "lattice." Each cell is assigned a set of instructions that allows it to respond to changes in the adjacent cells over a given unit of time; the interaction of cells models complex coevolution. It is also a primary device for constructing parallel processes.

Central processing unit (CPU)
The key component of a computer that actually executes the instructions.

Chaos
This is a dynamical system exhibiting aperiodic behavior. While appearing to be random, its behavior is deterministic. Chaotic systems are highly sensitive to initial conditions, and/or points quickly diverge from a linear path.

Closed system
A system that does not interact or exchange energy with its environment.

Coevolution
A pattern of systemic evolution by which systems and their environments evolve simultaneously. Neither Darwinian nor Lamarckian, it is predicated on inherent tendencies to create novelty.

Cognitive science
Hybrid field that unites physiologists, psychologists, and other behavioral theorists with computer scientists to explore the nature of human as well as machine intelligence.

Combinatorial explosion
Describes a pattern of choices where each choice engenders more choices exponentially. Generally speaking, cognitive processes cannot assimilate all of the choices generated.

Complementarity
Originally Bohr's notion that advanced "quantum theory." Now applied to describe various paradoxical yet instrumental combinations, such as change and necessity.

Complex adaptive system
A simulation approach that studies the coevolution of a set of interacting agents that have alternative sets of behavioral rules.

Complexity
The study of the simple behavior of systems exhibiting complex patterns of interactions, which in turn result from simple rules and responses distorted through self-organizing processes.

Cost-benefit analysis
Originally developed by the Army Corps of Engineers in the 1950s, it became a mainstay of economics in the program budgeting era of the 1960s. Essentially a method of projecting and then discounting (back to present value) a stream of future benefits to justify capital expenditures. It is an attempt to create market signals for "public goods."

Cybernetics
From the Greek, literally "the art of the steerman." It is the study of control dynamics that constantly adapt toward the achievement of particular goals.

Decision science
The psychological or sociological study of how individuals actually make decisions, in contrast with the "rational choice" or "economic man" theory. Decision science generates empirical evidence regarding various behavioral or institutional "anomalies," such as "sunk cost," "preference reversal," "framing effects," "altruism," and other forms of "bounded rationality."

Deterministic
A property of formal (mathematical) descriptions so that having met a set of relevant conditions, a particular event or set of events is assumed to occur with regularity.

Deviation amplifying feedback
A result of positive feedback in unstable evolutionary processes. The process begins as the difference between the value of a factor in the system and an environmental condition increases. The deviation amplifying feedback destroys the system or forces the system to adapt. In nature this process explains why certain species evolve past their survival niche.

Dialectical
A philosophical method generally associated with Hegal and Marx. It maintains that any given historical epoch is the product of a synthesis of a previous thesis and its challenge or antithesis. The synthesis then becomes the thesis to be challenged once again, and so on. This movement of ideas and ideology also holds that all of the elements of previous epochs are embedded in the current reigning synthesis.

Dissipative structure

A concept developed by Prigogine to explain a system maintaining itself "far from thermodynamic equilibrium" by structurally evolving to a higher level of complexity. In more general usage it refers to the process of qualitative state change involving bifurcations.

Double-loop learning

When a system self-consciously processes information from the environment to change its internal dominant schema. Double-loop learning enhances a system's ability to adapt, to reproduce, and to survive in its environment.

Dynamical system

A description of a system that changes over time. It also implies a system that actively participates in change via its internal structures.

Ecology

The scientific study of relationships between entities and their environments assessing the effects of complex interactions of internal and external stimuli and how entities evolve and survive over time.

Economics

From the Greek, literally "the affairs of the household." It is the most mathematically sophisticated field of social inquiry and is seen as a useful method for studying diverse patterns of behavior (nonmonetized as well as monetized).

Emergence

The process by which "behaviors" and "properties" arise within a given system. These entities are novel products of the interaction of the parts, and thus cnnot be inductively derived from the parts alone.

Entropy

A measurement of the level of disorder, energy loss, or noise in a given system. Also a measurement of the system's capacity for change.

Epistemology

The study of the origins and nature of knowledge itself.

Ergodic

The assumption that a given process is equally representative of the whole. It generally involves a probability that any state will recur. Thus, ergodicity equates to the probability that a system will return to a relatively stationary cycle.

Evolution

The ensemble of changes that a system undergoes in order to resist entropy; it generally involves adaptations to changes in the environment.

Evolutionarily stable strategy

The collection of behaviors or structures that resists replacement by new traits when those replacements are unlikely to yield successful reproduction.

Expert system

The polling and collection of diverse and often tacit knowledge into a computer program. A knowledge based system used to simulate collective human wisdom. The best example is the medical diagnostic program *Caduceus.*

FAT

The acronym for fuzzy approximation theorem. It is predicated on the belief that given enough rules a fuzzy system can model any continuous process. It is also a useful tool for filling in logical gaps in mathematics and computing.

Feedback

A mechanism in which information about the output of a process is used to reinforce the quality of a process (positive feedback) or to indicate a need to improve the process (negative feedback).

Fractal

From the Greek, literally "the broken path." A set of objects displaying patterns of scalar self-similarities; the design of each object is a pattern replicated in various scales and embedded in these replicas to form larger objects of similar design.

Fractal geometry

Developed by Mandelbrot, it is the geometry used to describe fractals which are often discontinuous and exhibit fractional attributes or dimensions.

Fuzzy logic

In mathematics and computing, a knowledge system that represents intrinsically imprecise notions that depend on their context (such as good/bad, tall/short, etc.).

Fuzzy system

A system in which inputs are converted to outputs using fuzzy rules. A fuzzy system manipulates inputs, produces outputs, learns from its own experiences, and, consequently, creates new fuzzy rules for future applications. Also called adaptive fuzzy system.

Gaia hypothesis

The proposition that all of the earth's living and nonliving entities form one system, which is maintained by complex feedback processes.

Game theory

A simple mathematical representation of competitive interaction derived from the work of von Neumann. Generally involves firms or agents as players attempting to maximize their utility but only achieving accommodation. Used in economics to posit a new concept of "strategic equilibrium" in the place of "general equilibrium." (See *Nash equilibrium*.)

General systems theory

The theoretical foundations for the "systems approach" generally associated with the work of von Bertalanffy. In addition to the basic concepts of holism, nonlinear interactions, and so on, this theory promotes the "unity of science," which seeks to identify common structural and behavioral features found in all forms of organization, especially in living organisms.

Genetic algorithm

A formal program that simulates genetic evolution to test hybrids (mutations and genetic learning) in search of a robust adaptation to facilitate organism survival. It makes use of "classifier systems" and "evolutionary programming."

Geometry
> The branch of mathematics concerned with spatial relationships and measurement of one-, two-, or three-dimensional problems or objects in space.

Gödel's theorem
> Originally applied to mathematic theory, it is now argued that any formal system is essentially "incomplete" since its "truth" cannot be a function of its own self-contained axioms. It maintains that a given formal system cannot be both consistent and decidable at the same time. The term is also applied to assert the limits of machine intelligence. Also known as Gödel's paradox.

Hermeneutics
> A science and method of inquiry that involve the investigator's values and perceptions in acquiring and interpreting phenomena during data collection and analysis.

Hierarchy
> A structure organized by grading or ranking levels of capacity, authority, or successive components.

Holism
> The doctrine of holism is "the whole is often greater than the sum of its parts." It is based upon the assumptions that the whole is irreducible (its parts cannot be understood alone) and the whole is understandable within its complex, contextual elements.

Information theory
> Developed by Shannon to separate "noise" from information carrying signals; currently it is used to trace the flow of information in complex systems and to compare information needs with the capacities of existing information processors. Information theory centers upon the level of statistical entropy in a given set of data or communication processes.

Innovation
> The introduction of a new dominant schema (potential innovation) or the successful adaptation of the new schema (actual innovation).

Institutional economics
> A tangent or subculture to mainstream economics that maintains an interest in the cultural and broader contextual elements of economic behavior. These elements include various "ceremonial" and "technological" indices. This approach adheres to an evolutionary model of economic and institutional change.

Intractable
> A problem so complex that it is nearly insolvable using normal (standard computational) methods.

Isomorphic
> Describes entities or systems with the same or similar forms, structures, processes, or functions.

Lattice
> A configuration with repeating patterns of points, lines, particles, or objects established by rules.

Learning
>A process whereby an entity receives information, processes it efficiently, and, thereby, acquires knowledge successfully.

Limit cycle
>A system with such low level or dampened oscillation that it appears to rapidly return to regular path.

Linear equation
>The mathematical representation of a constant relationship between two elements or variables; it produces a straight line when plotted on Cartesian axes.

Logical positivism
>The popular philosophy of science doctrine that maintains that conventional scientific methods may be strictly applied to all phenomena and that truth is "posited" to exist in observable reality. It maintains that all meaningful utterances are either analytical or deducible from observations.

Lyapunov exponent
>A mathematical tool for measuring an attractor's internal dynamics. A positive Lyapunov represents the level of sensitivity to initial conditions; a negative one indicates the eventual convergence of points.

Macroeconomics
>The field of social science that deals with economic policy at the level of industries and nation-states, such as monetary policy, fiscal policy, manpower policy, an so on, and concerns itself with inflation, taxation, government spending, and so forth. An example of a major approach to macroeconomics is Keynesianism, the use of government spending to stimulate private-sector spending during economic downturns.

Markov chain
>A process of successive events or information flows exhibiting an unequal distribution of transformational probabilities.

Markov machine
>A regulatory device governed by probabilistic states. Generally speaking, a search system using "hunt and stick" probabilistic simulations (rather than "trial and error" methods) to weave its way through a complex problem or maze.

Methodology
>The tools and concepts used to guide a given scientific inquiry. It specifies the objectives and approach of the particular discipline and their application to a specific problem.

Microeconomics
>A field of social science that deals primarily with the short-term optimization behavior of individuals and firms. Essentially it is concerned with marginal utility functions such as "marginal cost," "marginal revenue," "marginal rate of substitution," and so on.

Modeling
>A means of representing real world phenomena to facilitate understanding processes (decision making, problem solving).

Nash equilibrium

A game-theoretic situation involving a profile of strategies that forms "best responses" to another player's "optimal reactions." Generally, the notion of strategic equilibrium; it is most useful in normal-form games with complete information.

Natural selection

The process of certain entities or subsystems surviving and improving while others succumb to entropy; the survivors have adapted to changes in the environment.

Neoclassical economics

The reigning paradigm (mainstream approach) to economics, which resulted from a merger of classical (conservative) economic theory à la Adam Smith and modern "marginal utility theory." It applies differential calculus to compute first derivatives of particular functions; essentially, it is this approach that holds that economics can mirror the mathematical precision of physics.

Neural network

In natural systems the actual mesh within the brain; in artificial systems a mechanism for solving problems of a nonlinear dynamical sort patterned after neurons and synapses in the brain.

Nonequilibrium

A state of system behavior without an apparent equilibrium; thus, it is a system that will change over time.

Nonlinear

The mathematical property of complex relationships among two or more elements interacting. Nonlinear behavior is typical of most natural and many social situations. Generally speaking, it means getting more than one bargained for.

Nonlinearity

A property of feedback-driven systems such that actions generate more than one result and/or actions engender disproportional outcomes. Thus, they do not track on a simple causal path.

Open system

A system that exchanges energy and information with its environment; it changes its behavior in response to conditions outside its boundaries.

Operations research

Starting with the mobilized interaction of human and physical systems during the Second World War, operations research ("operational research" in Europe) is the attempt to apply the tools of modern science to complex situations: problems that arise in the direction and management of large systems of humans, machines, materials, and money in business, government, and defense. It incorporates measurements of factors such as change and risk with which to predict and compare the outcomes of alternative decisions, strategies, or controls.

Optimization

The theoretical achievement of the most ideal solution or condition for a particular problem. In reality, social interactions achieve suboptimization or satisficing, the best possible solution or outcome under the circumstances.

Parallel processing

A computer technique using multiple CPUs to facilitate simultaneous calculations (rather than serial calculations).

Perceptron

A simple machine model of a neuron comprising some input channels, a processing element, and a single output. Each input value is multipled by a channel weight, summed by the processor, passed through a nonlinear filter, and put into the output channel. Generally speaking, a method of decision making using the results of numerous small experiments.

Periodicity

The quality of recurring at regular intervals measured by time or number of computations between repetitions.

Phase plane

Allows the relationship between two mutually causal or overlapping variables to be plotted two-dimensionally on a Cartesian axis.

Positivism

See *logical positivism.*

Punctuated equilibrium

A term originally conceived as a device to explain the fits and starts of evolution as exhibited in the fossil record. Today it is generally used to describe systems of discontinuous change.

Random

Attribute of a process that is entirely or largely governed by chance.

Random walk

Where a past change in a variable has little or no effect on or relationship with former or future variable values.

Rational (economic) behavior

The economic assumption that individuals will maximize their utility within given circumstances. It logically excludes altruism and/or simple irrational behavior.

Recessive schema

A system's schema are sets of rules that model behavior; recessive schema are the rules not in use for a given process or action.

Reductionism

A doctrine stating that complex phenomena, knowledge, and experiences can be reduced to indivisible parts to facilitate explanation and understanding.

Redundancy

The variety within a system that exceeds the amount of information or variety in the environment. A device often used by natural systems to enhance resiliency.

Requisite variety

Thought of by Ashby as a lawlike property of systems that maintains that the level of control and regulation is delimited by the level of available information. Generally speaking, the level of variety must be roughly equal in both.

Self-organization

The spontaneous emergence of structural organization. Originally designed to study systems "far from equilibrium," it is now seen as a fundamental property of most (especially living) systems, whereby they maintain order through fluctuation.

Self-organized criticality

A pattern of nonequilibrium behavior in which there are characteristic long-range temporal and spatial regularities.

Self-similarity

A geometrical resemblance or physical correspondence between the parts of a system and the system as a whole. In fractal geometry, the composition of wholes and the parts participating in such wholes follow the same principles of construction, albeit on a smaller scale.

Simulated annealing

A notion borrowed from the heating and combining of metals. Based on systems that actually reheat up in order to gradually cool down, these models allow for a number of missteps in order to facilitate a better solution to a conflict-ridden situation.

Single-loop learning

When a system institutes an immutable dominant schema.

Social entropy

The deterioration of structures that govern a social system; anomie describes the extreme state.

Sociotechnical system

A system composed of social and technical subsystems or elements.

Statistical mechanics

The discipline that relates the properties of a system to its subsystem and elements.

Stochastic process

A process of change governed by probabilities where only statistical approximation is possible.

Sustainable development

A concept associated with a United Nations report about industrial practices in Europe, Canada, and a few other places around the globe. Essentially it maintains that resources can be utilized in such a way as to promote economic development while not denigrating the natural environment.

Synergistic or synergetic

A nonlinear system in which the summing of previously individual inputs produces an output which is greater than, or different from, the sum of the inputs.

Systems

A structure of interrelated elements which operate in such a way that their behavior cannot be reduced to any single element.

Systems approach

A holistic approach to problems of complex systems recognizing that the total system is greater in terms of variation than the simple sum of its parts.

Teleonomic

Describes a system designed to make choices self-consciously (rather than automatically or mechanically) to facilitate goal achievement.

Tragedy of the commons

Theory that the economic model of human behavior inevitably leads to the exploitation of the "common pool" (publically shared properties or resources). Based on the analogy to common grazing areas in England whereby each individual herder had an incentive to continue to use the commons until the grasses were exhausted. Thus, each individual gain generates a collective loss.

Uncertainty principle

The postulate stating it is impossible to precisely measure an entity because the observer and/or measurement process inevitably changes the entity. In the case of subatomic physics, once one isolates the location of a particle, its momentum becomes a matter of probability.

Whole

An irreducible pattern of interaction such that without recognition of its parts, a whole is essentially without structure and cannot be analyzed. It is a perceptual "gestalt." Moreover, when the parts are few, complex, different, and tenuously related, as in marriage, the properties of the parts may figure more prominently yet still cannot be used to explain the functioning of the whole.

Bibliography

Aase, K. K. 1993. A jump/diffusion consumption-based capital asset pricing model and the equity premium puzzle. *Mathematical Finance* 3 (2): 65–84.

Abegglen, J., and Stalk, G. 1985. *Kaisha: The Japanese corporation.* New York: Basic Books.

Abernathy, W., and Utterback, J. 1978. Patterns of innovation in technology. *Technology Review* 80 (7): 40–47.

Abraham, R., and Shaw, C. D. 1982. *Dynamics—The geometry of behavior.* 4 vols. Santa Cruz, CA: Aerial Press.

Ackoff, R. L. 1970. *A concept of corporate planning.* New York: Wiley.

Ackoff, R. L. 1981. On the use of models in corporate planning. *Strategic Management Journal* 2 (4): 353–59.

Adams, D. A. 1990. Parallel processing implications for management scientists. *Interfaces* 20 (3): 88–93.

Adams, R. N. 1988. *The eighth day: Social evolution as the self-organization of energy.* Austin: University of Texas Press.

Aggarwal, S. 1993. A quick guide to total quality management. *Business Horizons* 36 (3): 66–68.

Akerlof, G., and Yellen, J. 1985. Can small deviations from rationality make significant differences to economic equilibrium? *American Economic Review* 75 (September): 708–20.

Albert, A. (ed.). 1995. *Chaos and society.* Washington, D.C.: IOS Press.

Alchian, A. 1950. Uncertainty, evolution and economic theory. *Journal of Political Economy* 58 (3): 211–21.

Aldrich, H. 1979. *Organizations and environments.* Englewood Cliffs, NJ: Prentice-Hall.

Allen, P. M. 1982. Evolution, modelling and design in a complex world. *Environment and Planning* 9: 95–111.

Allen, P. M. 1983. Self-organization and evolution in urban systems. In R. W. Crosby (ed.), *Cities and regions as nonlinear decision systems,* 29–62. Boulder: Westview.

Allen, P. M. 1985. Towards a new synthesis in the modeling of evolving complex systems. *Environmental and Planning* 7: 65–84.

Allen, P. M. 1990. Why the future is not what it was: New models of evolution. *Futures* 22 (6): 555–70.

Allen, P. M., and McGlade, J. M. 1985. Modeling complexity: The dynamics of discovery and exploitation in a fisheries example. In I. Prigogine and M. Sanglier (eds.), *Laws of nature and human conduct,* 49–76. Brussels: Task Force of Research Information and Study on Science.

Allen, P. M., and McGlade, J. M. 1987. Modeling complex human systems: A fisheries example. *European Journal of Operational Research* 30: 147–67.

Allen, P. M., and Sanglier, M. 1978. Dynamic models of urban growth. *Journal of Social and Biological Structures* 1: 265–80.

Allen, P. M., and Sanglier, M. 1981. Urban evolution, self-organization, and decision-making. *Environment and Planning* 13: 167–83.

Allen, P. M., Sanglier, M., Engelen, G., and Boon, F. 1985. Towards a new synthesis in the modeling of evolving complex systems. *Environment and Planning* 12: 65–84.

Allison, G. T. 1962. *Essence of decision: Conceptual models and the Cuban missile crisis.* Boston: Little, Brown and Company.

Amburgey T. L., and Rao, H. 1996. Organizational ecology: Past, present, and future directions. *Academy of Management Journal* 39 (5): 1265–86.

Amit, R., and Shoemaker, P. 1990. Key success factors: Their foundation and application. Working paper, Policy Division, University of British Columbia, Vancouver.

Ansoff, H. I. 1979. *Strategic Management.* New York: Wiley.

Ansoff, H. I. 1987. The emerging paradigm of strategic behavior. *Strategic Management Journal* 8 (5): 501–15.

Aoki, M. and Dore, R. (eds.). 1994. *The Japanese firm: The sources of competitive strength.* New York: Oxford University Press.

Aranson, P. 1990. Methodological individualism against system: A confrontation. Working paper, Department of Economics, Emory University.

Arbib, M. A. 1964. *Algebraic theory of machines, languages, and semigroups.* New York: Academic Press.

Argyris, C. 1982. *Reasoning, learning and action.* San Francisco: Jossey-Bass.

Argyris, C. 1976. Organizational learning and effective management information systems. Working paper, Kennedy School of Government, Harvard University, Cambridge.

Argyris, C., and Schon, D. 1978. *Organizational learning: A theory of action perspective.* Reading, MA: Addison-Wesley.

Arifovic, J. 1995. Genetic algorithms and inflationary economies. *Journal of Monetary Economics* 36 (1): 219–27.

Arrow, K. J. 1994. Methodological individualism and social knowledge. *American Economic Review* 48 (2): 1–9.

Arrow, K. J., and Debreu, G. 1954. Existence of an equilibrium for a competitive economy. *Econometrica* 22: 265–90.

Arrow, K. J., and Hahn, F. 1971. *General competitive analysis.* San Francisco: Holden Day.

Arthur, W. B. 1983. Competing technologies and lock-in by historical events: The dynamics of allocation under increasing returns. Working paper, 89–90, International Institute for Applied Systems Analysis, Laxenburg, Austria.

Arthur, W. B. 1988. Competing technologies: An overview. In G. Dosi, C. Freeman, R. Nelson, G. Silverberg and L. Soete (eds.), *Technical change and economic theory,* 590–607. New York: Pinter.

Arthur, W. B. 1990. Positive feedbacks in the economy. *Scientific American* 262: 92–99.

Arthur, W. B. 1991. Designing economic agents that act like human agents: A behavioral approach to bounded rationality. *American Economic Review* 81 (2): 353–59.

Ashby, W. R. 1956. *An introduction to cybernetics.* London: Chapman and Hall.

Ashby, W. R. 1960. *Design for a brain: The origin of adaptive behavior.* New York: Wiley.

Ashmos, D. P., and Huber, G. P. 1987. The systems paradigm on organizational theory: Correcting the record and suggestions for the future. *Academy of Management Review* 12 (4): 607–21.

Attaran, M. 1996. The coming age of fuzzy logic in manufacturing and service. *Journal of Systems Management* 47 (2): 4–12.

Axelrod, R. 1984. *The evolution of cooperation.* New York: Basic Books.

Ayala, F. J. 1978. The mechanisms of evolution. *Scientific American* 239: 56–68.

Ayala, F. J. 1980. *Origin and evolution of man.* Madrid: Alianza.

Ayer, A. J. 1946. *Language, truth, and logic.* New York: V. Gollancz.

Ayers, C. E. 1944. *The theory of economic progress: A study of the fundamentals of economic development and cultural change.* New York: Schocken Books.

Ayres, I., and Braithwaite, J. 1992. *Responsive regulation: Transcending the deregulation debate.* New York: Oxford University Press.

Ayres, R. U. 1984. *The next industrial revolution: Reviving industry through innovation.* Cambridge, MA: Ballinger.

Ayres, R. U., Norberg-Bohm, V., Prince, J., Stigliani, W. M., and Yanowitz, I. 1989. Industrial metabolism. Working paper, RR-89–11, International Institute for Applied Systems Analysis, Laxenberg, Austria.

Backoff, R. W., and Mitnick, B. M. 1986. Reappraising the promise of general systems theory for the policy sciences. In W. N. Dunn (ed.), *Policy analysis: Perspectives, concepts, and methods,* 23–40. Greenwich, CT: JAI Press.

Bailey, K. D. 1994a. *Sociology and the new systems theory: Toward a theoretical synthesis.* Albany: State University of New York Press.

Bailey, K. D. 1994b. Talcott Parsons, social entropy theory, and living systems theory. *Behavioral Science* 39 (1): 25–45.

Bailey, M. T. 1992. Beyond reality: Decisionmaking in an interconnected world. In M. T. Baily and R. T. Mayer (eds.), *Public management in an interconnected world: Essays in the Minnowbrook tradition.* New York: Greenwood Press.

Bailyn, L. 1993. Patterned chaos in human resource management. *Sloan Management Review* 34 (2): 77–83.

Bak, P., and Chen, K. 1991. Self-organized criticality. *Scientific American* 264 (1, January): 46–53.

Baland, J. M., and Platteau, J. P. 1996. *Halting degradation of natural resources.* New York: Oxford University Press.

Barber, B. (ed.). 1970. *L. J. Henderson on social systems: Selected writings.* Chicago: The University of Chicago Press.

Barber, B. E. 1995. *Jihad vs. McWorld.* Boston: Ballentine.

Barley, S. R., and Kunda, G. 1992. Designs and devotion: Surges of rational and normative ideologies of control and managerial discourse. *Administrative Science Quarterly* 37: 363–99.

Barnett, W., and Chen, P. 1987. The aggregation-theoretic monetary aggregates are chaotic and have strange attractors. In W. Barnett, E. Berndt, and H. White (eds.), *Dynamic econometric modelling, Proceedings of the Third International Symposium in Economic Theory and Econometrics.* Cambridge: Cambridge University Press.

Barnett, W. A., Geweke, J., and Shell, K. (eds.). 1989. *Economic complexity: Chaos, sunspots, bubbles and nonlinearity.* New York: Cambridge University Press.

Barney, J. B. 1989. Firm resources and sustained competitive advantage. Working paper, 89–016, Department of Management, Texas A & M University, College Station.

Barton, S. 1994. Chaos, self-organization and psychology. *American Psychologist* 49 (1): 5–14.

Bateson, G. 1972. *Steps to an ecology of the mind.* Scranton, PA: Intext.

Bateson, G. 1980. *Mind and nature: A necessary unity.* New York: Bantam.

Batty, M., and Longley, P. 1994. *Fractal cities: A geometry of form and function.* San Diego, CA: Academic Press.

Bauman, Z. 1988. Is there a postmodern sociology? *Theory, Culture and Society* 5 (2/3): 217–37.

Baumol, W. J. 1972. On taxation and the control of externalities. *American Economic Review* 62: 307–22.

Baumol, W. J., and Benhabib, J. 1989. Chaos: Significance, mechanism, and economic applications. *Journal of Economic Perspectives* 3: 77–105.

Bechtel, W. 1991. *Connectionism and the mind: An introduction to parallel processing in networks.* Cambridge: B. Blackwell.

Bechtel, W., and Richardson, R. 1993. *Discovering complexity: Decomposition and localization as strategies in scientific research.* New Jersey: Princeton University Press.

Beer, M. 1992. Strategic-change research: An urgent need for usable rather than useful knowledge. *Journal of Management Inquiry* 1 (2): 111–16.

Beer, S. 1959. *Cybernetics and management.* London: English Universities Press.

Beer, S. 1979. *The heart of enterprise.* New York: Wiley.

Beer, S. 1985. *Diagnosing the system for organizations.* New York: Wiley.

Bellah, R., Madsen, R., Sullivan, W. M., Swidler, A., and Tipton, S. M. 1985. *Habits of the heart.* New York: Harper and Row.

Bendor, J. 1993. Uncertainty and the evolution of cooperation. *Journal of Conflict Resolution* 37 (4): 709–34.

Bendor, J. and Mookherjee, D. 1987. Institutional structure and the logic of ongoing collective action. *American Political Science Review* 81 (1): 129–54.

Benhabib, J., and Day, R. 1981. Rational choice and erratic behavior. *Review of Economic Studies* 48: 459–71.

Benhabib, J., and Day, R. 1982. A characterization of erratic dynamics in the overlapping generations model. *Journal of Economic Dynamics and Control* 4: 37–55.

Beniger, J. R. 1986. *Control revolution: Technological and economic origins of the information society.* Cambridge: Harvard University Press.

Bennett, J. W. 1993. *Human ecology as human behavior: Essays in environmental and development anthropology.* New Brunswick, NJ: Transaction.

Bennis, W. 1989. *On becoming a leader*. Reading, MA: Addison-Wesley.

Berlinski, D. 1976. *On systems analysis: An essay concerning the limitations of some mathematical methods in social, political, and biological sciences*. Cambridge, MA: The MIT Press.

Bernard, H. W. 1993. *Global warming unchecked: Signs to watch for*. Bloomington: Indiana University Press.

Berry, B. J. L. 1991. *Long-wave rhythms in economic development and political behavior*. Baltimore: Johns Hopkins University Press.

Berry, B. J. L. 1994. Long-wave chaos: A circumstantial web. Working paper, Political Economy Program, University of Texas at Dallas.

Bettis, R. A. 1991. Strategic management and the straightjacket: An editorial essay. *Organization Science* 2 (3): 315–19.

Bird, A., and Beecher, S. 1995. Links between business strategy and human resource management in U.S.-based Japanese subsidiaries: An empirical investigation. *Journal of International Business Studies* 26 (1): 23–46.

Black, M. 1937. Vagueness: An exercise in logical analysis. *Philosophy of Science* 4: 427–55.

Blackburn, R., and Rosen, B. 1993. Total quality and human resources management: Lessons learned from Baldridge Award winning companies. *Academy of Management Executive* 7 (3): 49–66.

Blank, S. C. 1991. "Chaos" in futures markets? A nonlinear dynamical analysis. *Journal of Futures Markets* 11 (6): 711–28.

Blinder, A. 1984. Reflections on the current state of macro-economic theory: Discussion. *American Economic Review* 74 (2): 417–19.

Bohm, D. 1980. *Wholeness and the implicate order*. London: Routledge and Kegan Paul.

Bohm, D., and Peat, F. D. 1987. *Science, order, and creativity*. New York: Bantam.

Bohr, N. 1934. *Atomic theory and the description of nature*. Cambridge, England: Cambridge University Press.

Bohr, N. 1958. *Atomic theory and human knowledge*. New York: Wiley.

Boldrin, M. 1990. Equilibrium models displaying endogenous fluctuations and chaos: A survey. *Journal of Monetary Economics* 25 (2): 189–222.

Borris, M., Tyson, L., and Zysman, J. 1984. Creating advantage: How government policies shape high technology trade. Working paper 13, Berkeley Roundtable on the International Economy, University of California, Berkeley.

Boulding, K. 1950. *A reconstruction of economics*. New York: Science Editions.

Boulding, K. 1964. General systems as a point of view. In M. D. Mesarovic (eds.), *View on general systems theory*. New York: Wiley.

Boulding, K. 1981. *Evolutionary economics*. Beverly Hills: Sage Publications.

Boulding, K. 1985. *The world as a total system*. Beverly Hills: Sage Publications.

Bown, W. 1992. Mathematicians learn how to control chaos. *New Scientist* 134 (1823): 16.

Boyd, R. and Richerson, P. J. 1988. The evolution of reciprocity in sizable groups. *Journal of Theoretical Biology* 132: 337–56.

Boyett, J. H., and Conn, H. P. 1991. *Workplace 2000: The revolution reshaping American business*. New York: Dutton.

Bracker, J. S. 1980. The historical development of the strategic management concept. *Academy of Management Review* 5 (2): 219–24.

Brand, S. 1974. *Il cybernetic frontiers*. New York: Random House.

Brandenburger, A., and Nalebuff, B. 1996. *Co-opetition*. New York: Doubleday.

Briggs, J., and Peat, D. F. 1989. *Turbulent mirror: An illustrated guide to chaos theory and the science of wholeness*. New York: Harper and Row.

Brock, W. A., Hsieh, D. A., and Lebaron, B. 1991. *Nonlinear dynamics, chaos, and instability: Statistical theory and economic evidence*. Cambridge, MA: The MIT Press.

Brock, W. A., and Sayers, C. L. 1988. Is the business cycle characterized by deterministic chaos? *Journal of Monetary Economics* 22: 71–90.

Brockman, J. 1995. *The third culture: Beyond the scientific revolution*. New York: Simon and Schuster.

Broekstra, G. 1991. Parts and wholes in management and organization. *Systems Research* 8 (3): 51–57.

Bromley, D. 1989. *Economic interests & institutions: The conceptual foundations of public policy*. New York: Basil Blackwell.

Brown, A. L., and Daneke, G. A. 1990. Adaptive systems and technological development within the Japanese political economy. In M. Lawless and L. R. Gomez-Mejia (eds.), *Strategic management in high technology firms*, 143–65. Greenwich, CT: JAI Press.

Brown, C. 1995. *Chaos and catastrophe theories: Sage quantitative applications #107*. Thousand Oaks: Sage Publications.

Brown, T. 1995. Nonlinear politics. Working paper, Department of Political Science, University of Missouri at Columbia.

Bruderer, E., and Singh, J. V. 1996. Organizational evolution, learning, and selection: A genetic-algorithm-based model. *Academy of Management Journal* 39 (5): 1322–48.

Brundtland, G. (ed.). 1987. *Our common future*. New York: Oxford University Press.

Buchanan, J., and Vanberg, V. 1990. The market as a creative process. Working paper, Center for the Study of Public Choice, George Mason University, Fairfax, VA.

Buckley, W. 1967. *Sociology and modern systems theory*. Englewood Cliffs, NJ: Prentice-Hall.

Buescher, K. L., and Kumar, P. R. 1993. Selecting model complexity in learning problems. Working paper, University of California, Los Alamos National Laboratory.

Bullard, J. 1993. Nonlinearity and chaos in economic models: Implications for policy decisions. *Economic Journal* 103 (419): 849–67.

Burgelman, R. A. 1988. Strategy making as a social learning process: The case of internal corporate venturing. *Interfaces* 18 (13): 74–85.

Burr, B. B. 1989. Chaos: New market theory emerges. *Pensions and Investment Age* 17 (15): 3–45.

Butler, A. 1990. A methodological approach to chaos: Are economists missing the point? *Federal Reserve Bank of St. Louis Review* 72 (2): 36–48.

Butz, M. R., Chamberlain, L. L., and McCown, W. G. 1997. *Strange attractors: Chaos, complexity and the art of family therapy*. New York: Wiley.

Buzzel, R. D., and Gale, B. T. 1987. *The PIMS principles: Linking strategy and performance.* New York: Macmillan.

Bygrave, W. D. 1989a. The entrepreneurship paradigm (I): A philosophical look at its research methodologies. *Entrepreneurship: Theory and Practice* 14 (1): 7–26.

Bygrave, W. D. 1989b. The entrepreneurship paradigm (II): Chaos and catastrophe among quantum jumps? *Entrepreneurship: Theory and Practice* 14 (2): 7–30.

Cairncross, F. 1991. *Costing the earth.* Boston: Harvard Business School Press.

Caldwell, B. 1982. *Beyond positivism: Economic methodology in the twentieth century.* Boston: George Allen and Unwin.

Çambel, A. B. 1993. *Applied chaos theory: A paradign for complexity.* San Diego: Academic Press.

Campbell, D. T. 1979. A tribal model of the social system vehicle carrying scientific knowledge. *Knowledge: Creation, Diffusion, Utilization* 1 (2): 181–99.

Campbell, D. T. 1988. Systems theory and social experimentation. Working paper, USSR-U.S. Conference of Systems Theory and Management, Moscow.

Candela, G., and Gardini, A. 1986. Estimation of a non-linear discrete-time macro model. *Journal of Economic Dynamics and Control* 10: 249–54.

Cannon, W. B. 1932. *Wisdom of the body.* New York: W.W. Norton.

Capezio, P., and Morehouse, D. 1993. *Taking the mystery out of TQM: A practical guide to total quality management.* New York: Career Press.

Capra, F. 1975. *The Tao of physics.* Berkeley: Shambhala.

Capra, F. 1982. *The turning point: Science, society and the rising culture.* New York: Bantam Books.

Capra, F. 1996. *The web of life: A new scientific understanding of living systems.* New York: Anchor Books.

Carley, K. M. 1998. Advances in the formal methods for representing and analyzing organizations. *Computational and Mathematical Organization Theory* 4 (1): 3–15.

Carneiro, R. L. 1982. Successive reequilibrations as the mechanism of cultural evolution. In W. Schieve and P. Allen (eds.), *Self-organization and dissipative structures: Applications in the physical and social sciences.* Austin: University of Texas Press.

Cascio, W. F. 1993. Downsizing: What do we know? What have we learned? *Academy of Management Executive* 7 (1): 95–104.

Castells, M. (ed.). 1985. *High technology, space and society: Sage Urban Affairs Annual Review,* no. 28. Beverly Hills, CA: Sage Publications.

Casti, J. L. 1989. *Alternate realities: Mathematical models of man and nature.* New York: Wiley.

Casti, J. L. 1990. *Searching for certainty: What scientists can know about the future.* New York: William Morrow.

Casti, J. L. 1994. *Complex-ification: Explaining a paradoxical world through the science of surprise.* New York: HarperPerennial.

Catanese, A. J., and Steiss, A. W. 1970. *Systemic planning: Theory and application.* Lexington, MA: D. C. Heath.

Caves, R. 1980. Corporate strategy and structure. *Journal of Economic Literature* 18 (1): 64–92.

Cespedes, F. V. 1990. Agendas, incubators, and marketing organization. *California Management Review* 33 (1): 27–53.

Chaitin, G. 1982. Gödel's theorem and information. *International Journal of Theoretical Physics* 21 (12): 941–54.

Chaitin, G. 1987. *Algorithmic information theory*. New York: Cambridge University Press.

Chaitin, G. 1988. Randomness in arithmetic. *Scientific American* 259 (1): 80–85.

Champy, J., and Nohria, N. 1996. *Fast forward: The best ideas on managing business change*. Boston, MA: Harvard Business School Press.

Chandler, A. D. 1962. *Strategy and structure: Chapters in the history of industrial enterprise*. Cambridge, MA: The MIT Press.

Checkland, P., and Scholes, J. 1990. *Soft systems methodology in action*. New York: Wiley.

Christensen, H. K., and Montgomery, C. A. 1981. Corporate economic performance: Diversification strategy vs. market structure. *Strategic Management Journal* 3 (2): 327–43.

Christensen, S. L. 1994. Management for reality. *Proceedings of the International Conference on Advances in Management*. Bowling Green, KY: ICAM.

Chung, K. 1992. A fuzzy set-theoretic method for public facility location. *European Journal of Operational Research* 58 (1): 90–98.

Churchland, P. M. 1990. *Neurocomputational perspective: The nature of mind and the structure of science*. Cambridge, MA: The MIT Press.

Clapham, W. B. 1981. *Human ecosystems*. New York: Macmillan.

Clark, W. C. 1988. The human dimensions of global environmental change. In *U.S. Committee on Global Change, Toward understanding of global change*, 134–96. Washington, D.C.: National Academy Press.

Clark, W. C., and Munn, R. E. (eds.). 1986. *Sustainable development of the biosphere*. New York: Cambridge University Press.

Cline, W. R. 1992. *The economics of global warming*. Washington, D.C.: Institute for International Economics.

Coase, R. H. 1937. The nature of the firm. *Economica* 4: 386–405.

Coase, R. H. 1960. The problem of social cost. *Journal of Law and Economics* 3 (1): 1–44.

Cochrane, R. 1993. Chaos theory and spatial dynamics: A comment. *Journal of Transport Economics and Policy* 26 (2): 197–201.

Cohen, J., and Stewart, I. 1994. *The collapse of chaos: Discovering simplicity in a complex world*. New York: Penguin.

Cohen, M., and Levinthal, D. 1990. Absorptive capacity: A new perspective on learning and innovation. *Administrative Science Quarterly* 35: 128–52.

Cohen, M., and March, J. 1986. *Leadership and ambiguity*. 2d ed. Boston: Harvard Business School Press.

Cohen, M., March, J., and Olsen, J. 1972. A garbage can model of organizational choice. *Administrative Science Quarterly* 17 (1): 1–25.

Coleman, J. S. 1989. Editor's introduction. *Rationality and Society* 1 (1): 5–9.

Commons, J. R. 1950. *The economics of collective action*. New York: Macmillan.

Commons, J. R. 1961. *Institutional economics.* Madison: University of Wisconsin Press.

Commons, J. R. 1968. *Legal foundations of capitalism.* Madison: University of Wisconsin Press.

Conley, P. 1970. *Experience curves as a planning tool.* Boston: The Boston Consulting Group.

Cook, K. S., and Levi, M. (eds.). 1990. *The limits of rationality.* Chicago: The University of Chicago Press.

Cooper, W., Sinha, K., and Sullivan, R. 1996. Accounting for complexity in costing high technology manufacturing. *Operations Research/Management Science* 36 (1): 75–83.

Cooperrider, D., and Pasmore, W. 1991. Global social change: A new agenda for social science. *Human Relations* 44 (10): 1037–55.

Corcoran, E. 1991. Ordering chaos. *Scientific American* 265 (2): 96–98.

Corning, P. 1983. *The synergism hypothesis.* New York: McGraw-Hill.

Costanza, R. (ed.). 1991. *Ecological economics: The science and management of sustainability.* New York: Columbia University Press.

Cournot, A. A. 1960. *Research in the mathematical principles of wealth.* Translated by Nathaniel T. Bacon. New York: Kelley.

Coveney, P., and Highfield, R. 1990. *The arrow of time: A voyage through science to solve time's greatest mystery.* New York: Ballantine Books.

Coveney, P., and Highfield, R. 1995. *Frontiers of complexity: The search for order in a chaotic world.* New York: Ballantine Books.

Cowan, R. 1988. Nuclear power reactors: A study in technological lock in. Working paper, Starr Center for Applied Economics, New York University.

Cox, E. 1993. Adaptive fuzzy systems. *IEEE Spectrum* 30 (2): 27–33.

Crichton, M. 1990. *Jurassic Park.* New York: Ballantine Books.

Cronbach, L. J. 1982. Prudent aspirations for social inquiry. In W. Kruskal (ed.), *The social sciences: Their nature and uses,* 125–31. Chicago: University of Chicago Press.

Crowley, R. 1993. The meaning of TQM. Working paper, Oregon Utility Regulatory Commission, Salem.

Crozier, M. 1964. *The bureaucratic phenomenon.* London: Tavistock.

Csikszentmihalyi, M. 1993. *The evolving self.* New York: HarperCollins Publishers.

Cyert, R. M., and March, J. G. 1963. *A behavioral theory of the firm.* Englewood Cliffs, NJ: Prentice-Hall.

Daft, R. L., and Buenger, V. 1990. Hitching a ride on the fast train to nowhere: The past and future of strategic management research. In I. Fredrickson (ed.), *Perspectives on strategic management.* New York: Harper Business.

Daft, R. L., and Lewin, A. Y. 1990. Can organization studies begin to break out of the normal science straight jacket? *Organization Science* 1 (1): 1–9.

Damanpour, F. 1996. Organizational complexity and innovation: Developing and testing multiple contingency models. *Management Science* 42 (5): 693–703.

Daneke, G. A. 1985a. U.S. technology at the crossroads. Working paper, Terman Engineering Center, Stanford University.

Daneke, G. A. 1985b. Regulation and the sociopathic firm. *Academy of Management Review* 10 (1): 15–20.

Daneke, G. A. 1986. Revitalizing U.S. technology: A review essay. *Public Administration Review* 44 (6): 668–72.

Daneke, G. A. 1988. On paradigmatic progress in public policy and administration. *Policy Studies Journal* 17: 277–96.

Daneke, G. A. 1989. Short-stack chasing: The prospects and perils of state and local high tech development. In R. Rist (ed.), *Annual review of public policy,* 283–99. Beverly Hills, CA: Sage Publications.

Daneke, G. A. 1990a. A science of public administration. *Public Administration Review* 50: 383–92.

Daneke, G. A. 1990b. Beyond the bureautization of U.S. biotechnology. *Technology Analysis and Strategic Management* 2 (2): 129–42.

Daneke, G. A. 1991. Reconciling systems theory and rational choice? In *National Public Management Research Conference Proceedings,* 92–99. Syracuse: The Maxwell School of Citizenship and Public Affairs, Syracuse University.

Daneke, G. A. 1992. Changing the context for university research: Toward a new political economy of technology. In C. R. Haden and J. R. Brink (eds.), *Innovative models for university research.* New York: North-Holland.

Daneke, G. A. 1994. Coming full circle: On the return of systems thinking to strategic management. *Journal of Business and Management* 1 (1): 8–44.

D'Angelo, D. J., Howard, L. M., and Ashkenas, L. R. 1995. Ecological uses for genetic algorithms: Predicting fish distributions in complex physical habitats. *Canadian Journal of Fisheries and Aquatic Science* 52 (9): 1893–1901.

Darling, J. R. 1989. A model for reducing internal resistance to change in a firm's international marketing strategy. *European Journal of Marketing* 23 (7): 34–41.

David, P. 1975. *Technical choice, innovation and economic growth.* Cambridge, MA: Cambridge University Press.

David, P. 1985. Cliometrics and QWERTY. *American Economic Review, Papers and Proceedings.*

David, P. 1992. Path dependence and predictability in dynamic systems with local network externalities: A paradigm for historical economics. In D. Foray and C. Freeman (eds.), *Technology and the wealth of nations.* London: Pinter.

David, P., and Greenstein, S. 1990. The economics of compatibility standards: An introduction to recent research. Working paper, Center for Economic Policy Research, Stanford University.

Davies, P. 1987. *The cosmic blueprint.* New York: Heinemann.

de Bono, E. 1971. *Lateral thinking for management.* New York: American Management Association.

de Bono, E. 1985. *Tactics: The art and science of success.* Boston: Little, Brown and Company.

De Geus, A. 1997. *The living company.* Boston: Harvard Business School Press.

De Gregori, T. R. 1987. Resources are not; they become: An institutional theory. *Journal of Economic Issues* 21 (4): 1241–63.

Dean, J. W., and Bowen, D. E. 1994. Total quality and management theory: Improving research and practice through theory development. *Academy of Management Review* 19 (2): 392–418.

Dean, J. W., and Goodman, P. S. 1994. Toward a theory of total quality integration. Working paper, College of Business, University of Cincinnati.

Debreu, G. 1959. *The theory of value.* New Haven, CT: Yale University Press.

De Greene, K. B. 1982. *The adaptive organization: Anticipation and management of crisis.* New York: Wiley.

De Greene, K. B. 1990. Nonlinear management in technologically induced fields. *Systems Research* 7 (3): 159–68.

DeJong, K. A. 1975. Analysis of the behavior of a class of genetic adaptive systems. Ph.D. diss., University of Michigan.

DeMarzo, P. M. 1989. Coalition, leadership, and social norms: The power of suggestion in games. *Games and Economic Behavior* 4 (1): 72–100.

Deming, W. E. 1986. *Out of the crisis.* New York: Cambridge University Press.

Deming, W. E. 1993. *The new economics for industry, government, and education.* Cambridge, MA: MIT, Center for Advanced Engineering.

Dess, G., and Davis, P. 1984. Porter's (1980) generic strategies as determinants of strategic group membership and organizational performance. *Academy of Management Journal* 27 (3): 467–88.

Deutsch, K. 1986. What do we mean by advances in the social sciences? In K. W. Deutsch, A. S. Markovits, and J. Platt (eds.), *Advances in the social sciences from 1900 to 1980.* Lanham, MD: University Press of America.

Diesing, P. 1982. *Science and ideology in the policy sciences.* Chicago: Aldine Publishing.

Ditto, W. L. 1993. Mastering chaos. *Scientific American* 269 (2): 78–84.

Dixit, A. K., and Nalebuff, B. J. 1991. *Thinking strategically: The competitive edge in business, politics, and everyday life.* New York: W.W. Norton.

Dobuzinskis, L. 1987. *The self-organizing polity: An epistemological analysis of political life.* Boulder, CO: Westview Press.

Dooley, K. J. 1994. Methods for studying chaos. *Teaching notes.* Department of Mechanical Engineering, University of Minnesota at Minneapolis.

Dooley, K. J., and Bush, D. H. 1994. TQM and chaos. Working paper, Department of Mechanical Engineering, University of Minnesota at Minneapolis.

Dooley, K., and Van de Ven, A. 1998. Explaining complex organizational dynamics. Working paper, Department of Management, Arizona State University, Tempe.

Dooley, K. J., et al. 1993. Some relationships between chaos, randomness, and statistics. Working paper, Department of Mechanical Engineering, University of Minnesota at Minneapolis.

Dorfman, J. 1969. Heterodox economic thinking and public policy. In W. Samuals (ed.), *The methodology of economic thought,* 38–59. New Brunswick, NJ: Transaction Books.

Dornbusch, R., Fischer, S., and Bossons, J. (eds.). 1987. *Macroeconomics and finance: Essays in honor of Franco Modigliani.* Cambridge, MA: The MIT Press.

Dosi, G. 1984. *Technical change and industrial transformation.* London: Macmillan.

Dosi, G. 1988. How well does established theory work: Preface to part III. In G. Dosi, C. Freeman, R. Nelson, G. Silverberg, and L. Soete (eds.), *Technical change and economic theory,* 120–23. New York: Pinter.

Dosi, G., Freeman, C., Nelson, R., Silverberg, G., and Soete, L. (eds.). 1988. *Technical change and economic theory.* New York: Pinter.

Dosi, G., and Orsenigo, S. 1988. Coordination and transformation: An overview of structures, behaviors and change in evolutionary environments. In G. Dosi, C. Freeman, R. Nelson, G. Silverberg, and L. Soete (eds.), *Technical change and economic theory,* 13–38. New York: Pinter.

Dosi, G., and Soete, L. 1988. Technical change and international trade. In G. Dosi, C. Freeman, R. Nelson, G. Silverberg, and L. Soete (eds.), *Technical change and economic theory,* 401–31. New York: Pinter.

Douglas, M. 1986. *How institutions think.* Syracuse, NY: Syracuse University Press.

Drucker, P. F. 1954. *The practice of management.* New York: Harper and Row.

Drucker, P. F. 1959. Long-range planning. *Management Science* 5 (3): 27–31.

Drucker, P. F. 1971. What we can learn from Japanese management. Reprinted in: F. Hearn (ed.), *Issues in industrial organization.* Belmont, CA: Wadsworth, 1988.

Drucker, P. F. 1985. *The practice of management.* New York: Harper and Row.

Drucker, P. F. 1993. *The ecological vision: Reflections on the American condition.* New Brunswick, NJ: Transaction Publishers.

Drucker, P. F. 1994. The age of social transformation. *Atlantic Monthly* 274 (5): 53–80.

Duchin, F., and Lange, G. M. 1995. *The future of environmental and technological change.* New York: Oxford University Press.

Dumas, L. J. 1986. *The overburdened economy.* Berkeley: University of California Press.

Dunn, E. S. 1971. *Economic and social development: A process of social learning.* Baltimore: Johns Hopkins University Press.

Dwyer, G. P. Jr. 1992. Stabilization policy can lead to chaos. *Economic Inquiry* 30 (1): 40–46.

Dyke, C. 1988. *The evolutionary dynamics of complex systems: A study in biosocial complexity.* New York: Oxford University Press.

EC. 1992. *Towards sustainability: A European community programme of policy and action in relation to the environment and sustainable development.* Brussels, Belgium: The European Community, DGXI.

Eckman, J. P. 1981. Roads to turbulence in dissipative dynamical systems. *Review of Modern Physics* 53: 643–54.

Eckman, J. P., and Ruelle, D. 1985. Ergodic theory of chaos and strange attractors. *Reviews of Modern Physics* 57 (3): 617–56.

Edelman, G. 1989. *Neural Darwinism.* New York: Basic Books.

Edwards, F. R. 1996. *The new finance: Regulation and financial stability.* Washington, D.C.: AEI Press.

Eggertsson, T. 1990. *Economic behavior and institutions.* New York: Cambridge University Press.

Eigen, M. 1979. *Hypercycle: A natural principle of self-organization.* New York: Springer-Verlag.

Eiler, R. 1990. Managing complexity. *Ohio CPA Journal* 49 (1): 45–47.

Einstein, A., Podolsky, B., and Rosen, N. 1935. Can quantum-mechanical description of physical reality be considered complete? *Physical Review* 47: 777–90.

Einstein, A., and Infeld, L. 1938. *The evolution of physics.* New York: Simon and Schuster.

Eisenhardt, K. 1989. Agency theory: An assessment and review. *Academy of Management Review* 14 (1): 57–74.

Elridge, M. 1998. *Transforming experience: John Dewey's cultural instrumentalism.* Nashville, TN: Vanderbilt University Press.

Ellis, C. D. 1992. A new paradigm: The evolution of investment management. *Financial Analysis Journal* 48 (2): 16–18.

Elster, J. (ed.). 1986. *Rational choice.* New York: New York University Press.

Emery, F. E., and Trist, E. 1965. Casual texture in organizational environments. *Human Relations* 18 (1): 21–23.

Emery, F. E., and Trist, E. 1969. Socio-technical systems, In F. E. Emery (ed.), *Systems thinking,* 281–96. London: Penguin Books.

Emery, F. E., and Trist, E. 1973. *Towards a social ecology.* New York: Plenum Press.

Engelen, G. 1988. The theory of self-organization and modelling complex urban systems. *European Journal of Operational Research* 37 (1): 42–57.

Epstein, J. M., and Axtell, R. L. 1996. *Growing artificial societies: Social sciences from the bottom up.* Washington, D.C.: The Brookings Institution.

Eskildson, L. 1995. TQM's role in corporate success: Analyzing the evidence. *National Productivity Review* 14 (1): 25–38.

Espejo, R., and Harnden, R. 1989. *Viable systems model.* New York: Wiley.

Etzioni, A., and Lawrence, P. R. (eds.). 1991. *Socioeconomics: Towards a new synthesis.* New York: M. E. Sharpe.

Fama, E. 1980. Agency problems and the theory of the firm. *Journal of Political Economy* 88 (2): 288–307.

Farmer, J. D., Ott, E., and Yorke, J. A. 1983. The dynamics of chaotic attractors. *Physica* 7D: 153–80.

Farmer, J. D., and Sidorovich, J. 1988. Exploiting chaos to predict the future. In Y. C. Lee (ed.), *Evolution, learning, and cognition.* New York: World Scientific Press.

Feichtinger, G., and Kopel, M. 1993. Chaos in nonlinear dynamical systems exemplified by an R&D model. *European Journal of Operational Research* 68 (2): 145–59.

Feichtinger, G., Novak, A., and Wirl, F. 1994. Limit cycles in intertemporal adjustment models: Theory and applications. *Journal of Economic Dynamics and Control* 18 (2): 353–80.

Feigenbaum, A. V. 1961. *Total quality control.* New York: McGraw-Hill.

Feigenbaum, M. 1978. Quantitative universality for a class of nonlinear transformations. *Journal of Statistical Physics* 19: 25–33.

Feigenbaum, M. 1980. Universal behavior in nonlinear systems. *Los Alamos Science* 1 (1): 4–27.

Feynman, R. P. 1948. Space-time approach to non-relativistic quantum mechanics. *Review of Modern Physics* 20: 367–71.

Field, M., and Golubitsky, M. 1993. Symmetries on the edge of chaos. *New Scientist* 137 (1855): 32–35.

Finney, R. G. 1993. Defining your organization's work. *Management Review* 82 (11): 34–37.

Fisher, R. A. 1930. *The genetical theory of natural selection.* Oxford: Clarendon Press.

Florida, R. L. 1990. *The breakthrough illusion: Corporate America's failure to move from innovation to mass production.* New York: Basic Books.

Fogel, D. 1995. A comparison of evolutionary programming and genetic algorithms on selected constrained optimization problems. *Simulation* 64 (6): 397–404.

Forrester, J. W. 1961. *Industrial dynamics.* Cambridge, MA: The MIT Press.

Forrester, J. W. 1968. *Urban dynamics.* Cambridge, MA: The MIT Press.

Forrester, J. W. 1973. *Principles of systems.* Cambridge, MA: Wright-Allen.

Forrester, J. W. 1987. Nonlinearity in high-order models of social systems. *European Journal of Operational Research* 30: 104–09.

Foster, C. C. 1976. *Content addressable parallel processors.* New York: Van Nostrand Reinhold.

Foxall, G. R. 1992. An evolutionary model of technological innovation as a strategic management process. *Technovation* 12 (3): 191–202.

Frank, M., and Stengos, T. 1988. Chaotic dynamics in economic time-series. *Journal of Economic Surveys* 2 (2): 103–133.

Freeman, C. 1982. *The economics of industrial innovation.* Cambridge, MA: The MIT Press.

Freeman, C., and Perez, C. 1988. Structural crises of adjustment: Business cycles and investment behavior. In G. Dosi, C. Freeman, R. Nelson, G. Silverberg, and L. Soete (eds.), *Technical change and economic theory.* London: Pinter Publishers.

Frey, B. S., and Eichenberger, R. 1989. Anomalies and institutions. *Journal of Institutional and Theoretical Economics* 145 (September): 423–37.

Fudenberg, D., and Tirole, J. 1991. *Game theory.* Cambridge, MA: The MIT Press.

Fulkerson, B., and Staffend, G. 1997. Decentralized control in customer focused enterprise. *Annals of Operations Research* 77: 325–33.

Funtowicz, S. O., and Ravetz, J. R. 1990. *Uncertainty and quality in science for policy.* Dordrecht, Netherlands: Kluwer.

The future of Silicon Valley: Do we need a high-tech industrial policy? 1990. *Business Week,* February 5, 54–60.

Galbraith, J. K. 1973. *The new industrial state.* Boston: Houghton-Mifflin.

Galbraith, J. 1975. *Organization design.* Reading, MA: Addison-Wesley.

Gardner, M. 1983. *Wheels, life and other mathematical amusements.* San Francisco: Freeman.

Garfinkel, A. 1987. The slime mold dictyostelium as a model of self-organization in social systems. In F. E. Yates (ed.), *Self-organizing systems.* New York: Plenum.

Gauci, B., and Baumgartner, T. 1989. Inaccurate financial forecasts and societal complexity: Unique-model and multiple-model representation of reality. *Human Systems Management* 8 (2): 145–54.

Gawthorp, L. C. 1984. *Public sector management, systems, and ethics.* Bloomington: Indiana University Press.

Gell-Mann, M. 1994. *The quark and the jaguar: Adventures in the simple and the complex.* New York: W.H. Freeman.

Gemmill, G., and Smith, C. 1985. A dissipative structure model of organization transformation. *Human Relations* 38: 751–66.

Georgescu-Roegen, N. 1976. *Energy and economic myths.* New York: Pergamon.

Ghemawat, P. 1985. Sustainable advantage. *Harvard Business Review* 64 (1): 53–58.

Ghemawat, P. 1991. *Commitment: The dynamic of strategy.* New York: The Free Press.

Giarini, O. 1985. Notes on the limits of certainty: Risk, uncertainty, and economic value. In I. Prigogine and M. Sanglier (eds.), *Laws of nature and human conduct,* 285–96. Brussels: Task Force of Research Information and Study on Science.

Gibbons, R. 1992. *Game theory for applied economists.* Princeton, NJ: Princeton University Press.

Gilder, G. 1988. The revitalization of everything: The law of microcosm. *Harvard Business Review* 88 (1): 57–59.

Gladwin, T. N., Kennelly, J. J., and Krause, T. S. 1995. Shifting paradigms for sustainable development: Implications for management theory and research. *Academy of Management Review* 20 (4): 874–907.

Glance, N. S., and Huberman, B. 1993. The outbreak of cooperation. *Journal of Mathematical Sociology* 17 (4): 281–302.

Glance, N. S., and Huberman, B. 1994. The dynamics of social dilemmas. *Scientific American* 270 (3): 76–81.

Glass, L., and Mackey, M. C. 1988. *From clocks to chaos: The rhythms of life.* Princeton, NJ: Princeton University Press.

Gleick, J. 1987. *Chaos: Making a new science.* New York: Viking.

Gleick, J. 1992. *Genius: The life and science of Richard Feynman.* New York: Pantheon.

Glynn, M. A., Miliken, F. J., and Lant, T. K. 1992. Learning about organizational learning theory: An umbrella of organizing processes. Working paper, School of Organization and Management, Yale University, New Haven, CT.

Goertzel, B. 1994. *Chaotic logic language, thought, and reality from the perspective of complex systems science.* New York: Plenum Press.

Goleman, D., Kaufman, P., and Ray, M. 1992. *The creative spirit: A companion to the PBS television series.* New York: Dutton.

Gordon, T. J. 1991. Notes on forecasting a chaotic series using regression. *Technological Forecasting and Social Change* 39: 337–48.

Gordon, T. J. 1992. Chaos in social systems. *Technological Forecasting and Social Change* 42 (1): 1–16.

Gorman, R. E., and Krehbiel, T. C. 1997. Quality management and sustainability. *Quality Management Journal* 4 (4): 8–15.

Gould, S. J. 1989. *Wonderful life: The Burgess shale and the nature of history.* New York: W.W. Norton.

Grabher, G. (ed.). 1993. *The embedded firm: On the socioeconomics of industrial networks.* New York: Routledge.

Granger, C. W. J., and Westlund, A. H. 1991. Developments in the nonlinear analysis of economic series. *Scandinavian Journal of Economics* 93 (20): 263–81.

Granovetter, M. 1985. Economic action and social structure: The problem of embeddedness. *American Journal of Sociology* 91 (8): 481–510.

Grant, R. B., and Boardman, A. E. 1990. Realizing the potential of corporate resources and capabilities: A resource-based approach to strategic analysis. Working paper, Policy Division, University of British Columbia, Vancouver.

Grant, R. M., Shani, R., and Krishnan, R. 1994. TQM: Challenge to management theory and practice. *Sloan Management Review* (winter): 25–35.

Greenwood, R., and Hinings, C. R. 1988. Organizational design types, tracks and the dynamics of strategic change. *Organization Studies* 9 (3): 293–316.

Gregersen, H., and Sailer, L. 1993. Chaos theory and its implications for social science research. *Human Relations* 46 (7): 777–802.

Gresser, J. 1984. *Partners in prosperity: Strategic industries for the U.S. and Japan.* New York: McGraw-Hill.

Gribbin, J. 1984. *In search of Schrödinger's cat: Quantum physics and reality.* New York: Bantam Books.

Gronovetter, M. 1985. Economic action and social structure: The problem of embeddedness. *American Journal of Sociology* 91: 481–510.

Grossberg, S. 1982. *Studies of mind and brain.* Boston: Reidel.

Gruchy, A. G. 1987. *The reconstruction of economics: An analysis of the fundamentals of institutional economics.* Westport, CT: Greenwood Press.

Guastello, S. J. 1981. Catastrophe modeling of equity in organizations. *Behavioral Science* 26: 63–74.

Guastello, S. J. 1988. The organizational security subsystem: Some potentially catastrophe events. *Behavioral Science* 33: 48–58.

Guastello, S. J. 1992. Clash of the paradigms: A critique of an examination of the polynomial regression technique for evaluating catastrophe theory hypotheses. *Psychological Bulletin* 111: 375–79.

Guastello, S. J. 1993. Review of organizations and chaos: Defining the methods of nonlinear management by H. Richard Priesmeyer. *Chaos Network* 2: 7–10.

Guastello, S. J. 1995. *Chaos, catastrophe, and human affairs: Applications of nonlinear dynamics to work, organizations, and social evolution.* Mahwah, NJ: Lawrence Erlbaum Associates.

Guastello, S. J. et al. 1994. Chaos, organizational theory, and organizational development. Working paper, Department of Psychology, Marquette University, Milwaukee, WI.

Habermas, J. 1979. *Communication and the evolution of society.* London: Heinemann.

Habermas, J. 1987. *Lectures on the philosophical discourse of modernity.* Cambridge, MA: The MIT Press.

Hackett, S., Schlager, E., and Walker, J. 1994. The role of communication in resolving common dilemmas: Experimental evidence with heterogeneous appropriators. *Journal of Environmental Economics and Management* 27 (1): 99–126.

Haken, H. 1978. *Synergetics: An introduction.* New York: Springer-Verlag.

Haken, H. 1983. *Advanced synergetics.* New York: Springer-Verlag.

Hall, N. 1991. On the complexity of generalized due date scheduling problems. *European Journal of Operational Research* 51 (1): 100–9.

Hall, N. (ed.). 1993. *Exploring chaos: A guide to the new science of disorder.* New York: W.W. Norton.

Hamilton, W. R. 1834. On a general method in dynamics. *Philosophical Transactions of the Royal Society* 2: 247–57.

Hamilton, J. O. C. 1994. A little dose of government won't kill biotech. *Business Week* (Industrial/Technology Edition), February 28, 65.

Hammer, M. 1990. Reengineering work: Don't automate, obliterate. *Harvard Business Review* 90 (4): 104–12.

Hammer, M., and Champy, J. 1993. *Reengineering the corporation: A manifesto for business revolution.* New York: HarperCollins Publishers.

Hammershlag, C. 1988. *The dancing healers: A doctor's journey of healing with native Americans.* New York: Harper and Row.

Hammitt, J. K. 1992. Outcome and value uncertainties in global-change policy. Working paper, RAND Graduate School, Santa Monica, CA.

Hampden-Turner, C. 1990a. *Charting the corporate mind.* New York: The Free Press.

Hampden-Turner, C. 1990b. *Creating corporate culture.* Reading, MA: Addison-Wesley.

Handy, C. 1994. *The age of paradox.* Cambridge, MA: Harvard University Press.

Hannan, M. T., and Freeman, J. 1989. *Organizational ecology.* Cambridge, MA: Harvard University Press.

Hanson, P. 1989. A short discussion of the OR crisis. *European Journal of Operational Research* 38 (3): 277–81.

Hardin, G. 1968. The tragedy of the commons. *Science* 162: 1243–48.

Harrington, J. H. 1995. The new model for improvement: Total quality management. *Management Decision* 33 (3): 17–24.

Harsanyi, J. 1967–68. Games with incomplete information played by "Bayesian Players." Parts I–III. *Management Science* 14: 159–82, 320–34, 486–502.

Hart, S., and Banbury, C. 1992. Strategy-making process capability. Paper presented at the Academy of Management Meeting, Las Vegas, NV.

Hasslacher, B. 1992. Parallel billiards and monster systems. *Daedalus* 121 (1): 53–66.

Hatten, K. J., and Schendel, D. E. 1977. Heterogeneity within an industry. *Journal of Industrial Economics* 26 (4): 97–113.

Haugeland, J. 1985. *Artificial intelligence: The very idea.* San Francisco: Freeman.

Hawken, P. 1993. *The ecology of commerce.* New York: HarperCollins Publishers.

Hawley, A. H. 1950. *Human ecology: A theory of community structure.* New York: Ronald Press.

Hawley, A. H. 1986. *Human ecology: A theoretical essay.* Chicago: University of Chicago Press.

Hax, A. C., and Majluf, N. S. 1984. *Strategic management: An integrative perspective.* Englewood Cliffs, NJ: Prentice-Hall.

Hayles, N. K. (ed.). 1991. *Chaos and order: Complex dynamics in literature and science.* Chicago: University of Chicago Press.

Hearn, F. (ed.). 1988. *Issues in industrial organization.* Belmont, CA: Wadsworth.

Hechter, M. 1989. The emergence of cooperative social institutions. In M. Hechter, K. D. Opp, and R. Wippler (eds.), *Social institutions: Their emergence, maintenance and effects.* New York: Aldine de Gruyter.

Hechter, M. 1990. On the inadequacy of game theory for the solution of real-world collective action problems. In K. S. Cook and M. Levi (eds.), *The limits of rationality,* 240–48. Chicago: University of Chicago Press.

Heckathorn, D., and Maser, S. 1990. The contractual architecture of public policy: A critical reconstruction of Lowi's typology. *Journal of Politics* 52 (4): 1101–23.

Heiner, R. A. 1983. The origin of predictable behavior. *American Economics Review* 73: 560–95.

Heisenberg, W. 1958. *Physics and philosophy.* New York: Harper and Row.

Heisenberg, W. 1974. *Across the frontiers.* New York: Harper and Row.

Henderson, B. 1980. *The experience curve revisited.* Boston: The Boston Consulting Group.

Henderson, H. 1991. *Paradigms in progress: Life beyond economics.* Indianapolis, IN: Knowledge Systems.

Henderson, R. M., and Clark, K. 1990. Architectural innovation: The reconfiguration of existing product technologies and the failure of established firms. *Administrative Science Quarterly* 35 (11): 9–30.

Herbig, P. A. 1991. A Cusp catastrophe model of the adoption of an industrial innovation. *Journal of Product Innovation* 8 (2): 127–37.

Herman, S. 1994. *The force of ones: Reclaiming individual power in a time of teams, work groups, and other crowds.* San Francisco: Jossey-Bass.

Herriott, S., Levinthal, D., and March, J. 1985. Learning from experience in organizations. In J. March (ed.), *Decisions and organizations,* 219–27. Cambridge, MA: Basil Blackwell.

Hershey, D., Patel, V., and Hahn, J. 1990. Speculation on the relationship between organizational structure, entropy, and organizational function. *Systems Research* 7 (3): 207–08.

Hicks, J. R. 1939. *Value and capital.* Oxford: Oxford University Press.

Hinnings, C. R., and Greenwood, R. 1990. *The dynamics of strategic change.* New York: Blackwell.

Hirschman, A. O. 1984. Against parsimony: Three easy ways of complicating some categories of economic discourse. *Bulletin: The American Academy of Arts and Sciences* 37 (8): 11–28.

Hirshleifer, J. 1982. Evolutionary models in economics and law. In R. O. Zerbe Jr. and P. H. Rubin (eds.), *Research in law and economics,* vol. 4, 1–60. Greenwich, CN: JAI Press.

Hofstadter, D. R. 1979. *Gödel, Escher, Bach: An eternal golden braid.* New York: Basic Books.

Hogarth, R. M., and Reder, M. W. (eds.). 1986. *Rational choice.* Chicago: The University of Chicago Press.

Holland, J. H. 1987. Genetic algorithms and classifier systems: Foundations and future directions. In J. J. Grefenstette (ed.), *Genetic algorithms and their applications.* Hillsdale, NJ: Lawrence Erlbaum.

Holland, J. H. 1988. The global economy as an adaptive process. In P. W. Anderson, K. J. Arrow, and D. Pines (eds.), *The Economy as an Evolving Complex System,* 117–24. Menlo Park, CA: Addison-Wesley.

Holland, J. H. 1992. *Adaptation in natural and artificial systems.* Cambridge, MA: The MIT Press.

Holland, J. H. 1995. *Hidden order: How adaptation builds complexity.* Menlow Park, CA: Addison-Wesley.

Holland, J. H., and Miller, J. 1991. Artificial adaptive agents in economic theory. *American Economic Review* 81 (2): 365–70.

Holling, C. S. 1973. Resilience and stability of ecological systems. *Annual Review of Ecological Systems* 4: 1–23.

Holling, C. S. (ed.). 1978. *Adaptive environmental assessment and management.* New York: Wiley.

Holling, C. S. 1986. Resilience of ecosystems; local surprises and global changes. In W. C. Clark and R. E. Munn (eds.), *Sustainable Development of the Biosphere.* New York: Cambridge University Press.

Holling, C. S. 1987. Simplifying the complex: The paradigm of ecological function and structure. *European Journal of Operations Research* 30: 139–46.

Holling, C. S., and Clark, W. 1973. Notes toward a science of ecological management. In W. Van Dobben and R. H. Lowe-McConnel (eds.), *Unifying Concepts in Ecology.* The Hague: W. Junk.

Hoos, I. 1972. *Systems analysis of public policy: A critique.* Berkeley: University of California Press.

Horgan, J. 1995. From complexity to perplexity. *Scientific American* 274 (June): 104–9.

Hotelling, H. 1929. Stability in competition. *Economic Journal* 39 (1): 41–57.

Hsieh, D. A. 1991. Chaos and nonlinear dynamics: Application to financial markets. *Journal of Finance* 46 (5): 1839–77.

Hsieh, D. A. 1993. Chaos and order in capital markets: A new view of cycles, prices and market volatility. *Journal of Finance* 48 (5): 2041–44.

Huffman, G. 1992. Information, assets, prices and the volume of trade. *Journal of Finance* 47 (4): 1575–82.

Imai, M. 1986. *Kaizen, the key to Japan's competitive success.* New York: Random House Business Division.

Imai, K., Nonaka, I., and Takeuchi, H. 1985. Managing the new product development process: How Japanese companies learn and unlearn. In K. Clark, R. H. Hayes, and C. Lorenz (eds.), *The uneasy alliance: Managing the productivity-technology dilemma.* Boston, MA: Harvard Business School Press.

Ingrao, B., and Georgio, I. 1990. *The invisible hand: Economic equilibrium in the history of science.* Cambridge, MA: The MIT Press.

Ishikawa, K. 1984. *Quality control circles at work: Cases from Japan's manufacturing and service sectors.* Tokyo: Asian Productivity Organization.

It's only a game. 1996. *Economist,* June 15, 57.

Jablonowski, M. 1991. Fuzzy logic and insurance decisions. *CPCU Journal* 44 (3): 181–87.

Jackson, E. A. 1989. *Perspectives of nonlinear dynamics.* Cambridge, UK: Cambridge University Press.

Jackson, M. C. 1991. Origins and nature of critical systems thinking. *Systems Practice* 4: 131–49.

Jackson, M. C., Mansell, G. T., Flood, R. L., Blackham, R. B., and Probert, S. V. E. 1991. *Systems thinking in Europe.* New York: Plenum.

Jacob, R. 1993. TQM: More than a dying fad? *Fortune* 128 (9): 66–72.

Jacobs, B. I. 1989. The complexity of the stock market. *Journal of Portfolio Management* 16 (1): 19–27.

Jacobs, J. 1969. *The economy of cities.* New York: Random House.

Jacobs, J. 1984. *Cities and the wealth of nations.* New York: Random House.

Jacques, E. 1989. *Requisite organization.* Arlington, VA: Carson Hall.

Jankowski, R. 1990. Public policy and global climactic change: Public policy as insurance. In F. N. Burkhead, C. F. Hutchinson, and M. Saint-Germain (eds.), *Global climate change: The meeting of science and policy.* Tucson: Udall Center, University of Arizona.

Jantsch, E. 1975. Design for evolution: Self-organization and planning. New York: Braziller.

Jantsch, E. 1976. Introduction and summary. In E. Jantsch and C. H. Waddington (eds.), *Evolution and consciousness: Human systems in transition,* 1–8. Reading, MA: Addison-Wesley.

Jantsch, E. 1980. *The self-organizing universe: Scientific and human implications of the emerging paradigm of evolution.* Oxford: Pergamon Press.

Jantsch, E., and Waddington, C. H. (eds.). 1976. *Evolution and consciousness: Human systems in transition.* Reading, MA: Addison-Wesley.

Jelinek, M., and Schoonhoven, C. B. 1990. *The innovation marathon: Lessons from high technology firms.* New York: Basil Blackwell.

Jennings, P. D., and Zandbergen, P. A. 1995. Ecologically sustainable organizations: An institutional approach. *Academy of Management Review* 20 (4): 1015–52.

Jewkes, J., Sawers, D., and Stillerman, R. 1969. *Sources of innovation.* 2d ed. New York: W.W. Norton.

Johnson, C. 1982. *MITI and the Japanese miracle.* Stanford, CA: Stanford University Press.

Johnson, G. 1996. *Fire in the mind: Science, faith, and the search for order.* New York: Alfred A. Knopf.

Johnson, R. A. 1991. Loss of stability and emergence of chaos in dynamical systems. *Journal of Economic Behavior and Organization* 16 (1, 2): 93–113.

Jones, P. O., and Wigley, T. M. L. 1990. Global warming trends. *Scientific American* (August): 84–91.

Jost, A. 1993. Neural networks: A logical progression in credit and marketing decision systems. *Credit World* 81: 26–33.

Jowett, B. 1972. *The Republic: A translation.* London: Grolier.

Juran, J. M., and Barish, N. 1951. Case studies in industrial management. New York: McGraw-Hill.

Kahneman, D., Slovic, P., and Tversky, A. 1982. *Judgment under uncertainty: Heuristics and biases.* Cambridge, NY: Cambridge University Press.

Kalberg, S. 1980. Max Weber's types of rationality: Cornerstones for the analysis of rationalization processes in history. *American Journal of Sociology* 85 (5): 1145–79.

Kanter, R. B. 1983. *The changemasters.* New York: Simon and Schuster.

Karsten, S. F. 1990. Quantum theory and social economics: The holistic approach of modern physics serves better than newton's mechanics in approaching reality. *American Journal of Economics and Sociology* 49 (4): 385–399.

Katayama, R. 1993. Developing tools and methods for applications incorporating neuro, fuzzy and chaos technology. *Computers and Industrial Engineering* 24 (4): 579–92.

Katz, D., and Kahn, R. L. 1968. *The social psychology of organizations.* New York: Wiley.

Katz, M., and Shapiro, C. 1985. Network externalities, competition and compatibility. *American Economic Review* 75: 424–40.

Kaufman, H. 1991. *Time, chance, and organization.* 2d ed. Chatham, NJ: Chatham House.

Kauffman, S. 1993. *The origins of order: Self-organization and selection in evolution.* New York: Oxford University Press.

Kauffman, S. 1995. *At home in the universe: The search for laws of self-organization and complexity.* New York: Oxford University Press.

Keenan, D. G. 1993. Competition, collusion, and chaos. *Journal of Economic Dynamics and Control* 17 (3): 327–53.

Kellert, S. 1993. *In the wake of chaos.* Chicago: University of Chicago Press.

Kelly, S., and Allison, M. 1999. *The complexity advantage: How the science of complexity can help your business achieve prak performance.* New York: McGraw-Hill.

Kennedy, P. 1993. *Preparing for the twenty-first century.* New York: Random House.

Kent, S. 1986. *The story of the Challenger disaster.* Chicago: Childrens Press.

Kiel, L. D. 1994. *Managing chaos and complexity in government.* San Francisco: Jossey-Bass.

Kiel, L. D., and Elliott, E. 1992. Budgets as dynamic systems: Time, chance, variation and budgetary heuristics. *Journal of Public Administration Research and Theory* 2 (2): 139–56.

Kiel, L. D., and Elliott, E. 1993. Economic cycles and reform in public administration. Working paper, Political Economy Program, University of Texas, Dallas.

Kiel, L. D., and Elliott, E. W. (eds.). 1996. *Chaos theory in social sciences: Foundations and applications.* Ann Arbor: The University of Michigan Press.

Kim, S. H. 1990. *Essence of creativity: A guide to tackling difficult problems.* New York: Oxford University Press.

King, J. B. 1989. Confronting chaos. *Journal of Business Ethics* 8 (1): 39–50.

Kirkwood, C. W. 1992. An overview of methods for applied decision analysis. *Interfaces* 22 (6): 28–39.

Kirzner, I. M. 1979. *Perception, opportunity and profit: Studies in the theory of entrepreneurship.* Chicago: The University of Chicago Press.

Kline, S. 1987. The logical necessity of multi-disciplinarity: A consistent view of the world. Working paper, Stanford University.

Kline, S. 1994. *The logical necessity of multi-disciplinarity.* Palo Alto: Stanford University Press.

Kondo, T. 1990. Some notes on rational behavior, normative behavior, moral behavior, and cooperation. *Journal of Conflict Resolution* 34 (3): 495–530.

Kondratieff, N. D. 1935. The long waves in economic life. *Review of Economic Statistics* 17: 105–15.

Koontz, H. 1961. The management theory jungle. *Journal of the Academy of Management* 4 (3): 174–88.

Koput, K. W. 1997. A chaotic model of innovative search: Some answers, many questions. *Organization Science* 8 (5): 528–43.

Korten, D. 1995. *When corporations rule the world.* San Francisco: Berret-Koehler.

Kosko, B. 1993. *Fuzzy thinking: The new science of fuzzy logic.* New York: Hyperion.

Koza, J. 1992. *Genetic programming: On the programming of machines by means of natural selection.* Cambridge, MA: The MIT Press.

Koza, J. 1994. *Genetic programming II: Automatic discovery of reusable programs.* Cambridge, MA: The MIT Press.

Koza, J., Goldber, D. E., Fogel, D. B., and Riolo, R. L. 1996. *Genetic programming.* Cambridge, MA: The MIT Press.

Krasner, S. (ed.). 1990. *The ubiquity of chaos.* Washington, D.C.: American Association for the Advancement of Science.

Kreps, D. M. 1990. *A course in microeconomic theory.* Princeton, NJ: Princeton University Press.

Krohm, K., Gunter, K., and Nowothy, H. (eds.). 1990. *Self-organization: Portrait of a scientific revolution.* New York: Kluwer.

Krugman, P. 1996. *The self-organizing economy.* Cambridge, MA: Blackwell.

Kryzanowski, L. 1995. Analysis of small-business financial statements using neural nets. *Journal of Accounting, Auditing, and Finance* 10 (1): 147–72.

Kryzanowski, L., Guller, M., and Wright, D. M. 1993. Using artificial neural networks to pick stocks. *Financial Analysts Journal* 49 (July/August): 21–27.

Kuhn, T. S. 1962. *The structure of scientific revolutions.* Chicago: University of Chicago Press.

Kumar, P., and Narendran, T. T. 1991. A nonlinear goal programming model for multistage, multi-objective decision problems with application to grouping and loading problem in a flexible manufacturing system. *European Journal of Operational Research* 53 (2): 166–171.

Kuttner, R. K. 1991. *The end of laissez-faire.* New York: Random House.

Kuznets, S. S. 1930. *Secular movements in production and prices.* New York: Houghton Mifflin.

Kuznets, S. S. 1953. *Economic change.* New York: W. W. Norton.

Laing, J. R. 1991. Efficient chaos: Or, things they never taught in business school. *Barron's* 71 (30): 12–13.

Lampe, M., and Gazda, G. M. 1992. Green marketing in Europe and the United States: An evolving business and society interface. Paper presented at the 1992 conference of the International Association for Business and Society, Leuven, Belgium.

Lancaster, E. 1998. Research publications of the swarm user-community. *OnLine List.* Santa Fe, NM: The Santa Fe Institute.

Langlois, R. H. 1992. Complexity, genuine uncertainty, and the economics of organization. *Human Systems Management* 11 (2): 67–75.

Langton, C. (ed.). 1989. *Artificial life.* Redwood City, CA: Addison-Wesley for the Santa Fe Institute.

Langton, C., Minor, N., Askenzai, M., and Burkhart, R. 1995. *SWARM.* Santa Fe, NM: The Santa Fe Institute.

Laverty, K. 1989. Market share-profitability puzzle: A structural equations approach. Paper presented at the Meeting of the Strategic Management Society, San Francisco.

Lawler, E. E., Mohrman, S. A., and Ledford, G. E. 1992. *Employee involvement and total quality management.* San Francisco: Jossey-Bass.

Lee, M. 1994. A conceptual framework of technological innovation management. *Technovation* 14 (1): 7–16.

Leifer, R. 1989. Understanding organizational transformation using a dissipative structure model. *Human Relations* 42: 899–916.

Levitan, H. 1988. *Chaos and fractals: Basic concepts demonstrated by the logistic model of population ecology.* College Park, MD: University of Maryland.

Levitt, B. 1988. Institutional constraints and decision-making in the textbook industry. Ph.D. diss., Department of Sociology, Stanford University.

Levitt, B., and March, J. G. 1988. Organizational learning. *Annual Review of Sociology* 14: 319–40.

Lewin, R. 1992. *Complexity: Life at the edge of chaos.* New York: Macmillan.

Leydesdorff, L. 1995. The operation of the social system in a model based on cellular automata. *Social Science Information* 34 (3): 413–19.

Likert, R. 1961. *New patterns of management.* New York: McGraw-Hill.

Linden, R. M. 1990. *From vision to reality.* Charlottesville, VA: LEL Enterprises.

Linster, B. G. 1992. Evolutionary stability in the infinitely repeated prisoners' dilemma played by two-state Moore machines. *Southern Economic Journal* 58 (4): 880–903.

Linstone, H. A. 1989. Multiple perspectives: Concept, applications and user guidelines. *Systems Practice* 2 (3): 307–31.

Lissack, M. R. 1997. Chaos and complexity: What does that have to do with knowledge management? In J. F. Schreinemakers (ed.), *Knowledge management: Organization, competence and methodology,* 62–81. Wurzburg, Germany: Verlog.

Lorange, P., and Probst, G. J. B. 1987. Joint ventures as self-organizing systems: A key to successful joint ventures. *Columbia Journal of World Business* 22 (2): 71–77.

Lorenz, E. N. 1963. Deterministic nonperiodic flow. *Journal of the Atmospheric Sciences* 20: 130–41.

Lorenz, E. N. 1984. Irregularity: A fundamental property of the atmosphere. *Tellus* 36 (1): 98–110.

Lorenz, H. W. 1987. Strange attractors in a multisector business cycle model. *Journal of Economic Behavior and Organization* 8: 397–411.

Lotka, A. J. 1925. *Elements of mathematical biology.* New York: Dover.

Lovelock, J. E. 1979. *Gaia: A new look at life on earth.* London: Oxford University Press.

Loye, D., and Eisler, R. 1987. Chaos and transformation: Implications of nonequilibrium theory for social science and society. *Behavioral Science* 32: 53–65.

Luce, R. D., and Raiffa, H. 1957. *Games and decisions.* New York: Wiley.

Lyapunov, A. M. 1950. *The general stability of motion.* Moscow: Gosteklhizdat.

Maccoby, M. 1988. *Why work: Motivating and leading the new generation.* New York: Simon and Schuster.

Machina, M. J. 1989. Dynamic consistency and non-expected utility models of choice under uncertainty. *Journal of Economic Literature* 28 (4): 1622–94.

Mackness, J. 1992. A systems view of top management commitment. *International Journal of Technology Management* 7 (4, 5): 219–24.

Macy, M. W. 1991. Chains of cooperation: Threshold effects in collective action. *American Sociological Review* 56: 730–47.

Mainzer, K. 1994. *Thinking in complexity: Complex dynamics of matter, mind, and mankind.* New York: Springer-Verlag.

Malaska, P., and Kinnunen, T. 1986. A model of management goal setting and its dissipative structure. *European Journal of Operational Research* 25: 75–84.

Maltz, M. 1960. *Psycho-cybernetics: A new technique for using your subconscious power.* North Hollywood, CA: Wilshire Book Company.

Mandelbrot, B. 1963. The variation of certain speculative prices. *Journal of Business* 36: 394–419.

Mandelbrot, B. 1983. *The fractal geometry of nature.* New York: W.H. Freeman.

Mansfield, G. 1968. *The economics of technical change.* New York: W.W. Norton.

Manz, C. C., and Stewart, G. L. 1997. Attaining flexible stability by integrating total quality management and socio-technical systems theory. *Organization Science* 8 (1): 59–70.

March, J. G. 1986. Bounded rationality, ambiguity, and the engineering of choice. In J. Elster (ed.). *Rational choice,* 142–70. New York: New York University Press.

March, J. G. 1987. Ambiguity and accounting: The elusive link between information and decision making. *Accounting, Organizations, and Society* 12: 153–68.

March, J. G., and Olsen, J. F. 1989. *Rediscovering institutions: The organizational basis of politics.* New York: Free Press.

March, J. G., and Simon, H. A. 1958. *Organizations.* New York: Wiley.

Marimon, R. 1993. Adaptive learning, evolutionary dynamics and equilibrium selection in games. *European Economic Review* 37 (2, 3): 603–11.

Marshall, A. 1898. Mechanical and biological analogies in economics. Reprinted in A. C. Pigou (ed.), *Memorials of Alfred Marshall.* New York: Macmillian, 1956.

Marshall, A. 1920. *Principles of economics.* London: Macmillan.

Maruyama, M. 1978. Prigogine's epistemology and its implications for the social sciences. *Current Anthropology* 19 (2): 453–54.

Maruyama, M. 1982. Mindscapes, management, business policy and public policy. *Academy of Management Review* 7 (4): 612–19.

Masuch, M., and LaPotin, P. 1989. Beyond garbage cans: An AI model of organizational choice. *Administrative Science Quarterly* 34 (1): 38–67.

Maturana, H., and Varela, F. 1975. The organization of the living: A theory of the living organization. *International Journal of Man-Machine Studies* 7: 313–32.

Maturana, H., and Varela. F. 1992. *The tree of knowledge.* Boston: Shambala.

May, R. M. 1973. *Stability and complexity in model ecosystems.* Princeton, NJ: Princeton University Press.

May, R. M. 1976. Simple mathematical models with very complicated dynamics. *Nature* 261: 459–67.

Mayer-Kress, G. 1986. *Dimensions and entropies in chaotic systems.* Berlin: Springer-Verlag.

Mayer-Kress, G. 1994. Messy futures and global brains. Working paper, Center for Complex Systems Research, University of Illinois at Urbana-Champaign.

Mayer-Kress, G. et al. 1994. A tele-conferencing experiment with WWW/mosaic. Working paper, Center for Complex Systems Research, University of Illinois at Urbana-Champaign.

Maynard Smith, J. 1982. *Evolution and the theory of games.* Cambridge, UK: Cambridge University Press.

Maynard Smith, J. and Price, G. 1973. The logic of animal conflicts. *Nature* 246: 15–18.

Mayr, E. 1982. *Toward a new philosophy of biology.* Cambridge, MA: Harvard Belknap.

McGregor, D. 1960. *The human side of enterprise.* New York: McGraw-Hill.

McMillan, C. J. 1985. *The Japanese industrial system.* 2d ed. New York: Walter de Gruyter.

Meadows, D. H., Meadows, D., and Randers, J. 1972. *The limits to growth, a report for the Club of Rome's project on the predicament of mankind.* New York: Universe Books.

Meadows, D. H., Meadows, D., and Randers, J. 1992. *Beyond the limits: Confronting global collapse, envisioning a sustainable future.* Post Mills, VT: Chelsea Green Publishing.

MEB. 1993. *Environmental progress report: The role of business schools.* Washington, D.C.: The Management Institute for Environment and Business.

Mensch, G. 1979. *Stalemate in technology.* Cambridge, MA: Ballinger.

Merkle, J. A. 1980. *Management and ideology: The legacy of the international scientific management movement.* Berkeley, CA: University of California Press.

Merton, R. K. 1940. Bureaucratic structure and personality. *Social Forces* 18: 560–68.

Meyer, D. A. 1999. Quantum strategies. *Physical Review Letters* 82: 1052–1055.

Meyer, M. W., Stevenson, W., and Webster, S. 1985. *Limits to bureaucratic growth.* New York: Walter de Gruyter.

Michael, D. 1973. *On learning to plan and planning to learn.* San Francisco: Jossey Bass.

Micklethwait, J., and Wooldridge, A. 1996. *The witch doctors.* New York: Times Books.

Milbraith, L. W. 1989. *Envisioning a sustainable society.* Albany, NY: State University of New York Press.

Milgram, P., and Roberts, J. 1991. *Economics, organization and management.* Englewood Cliffs, NJ: Prentice-Hall.

Miller, D. 1993. The architecture of simplicity. *Academy of Management Journal* 18 (1): 116–38.

Miller, D., and Friesen, P. H. 1982. The longitudinal analysis of organizations: A methodological perspective. *Management Science* 28: 1013–34.

Miller, J. H. 1988. The evolution of automata in the repeated prisoner's dilemma. Ph.D. diss. University of Michigan, Ann Arbor.

Miller, J. H. 1989. The coevolution of automata in the repeated prisoner's dilemma. Working paper, Santa Fe Institute Economics Research Program.

Minsky, M. L. 1985. *The society of mind.* New York: Simon and Schuster.

Mintzberg, H. 1990. *Mintzberg on management: Inside our strange world of organizations.* New York: The Free Press.

Mirowski, P. 1989. *More heat than light: Economics as social physics, physics as nature's economics.* New York: Cambridge University Press.

Mirowski, P. 1990. From Mandelbrot to chaos in economic theory. *Southern Economic Journal* 57 (2): 289–307.

Mishra, R. K., Mass, E., and Wierlein, Z. (eds.). 1994. *On self-organization: An interdisciplinary search for unifying principles.* New York: Springer-Verlag.

Mitchell, W. C. 1913. *Business cycles.* New York: National Bureau of Economic Research.

Mitroff, I. I., and Linstone, H. A. 1993. *The unbounded mind: Breaking the chains of traditional business thinking.* New York: Oxford University Press.

Moe, T. 1984. The new economics of organization. *American Journal of Political Science* 28 (4): 739–77.

Monroe, K. R. 1983. Altruism and rationality: The challenge for political economy and empirical political theory. Working paper, University of California at Irvine.

Montgomery, C.A., and Singh, H. 1984. Diversification and strategic risk. *Strategic Management Journal* 5 (2): 181–91.

Moore, B. J. 1997. An interpretive analysis of the ELSI program: Closing the loop. DPA diss., Arizona State University, Tempe.

Moore, J. C. 1990. Optimal decision processes and algorithms. *Journal of Economic Dynamics and Control* 14 (2): 375–417.

Moore, J. F. 1996. *The death of competition: Leadership and strategy in the age of business ecosystems.* New York: HarperBusiness.

Morgan, G. 1983. Rethinking corporate strategy: Cybernetics perspective. *Human Relations* 36 (4): 345–60.

Morgan, G. 1986. *Images of organization.* Beverly Hills: Sage Publications.

Morgenstern, R. D. 1991. Toward a comprehensive approach to global climate change mitigation. *American Economic Review* 82 (2): 140–45.

Mosekilde, E., Aracil, J., and Allen, P. M. 1988. Instabilities and chaos in nonlinear dynamic systems. *Systems Dynamics Review* 4: 14–55.

Mosekilde, E., Larsen, E., and Sterman, J. 1991. Coping with complexity: Deterministic chaos in human decisionmaking behavior. In J. L. Casti and A. Karlqvist (eds.), *Beyond belief: Randomness, prediction and explanation in science.* Boca Raton: CRC Press.

Mowery, D. C., and Rosenberg, N. 1982. The influence of market demand upon innovation: A critical review of some recent empirical studies. In N. Rosenberg (ed.), *Inside the black box: Technology and economics,* 193–243. New York: Cambridge University Press.

Mueller, D. 1989. *Public choice II.* Cambridge: Cambridge University Press.

Mukherjee, A. 1993. A stochastic cellular automata model of innovation diffusion. *Technological Forecasting and Social Change* 44 (1): 87–95.

Mukherjee, T. K. 1991. Reducing the uncertainty-induced bias in capital budgeting decisions—A hurdle rate approach. *Journal of Business Finance & Accounting* 18 (5): 747–53.

Mulvey, J. M., and Ziemba, W. T. (eds.). 1998. *Worldwide asset liability management.* New York: Cambridge University Press.

Myrdal, G. 1958. *Value in social theory.* London: Routledge and Kegan Paul.

Myrdal, G. 1960. *Beyond the welfare state.* New Haven, CT: Yale University Press.

Myrdal, G. 1969. *The political element in the development of economic theory.* Cambridge, MA: Harvard University Press.

Nakicenovic, N., Grubler, A., Inaba, A., Messner, S., Nilsson, S., Nishimura, Y., Rogner, H., Schafer, A., Schrattenholzer, L., Strubegger, M., Swisher, J., Victor, D., and Wilson, D. 1993. Long-term strategies for mitigating global warming. Special Issue, *Energy—The International Journal* 18 (5): 409–601.

Nash, J. 1950. Equilibrium points in *n*-person games. In *Proceedings of the National Academy of Sciences of the United States of America,* vol. 36, 48–49.

Nash, J. 1951. Non-cooperative games. *Annals of Mathematics* 54: 286–95.

NCM. 1991. Environmental labelling in the Nordic countries. *Position Report.* Copenhagen: Nordic Council of Ministers.

Neitzel, L. A., and Hoffman, L. 1980. Fuzzy cost-benefit analysis. In P. P. Wang and S. K. Chang (eds.), *Fuzzy sets: Theory and applications to policy analysts and information systems,* 276–88. New York: Plenum Press.

Nelson, R. R. 1985. *High-technology policies: A five nation comparison.* Washington, D.C.: American Enterprise Institute.

Nelson, R. R., and Winter, S. G. 1973. Toward an evolutionary theory of economic capabilities. *American Economic Review* 63: 440–49.

Nelson, R. R., and Winter, S. G. 1977. In search of useful theory of innovation. *Research Policy* 5: 36–76.

Nelson, R. R., and Winter, S. G. 1982. *An evolutionary theory of economic change.* Cambridge, MA: The Belknap Press of Harvard University Press.

The new breed of strategic planner. 1984. *Business Week,* September 17, 62–68.

Nicolis, G., and Prigogine, I. 1971. Biological order, structures and instabilities. *Quarterly Review of Biophysics* 4: 107–48.

Nicolis, G., and Prigogine, I. 1977. *Self-organization in nonequilibrium systems: From dissipative structures to order through fluctuation.* New York: Wiley-Interscience.

Nicolis, G., and Prigogine, I. 1989. *Exploring complexity: An introduction.* New York: W.H. Freeman.

Nichols, N. 1993. Efficient? Chaotic? What's the new finance? *Harvard Business Review* 71 (2): 50–60.

Nonaka, I. 1988. Creating organizational order out of chaos: Self-renewal in Japanese firms. *California Management Review* 30 (3, spring): 57–73.

Nonaka, I. 1990. Redundant, overlapping organization: A Japanese approach to innovation. *California Management Review* 32 (3): 27–38.

Nooteboom, B. 1992. A postmodern philosophy of markets. *International Studies of Management and Organization* 22 (2): 53–59.

Nordhaus, W. D. 1990. Greenhouse economics: Count before you leap. *Economist* (July 7): 21–24.

Nordhaus, W. D. 1991. The cost of slowing climate change: A survey. *Energy Journal* 12 (1): 37–66.

Norgaard, R. B., and Howarth, R. B. 1991. Sustainability and discounting the future. In R. Costanza (ed.), *Ecological economics: The science and management of sustainability,* 88–101. New York: Columbia University Press.

North, D. C. 1990. *Institutions, institutional change and economic performance.* New York: Cambridge University Press.

Nowak, M. 1993. Chaos and the evolution of cooperation. *Proceedings of the National Academy of Sciences of the United States of America* 90 (11): 5091–94.

NSF. 1995. *Transformation to quality organizations: Program description.* Washington, D.C.: National Science Foundation.

Nutt, P. C., and Backoff, R. W. 1992. *Strategic management of public and third sector organizations.* San Francisco, CA: Jossey-Bass.

NWF. 1989. *The natural environment: Issues for management.* Washington, D.C.: National Wildlife Federation, Corporate Conservation Council, Curriculum Planning Report I.

NWF. 1990. *The natural environment: Issues for management.* Washington, D.C.: National Wildlife Federation, Corporate Conservation Council, Curriculum Planning Report II.

Olson, M. 1965. *The logic of collective action.* Cambridge, MA: Harvard University Press.

Olson, M. 1982. *The rise and decline of nations: Economic growth, stagflation, and social rigidities.* New Haven, CT: Yale University Press.

Olson, M. 1990. Toward a unified view of economics and the other social sciences. In J. E. Alt and K. A. Shepsle (eds.), *Perspectives on positive political economy,* 212–32. New York: Cambridge University Press.

Ono, T. 1993. Chaos engineering. *Japan Times Weekly International Edition* 33 (4): 16–18.

OSTP. 1990. *U.S. technology policy.* Washington, D.C.: Office of Science and Technology Policy, Executive Office of the President.

Ostrom, E. 1990. *Governing the commons.* New York: Cambridge University Press.

Ostrom, E., Gardner, R., Walker, J., and Agrawal, A. 1994. *Rules, games, and common-pool resources.* Ann Arbor: University of Michigan Press.

OTA. 1984. *Technology, innovation and regional economic development.* Washington, D.C.: Office of Technology Assessment, U.S. Congress.

OTA. 1988. *Technology and American economic transition: Choices for the future.* Washington, D.C.: Office of Technology Assessment, U.S. Congress.

Ouchi, W. A. 1981. *Theory 2: How American business can meet the Japanese challenge.* Reading, MA: Addison-Wesley.

Ouchi, W. A. 1984. *The M Form Society.* Reading, MA: Addison-Wesley.

Padmanabhan, G. 1990. Analysis of multi-item inventory systems under resource constraints: A non-linear goal programming approach. *Engineering Costs and Production Economics* 2 (2): 121–27.

Pagels, H. 1988. *The dreams of reason.* New York: Simon and Schuster.

Papadimitriou, C. H. 1992. On players with a bounded number of states. *Games and Economic Behavior* 4 (1): 122–31.

Pareto, W. 1971. *Manual of political economy.* Translated by A. S. Schwier. New York: Augustus M. Kelley.

Pareto, W. 1935. *The mind of society.* New York: Harcourt and Brace.

Parsons, T. 1951. *The social system.* New York: The Free Press.

Pascale, R. 1990. *Managing on the edge.* New York: Simon and Schuster.

Patten, T. H. 1992. Beyond systems: The politics of managing in a TQM environment. *National Productivity Review* 11 (1): 9–19.

Patterson, D. M. 1993. Nonlinear dynamics, chaos and instability. *Journal of Finance* 48 (1): 404–7.

Payne, S. L. 1992. Critical systems thinking: A challenge or dilemma in its practice. *Systems Practice* 5 (3): 237–50.

Pearce, M., Ram, A., and Arkin, R. 1994. Using genetic algorithms to learn reactive control parameters for autonomous robotic navigation. *Adaptive Behavior* 2 (3): 277–88.

Pechersky, S., and Sobolev, A. 1995. Set-valued nonlinear analogues of the shapely value. *International Journal of Game Theory* 24 (1): 57–63.

Peet, J. 1992. *Energy and the ecological economics of sustainability.* Washington, D.C.: Island Press.

Penrose, R. 1989. *The emperor's new mind: Concerning computers, minds, and the laws of physics.* Oxford: Oxford University Press.

Pepper, S. C. 1942. *World hypotheses: A study in evidence.* Berkeley: University of California Press.

Pepper, S. C. 1966. *Concept and quality: A world hypothesis.* LaSalle, IL: Open Court Publishing.

Perrow, C. 1984. *Normal accidents: Living with high risk technologies.* New York: Basic Books.

Perrow, C. 1991. A society of organizations. *Theory and Society* 20: 725–62.

Perry, W. G. 1994. What is neural network software? *Journal of Systems Management* 45 (9): 12–15.

Peschel, M., and Mende, W. 1986. *The predator-prey model: Do we live in a Volterra world?* Wien, Austria: Springer-Verlag.

Peteraf, M. A. 1991. The cornerstone of competitive advantage: A resource-based view. Discussion paper 90–29, Kellogg Graduate School of Management, Northwestern University, Evanston, IL.

Peters, E. E. 1991. *Chaos and order in the capital markets: A new view of cycles, prices and market volatility.* New York: Wiley.

Peters, E. E. 1994. *Fractal market analysis: Applying chaos theory to investment and economics.* New York: Wiley.

Peters, T. 1987. *Thriving on chaos: Handbook for a management revolution.* New York: Knopf.

Peters, T. J., and Waterman, R. H. Jr. 1982. *In search of excellence: Lessons from America's best-run companies.* New York: Harper & Row.

Petr, J. 1984. Fundamentals of an institutionalist perspective on economic policy. In M. Tool (ed.), *An institutionalist guide to economics and public policy,* 1–18. Armonk, NY: M. E. Sharpe.

Pfeffer, J. 1994. Producing sustainable competitive advantage through effective management of people. *Academy of Management Executive* 9 (1): 55–72.

Philippe, P. 1993. Chaos, population biology, and epidemology: Some research implications. *Human Biology* 65 (4): 525–46.

Pinchot, G. 1985. *Intrapreneuring: Why you don't have to leave the corporation to become an entrepreneur.* New York: Harper and Row.

Plath, D. A., Krueger, T. M., and Jolly, S. A. 1992. A dynamical systems model of capital asset pricing. *Mid-Atlantic Journal of Business* 28 (1): 55–74.

Poincaré, H. 1890. *The calculus of probabilities.* Paris: Gauthier-Villars.

Polanyi, K. 1957. *The great transformation: The political and economic origins of our time.* Boston: Beacon Press.

Pole, A. 1990. Efficient Bayesian learning in non-linear dynamic models. *Journal of Forecasting* 9 (2): 119–36.

Polkinghorne, D. 1988. *Narrative knowing and the human sciences.* Albany: State University of New York Press.

Polley, D. 1997. Turbulence in organizations: New metaphors for organizational research. *Organization Science* 8 (5): 445–58.

Poole, M. S., Van de Ven, A. H., Hewes, D., and Dooley, K. 1997. Event time series regression. Working paper, Department of Communication, Texas A & M University, College Station.

Porter, M. 1980. *Competitive strategy.* New York: Free Press.

Porter, M. 1985. *Competitive advantage.* New York: Free Press.

Post, J. E. (ed.). 1992. *Research is corporate social performance policy.* Greenwich, CT: JAI Press.

Postrel, S. 1991. Burning your britches behind you: Can policy scholars bank on game theory? *Strategic Management Journal* 12: 153–60.

Powell, W. W., and DiMaggio, P. J. (eds.). 1991. *The new institutionalism in organizational analysis.* Chicago: University of Chicago Press.

Prahalad, C. K., and Hamel, G. 1990. The core competence of the corporation. *Harvard Business Review* 90 (1): 70–93.

Preston, A. 1987. Improvising order. In I. L. Mangham (ed.), *Organization analysis and development: A social construction of organizational behavior.* New York: Wiley.

Priesmeyer, H. R. 1989. Discovering the patterns of chaos—A potential new planning tool. *Planning Review* 17 (6): 14–21, 47.

Priesmeyer, H. R. 1992. *Organizations and chaos: Defining the methods of non-linear management.* Westport, CT: Quorum Books.

Prigogine, I. 1980. *From being to becoming.* New York: W. H. Freeman and Company.

Prigogine, I., and Allen, P. M. 1982. The challenge of complexity. In W. Schieve and P. M. Allen (eds.), *Self-organization and dissipative structures: Application in the physical and social sciences,* Austin, TX: University of Texas Press.

Prigogine, I., and Stengers, I. 1984. *Order out of chaos.* New York: Bantam.

Prokesch, S. E. 1993. Mastering chaos at the high-tech frontier: An interview with Silicon Graphic's Ed McCracken. *Harvard Business Review* 71 (6): 134–44.

Quandt, R. E. 1988. *The econometrics of disequilibrium.* New York: Blackwell.

Quinn, J. B. 1985. Managing innovation: Controlled chaos. *Harvard Business Review* 63: 73–84.

Radner, R., Myerson, R., and Maskin, E. 1986. An example of a repeated partnership game with discounting and with uniformly inefficient equilibria. *Review of Economic Studies* 53: 59–69.

Radsicki, M. J. 1990. Institutional dynamics, deterministic chaos, and self-organizing systems. *Journal of Economic Issues* 24 (1): 57–102.

Raduchel, W. J. 1988. Technostructure and technology: A modern theory of the firm and the implications for industrial competitiveness. *Journal of Business* 18 (1): 53–65.

Rand, D. 1976. Threshold in Pareto sets. *Journal of Mathematical Economics* 3: 139–54.

Rapoport, A., and Chammah, A. 1965. *Prisoner's dilemma.* Ann Arbor: University of Michigan Press.

Rasmussen, D. R., and Mosekilde, E. 1988. Bifurcations and chaos in a generic management model. *European Journal of Operational Research* 35: 80–88.

Ray, W. D. 1993. Nonlinear dynamics, chaos and instability statistical theory and economic evidence. *Journal of the Operational Research Society* 44 (2): 202–03.

Reed, R., and Luftman, G. A. 1986. Diversification: The growing confusion. *Strategic Management Journal* 7 (1): 29–35.

Reich, R. B. 1991. *The work of nations.* New York: Random House.

Resnick, M. 1994. Changing the centralized mind. *Technology Review* 97 (5, July): 32–40.

Richards, D. 1990. Is strategic decision-making chaotic? *Behavioral Science* 35: 219–32.

Richards, D., and Hays, J. A. 1998. Navigating a nonlinear environment: An experimental study of decision making in chaotic settings. *Journal of Economic Behavior and Organization* 35: 281–308.

Richardson, G. P. 1991. *Feedback thought in social science and systems theory.* Philadelphia: University of Pennsylvania Press.

Richardson, J., and Taylor, G. 1994. Strategic benchmaking: The co-evolution of competitor intelligence and quality management. Working paper, College of Business, University of Hawaii, Honolulu.

Richardson, L. F. 1926. Atmospheric diffusion shown on a distance-neighbour graph. *Proceedings of the Royal Society of London* A 110: 709–37.

Richardson, L. F. 1960. The problem of contiguity: An appendix to statistics of deadly quarrels. In L. von Bertalanffy and A. Rapoport, (eds.), *General systems—yearbook,* vol. 5, 139–87. Washington, D.C.: Society for General Systems Research.

Riordan, J., and Shannon, C. E. 1942. The numbers of two-terminal series-parallel networks. *Journal of Mathematical Physics* 21: 53–93.

Robinson, A. G., and Stern, S. 1997. *Corporate creativity: How innovation and improvement actually happen.* San Francisco: Berrett-Koehler.

Rogers, E., and Larsen, J. 1984. *Silicon Valley fever: Growth of high-technology culture.* New York: Basic Books.

Rogers, T. J., and Noyce, R. N. 1990. Debating George Gilder's microcosm. *Harvard Business Review* 90 (1): 24–37.

Rose, J. M. 1992. Humanities: A blessed rage for order: Deconstruction, evolution and chaos by Alexander J. Argyros. *Choice* 30 (4): 607.

Rosenberg, N. 1973. *Technology and American economic growth*. New York: Harper and Row.

Ross, J. E. 1993. *Total quality management*. Del Rey Beach, FL: St. Lucie Press.

Rosser, J. B. Jr. 1990. Chaos theory and the new Keynesian economics. *Manchester School* 58 (3): 265–91.

Rosser, J. B. Jr. 1991. *From catastrophe to chaos: A general theory of economic discontinuities*. Boston, MA: Kluwer Academic Publishers.

Rotemberg, J., and Saloner, G. 1990. Benefits of narrow strategies. Working paper 3217–90–EFA, Sloan School of Management, MIT, Cambridge, MA.

Roth, W. F. 1993. The evolution of management theory: Past, present and future. New York: Praeger.

Rothschild, M. R. 1990. *Bionomics: The inevitability of capitalism*. New York: Henry Holt and Company.

Rowlands, G. 1990. *Non-linear phenomena in science and engineering*. New York: E. Horwood.

Ruelle, D., and Takens, F. 1971. On the nature of turbulence. *Communications on Mathematical Physics* 20: 167–92; 23: 343–44.

Rugina, A. 1989. *Principia Methodologica* 1: A bridge from economics to all other natural sciences—Toward a methodological unification of all sciences. *International Journal of Social Economics* 16 (4): 3–76.

Rumelhart, D. E. 1986. *Parallel distributed processing: Exploration in the microstructure of cognition*. Cambridge, MA: The MIT Press.

Rumelt, R. P. 1974. *Strategy structure and economic performance*. Cambridge, MA: Harvard University Press.

Rumelt, R. P., Schendel, D., and Teece, D. J. 1994. Afterword. In R. Rumelt, D. Schendel, and D. J. Teece. (eds.), *Fundamental issues in strategy,* 527–55. Boston, MA: Harvard Business School Press.

Russo, M., and Fouts, P. A. 1993. The green carrot: Do markets reward corporate environmentalism? Working paper, Department of Management, University of Oregon, Eugene.

Saloner, G. 1991. Modeling, game theory, and strategic management. *Strategic Management Journal* 12 (Special Issue): 119–25.

Samdani, G. 1991. The simple rules of complexity. *Chemical Engineerimg* 98 (7): 30–35.

Saxenian, A. 1994. *Regional advantage: Culture and competition in Silicon Valley and Route 128*. Cambridge, MA: Harvard University Press.

Schein, E. 1985. *Organizational culture and leadership*. San Francisco: Jossey-Bass.

Schelling, T. 1992. Some economics of global warming. *American Economic Review* 82 (1): 1–14.

Schendel, D. E., and Cool, K. O. 1988. Development of the strategic management field: Some accomplishments and challenges. In J. M. Grant (ed.). *Strategic management frontiers,* 27–32. Greenwood, CT: JAI Press.

Schendel, D. E., and Hoffer, S. W. 1979. *Strategic management: A new view of business policy and planning.* Boston, MA: Little Brown.

Schieve, W., and Allen, P. M. (eds.). 1982. *Self-organization and dissipative structures: Applications in the physical and social sciences.* Austin: University of Texas Press.

Schmidheiny, S. 1992. *Changing course: A global business perspective on development and the environment.* Cambridge, MA: The MIT Press.

Schmookler, J. 1966. *Invention and economic growth.* Cambridge, MA: Harvard University Press.

Schneider A., and Ingram, H. 1988. Filling empty boxes. Working paper, College of Public Programs, Arizona State University, Tempe, AZ.

Schoemaker, P. J. H. 1990. Strategy, complexity and economic rent. *Management Science* 36 (10): 1178–92.

Schrödinger, E. 1943. *What is life?* Cambridge, UK: Cambridge University Press.

Schrödinger, E. 1951. *Science and humanism.* Cambridge, UK: Cambridge University Press.

Schuessler, R. 1989. The gradual decline of cooperation: Endgame effects in evolutionary game theory. *Theory and Decision* 26: 133–55.

Schuessler, R. 1990. Threshold effects and the decline of cooperation. *Journal of Conflict Resolution* 34 (3): 476–94.

Schulman, P. R. 1975. Nonincremental policy making: Notes toward an alternative paradigm. *American Political Science Review* 69 (4): 1354–70.

Schumacher, B. G. 1986. *On the origin and the nature of management.* Norman, OK: Eugnosis Press.

Schumpeter, J. A. 1934. *The theory of economic development.* Cambridge, MA: Harvard University Press.

Schumpeter, J. A. 1942. *Capitalism, socialism and democracy.* New York: Harper and Row.

Scott, W. R., and Meyer, J. 1994. *Institutional environments and organizations.* Thousand Oaks, CA: Sage Publications.

Searle, J. 1992. *The rediscovery of the mind.* Cambridge, MA: The MIT Press.

Seckler, D. W. 1975. *Thorstein Veblen and the Institutionalists: A study in the social philosophy of economics.* Boulder, CO: Colorado Associated University Press.

Sen, A. 1977. Rational fools: A critique of the behavioral foundations of economic theory. *Philosophy and Public Affairs* 6 (6): 317–44.

Senge, P. M. 1990. *The fifth discipline: The art and practice of the learning organization.* New York: Doubleday/Currency.

Senge, P. M., and Fulmer, R. M. 1993. Simulations, systems thinking and anticipatory learning. *Journal of Management Development* 12 (6): 21–33.

Seydel, R. 1988. *From equilibrium to chaos: Practical bifurcation and stability analysis.* New York: Elsevier.

Shackle, G. 1961. *Decision, order, and time in human affairs.* Cambridge: Cambridge University Press.

Shane, B., and Connor, P. 1993. A new tool for management theory: Parallel computing. Working paper, College of Business, Oregon State University, Corvallis.

Shannon, C. E. 1949. A mathematical theory of communication. *Bell System Journal* 27: 379–423, 623–56.

Shannon, C. E., and Weaver, W. 1963. *The mathematical theory of communication.* Urbana: University of Illinois Press.

Shapiro, C. 1987. Theories of oligopoly behavior. Discussion paper 126, Woodrow Wilson School, Princeton University.

Shetty, B. 1990. A parallel projection for the multicommodity network model. *Journal of the Operational Research Society* 41 (9): 837–42.

Shingo, S. 1986. *Zero quality control: Source imperfection and the Poka-Yoke system.* Stamford, CT: Productivity Press.

Silverberg, G. 1984. Embodied technical progress in a dynamic economic mode: The self-organization paradigm. In R. M. Goodwin, M. Kruger, and A. Vercel (eds.), *Nonlinear models of fluctuating growth.* New York: Springer-Verlag.

Silverberg, G. 1988. Modeling economic dynamics and technical change: Mathematical approaches to self-organization and evolution. In G. Dosi, C. Freeman, R. Nelson, G. Silverberg, and L. Soete (eds.), *Technical change and economic theory,* 531–59. New York: Pinter.

Silverberg, G., Dosi, G., and Orsenigo, L. 1988. Innovation, diversity and diffusion: A self-organization model. *Economic Journal* 98 (393): 1032–54.

Simon, H. A. 1957. *Models of man.* New York: Wiley.

Simon, H. A. 1969. *The sciences of the artificial.* Cambridge, MA: The MIT Press.

Simon, H. A. 1982. *Models of bounded rationality: Behavioral economics and business organization.* Cambridge, MA: The MIT Press.

Simon, H. A. 1985. Human nature in politics: The dialogue of psychology with political science. *American Political Science Review* 79: 293–304.

Simon, H. A. 1987. Making management decisions: The role of intuition and emotion. *Academy of Management Executive* 1 (1, February): 57–64.

Simon, H. A. 1990. A mechanism for social selection and successful altruism. *Science* 250 (4988): 1665–68.

Singer, B. 1994. Colors: Organizing processes in cellular automata. Working paper, Department of Management, University of Oregon, Eugene.

Singh, J. 1966. *The great ideas of information theory, language and cybernetics.* New York: Dover.

Sinyak, Y., and Nagano, K. 1992. Global energy and climate change. Laxenberg, Austria: International Institute for Applied Systems Analysis.

Smelzer, N. 1978. Re-examining the parameters of economic activity. In E. Epstein and D. Votari (eds.), *Rationality, legitimacy, and responsibility.* Santa Monica: Goodyear.

Smilor, R. W., and Feeser, H. 1991. Chaos and the entrepreneurial process: Patterns and policy. *Journal of Business Venturing* 6 (3): 165–72.

Smith, C. 1991. Change in the small group: A dissipative structure perspective. *Human Relations* 44 (7): 697–716.

Smith, K. G., Grimm, C. M., and Gannon, M. J. 1992. *Dynamics of competitive strategy.* Newbury Park, CA: Sage Publications.

Smith, L., and Thelen, E. (eds.). 1993. *A dynamic systems approach to development*: *Applications*. Cambridge, MA: The MIT Press.

Smith, R. L. 1972. *The ecology of man: An ecosystem approach*. New York: Harper and Row.

Smuts, J. C. 1926. *Holism and evolution*. London: MacMillan.

Solow, R. 1957. Technical change and the aggregate production functions. *Review of Economics and Statistics* 39 (3): 312–20.

Sommers, A. 1985. *The U.S. economy demystified.* Lexington, MA: Lexington Books.

Speidell, L. S. 1988. As a science, chaos can put things in order. *Pensions and Investment Age* 25: ???–??.

Spence, A. M. 1977. Entry, capacity, investment, and oligopolistic pricing. *Bell Journal of Economics* 8 (3): 534–44.

Stacey, R. D. 1992. *Managing the unknowable-strategic boundaries between order and chaos in organizations*. San Francisco, CA: Jossey-Bass Publishers.

Stacey, R. D. 1993. Strategy as an order emerging from chaos. *Long Range Planning* 26 (1): 10–17.

Stacey, R. D. 1995. The science of complexity: An alternative perspective for strategic change processes. *Strategic Management Journal* 16 (6): 477–95.

Stacey, R. D. 1996. *Complexity and creativity in organizations*. San Francisco: Berrett-Koehler.

Stanley, E. A. 1989. Mathematical models of the AIDS epidemic: A historical perspective. In D. L. Stein (ed.), *Lectures in the science of complexity*. Reading, MA: Addison-Wesley.

Steen, N. (ed.). 1994. *Sustainable development and the energy industries*. London: The Royal Institute of International Affairs.

Steenburg, D. 1991. Chaos at the marriage of heaven and hell. *Harvard Theological Review* 84 (4): 447–66.

Stein, D. L. 1989. *Lectures in the sciences of complexity*. Redwood City, CA: Addison-Wesley for the Santa Fe Institute.

Stevenson, H. 1990. Entrepreneurial management's need for a more "chaotic" theory. *Journal of Business Venturing* 5 (1): 1–14.

Steward, J. 1993. Rational choice theory, public policy and the liberal state. *Policy Science* 26: 317–30.

Stewart, I. 1989. *Does God play dice?: The mathematics of chaos*. Oxford: B. Blackwell.

Stigliani, W. M., and Jaffee, P. 1994. *Industrial metabolism and river basin studies: A new approach for the analysis of chemical pollution*. Laxenburg, Austria: International Institute for Applied Systems Analysis.

Strader, T., Lin, F. R., and Shaw, M. 1998. The impact of information sharing on order fulfillment in divergent differentiation supply chain. Working paper, The Beckman Institute, Urbana, IL.

Sullivan, J. J., and Nonaka, I. 1986. The application of organizational learning theory to Japanese and American management. *Journal of International Business Studies* 17 (3): 127–48.

Swedberg, R., Himmelstrand, U., and Göran, B. 1990. The paradigm of economic sociology. In S. Zukin and P. DiMagio (eds.), *Structures of capital: The social organization of the economy,* 57–86. New York: Cambridge University Press.

Swenson, D. 1991. General living systems theory and just-in-time manufacturing: A framework for change. *Industrial Management* 33 (5): 12–14.

Swieringa, J., and Wierdsma, A. F. M. 1992. *Becoming a learning organization.* Reading, MA: Addison-Wesley.

Taber, W. R. 1991. Knowledge processing with fuzzy cognitive maps. *Expert Systems Applications* 2 (1): 83–87.

Taguchi, G. 1987. *On-line quality control during production.* Tokyo: Japanese Standards Association.

Taguchi, G., and Clausing, D. 1990. Robust quality. *Harvard Business Review* 68 (1, January): 65–75.

Tainter, J. A. 1988. *The collapse of complex societies.* New York: Cambridge University Press.

Tam, K., and Yan-Kiang, M. Y. 1992. Managerial applications of neural networks: The case of bank failure predictions. *Management Science* 38 (7): 926–47.

Taormina, R. J. 1991. Organizational analysis of information processing using living systems theory. *Behavioral Science* 36 (3): 196–223.

Taylor, F. W. 1911. *The principles of scientific management.* New York: Harper and Brothers.

Taylor, G. 1993. Parallel processing: A design principle for system-wide total quality management. *Management International Review* 33 (Special Issue): 99–109.

Teece, D. 1984. Economic analysis and strategic management. In G. Carrol and D. Vogel (eds.), *Strategy and organization: A West Coast perspective,* 78–101. Boston, MA: Pittman.

Teske, P. and Johnson, R. 1994. Moving towards an American industrial technology policy. *Policy Studies Journal* 22 (2): 196–310.

Thaler, R. 1991. *Quasi rational economics.* New York: Russell Sage Foundation.

Thaler, S. 1996. Neural nets that create and discover. *PC AI* 10 (3): 16–20.

Theobald, R. 1972. *Habit and habitat.* Englewood Cliffs, NJ: Prentice-Hall.

Thom, R. 1972. *Structural stability and morphogenesis.* Reading, MA: Benjamin.

Thom, R. 1983. *Mathematical models of morphogenesis.* Chichester: Ellis Harwood, Ltd.

Thompson, d'A. 1917. *On growth and form.* Cambridge, UK: Cambridge University Press.

Thompson, J. M. T., and Stewart, H. B. 1986. *Nonlinear dynamics and chaos.* New York: Wiley.

Thurow, L. 1996. *The future of capitalism.* New York: Morrow.

Toffler, A. 1970. *Future shock.* New York: Random House.

Toffler, A. 1980. *The third wave.* New York: William Morrow and Company.

Toffler, A. 1984. Foreword: Science and change. In I. Prigogine and I. Stengers (eds.), *Order out of chaos.* New York: Bantam.

Toffler, A. 1985. New science of instability throws light on politics. In I. Prigogine and M. Sanglier (eds.), *Laws of nature and human conduct.* Brussels: Task Force of Research Information and Study on Science.

Toffoli, T., and Margolus, N. 1987. *Cellular automata machines*. Cambridge, MA: The MIT Press.

Toulmin, S. E. 1982. *The return to cosmology: Postmodern science and the theology of nature*. Berkeley: University of California Press.

Tracy, L. 1993. Applications of living systems theory to the study of management and organizational behavior. *Behavioral Science* 38 (3): 218–30.

Trist, E. L. 1979. New directions of hope: Recent innovations interconnecting organizational, industrial, community and personal development. *Regional Studies* 13: 440–54.

Trist, E. L. 1981. The evolution of socio-technical systems. Working paper, Ministry of Labor, Toronto.

Tsoukas, H. 1992. Panoptic reason and the search for totality: A critical assessment of the critical systems perspective. *Human Relations* 45 (7): 637–58.

Tsujimura, Y. 1992. A parallel processing algorithm for nonlinear programing problems. *Computers and Industrial Engineering* 23 (1–4): 305–7.

Tversky, A., and Kahneman, D. 1986. Rational choice and the framing of decisions. *Journal of Business* 59: 251–78.

Tyson, L. D. A. 1987. Creating advantage: Strategic policy for national competitiveness. Working paper 23, Berkeley Roundtable on the International Economy, University of California, Berkeley.

Tyson, L. D. A. 1992. *Who's bashing whom? Trade conflict in high-technology industries*. Washington, D.C.: Institute for International Economics.

UN IPCC. 1995. *Report on global climate change*. New York: United Nations.

Utterback, J. M., and Suárez, F. F. 1990. Innovation, competition, and industry structure. Working paper 29–91, International Center for Research on the Management of Technology, MIT, Cambridge.

Vaga, T. 1994. *Profiting from chaos: Using chaos theory for market timing, stock selection, and option valuation*. New York: McGraw-Hill.

van Duijn, J. J. 1983. *The long wave in economic life*. London: George Allen and Unwin.

Van de Vijver, G. 1992. *New perspectives on cybernetics: Self-organization, autonomy, and connectionism*. Netherlands: Kluwer Academic Publishers.

Vaugh, D. 1996. *The Challenger launch decision*. Chicago: The University of Chicago Press.

Veblen, T. 1898. Why is economics not an evolutionary science? *Quarterly Journal of Economics* 12: 373–97.

Veblen, T. 1919. *The place of science in modern civilization*. New York: B. W. Huebsch.

Veblen, T. 1934. *Essays in our changing orders*. (Collected by Leon Ardzrooni). New York: The Vilerny Press.

Venkatraman, N. 1990. Strategic orientation of business enterprises. *Management Science* 35 (8): 942–62.

Venugopal, V. 1992. A genetic algorithm approach to the machine-component grouping problem with multiple objectives. *Computers and Industrial Engineering* 22 (4): 469–80.

Venugopal, V., and Baets, W. 1994. Neural networks and their applications in marketing management. *Journal of Systems Management* 45 (9): 16–27.

Venugopal, V., and Narendran, T. 1992. A genetic algorithm approach to the machine-component grouping problem with multiple objectives. *Computers and Industrial Engineering* 22 (4): 469–80.

Vertinsky, I. 1987. An ecological model of resiliency decision-making: An application to the study of public and private sector decision-making. *Ecological Modelling* 38 (1): 141–58.

Vertinsky, I., Kira, D., and Kanetkar, V. 1990. A study of production decisions under extreme uncertainty in the wood products industry. *Managerial and Decision Economics* 11 (3): 155–65.

Voge, J. 1985. The Information economy and the restructuring of human organizations. In I. Prigogine and M. Sanglier (eds.), *Laws of nature and human conduct*. Brussels: Task Force of Research Information and Study on Science.

von Bertalanffy, L. 1933. *Modern theories of development: An introduction to theoretical biology*. Translated by J. H. Woodger. London: Oxford University Press.

von Bertalanffy, L. 1950. The theory of open systems in physics and biology. *Science* 111: 23–29.

von Bertalanffy, L. 1968. *General System Theory: Foundations, Development, Applications*. New York: Braziller.

von Foerster, H., and Zopf, G. W. (eds.). 1962. *Principles of Self-organization*. New York: Pergamon.

von Hayek, F. A. 1983. *Knowledge, evolution, and society*. London: Adam Smith Institute.

von Hippel, E. 1988. *The sources of innovation*. New York: Oxford University Press.

von Mises, L. 1949. *Human action: A treatise on economics*. New Haven: Yale University Press.

von Neumann, J. 1958. *The computer and the brain*. New Haven: Yale University Press.

von Neumann, J. 1968. The general and logical theory of automata. In W. Buckley (ed.), *Modern systems research for the behavioral scientist*. Chicago: Aldine.

von Neumann, J., and Morgenstern, O. 1944. *Theory of games and economic behavior*. New York: Wiley.

von Stackelberg, H. 1934. *Marktform und Gleichgewicht*. Vienna, Austria: Springer.

Waldrop, M. M. 1992. *Complexity: The emerging science at the edge of order and chaos*. New York: Simon and Schuster.

Wallerstein, I. 1987. Historical systems as complex systems. *European Journal of Operational Research* 30: 203–207.

Walras, L. 1954. *Elements of Pure Economics*. Translated by W. Jeffe from 1874 text. London: Allen S. Unwin.

Walters, J. 1992. The cult of total quality. *Governing* 5 (8): 38–42.

Wang, P. P., and Chang, S. K. (eds.). 1980. *Fuzzy sets: Theory and applications to policy analysis and information systems*. New York: Plenum Press.

Watson, F. D. 1994. TQM; bah, humbug. *Proceedings of the International Conference on Advances in Management*. Bowling Green, KY: ICAM.

Weber, M. 1947. *The theory of social and economic organization*. Translated by A. M. Henderson and T. Parsons. New York: Free Press.

Weick, K. E. 1976. Educational organizations as loosely coupled systems. *Administrative Sciences Quarterly* 21 (1): 1–19.

Weick, K. E. 1979. *The social psychology of organizing.* 2d ed. Reading, MA: Addison-Wesley.

Weiss, G. 1992. Chaos hits Wall Street—The theory, that is. *Business Week,* November 2, (Technology Edition), 138–40.

Wells, D. 1996. *Environmental Policy.* Upper Saddle River, NJ: Prentice Hall.

West, B. J., and Salk, J. 1985. Human conduct and natural laws: Laws of simple and complex systems. In I. Prigogine and M. Sanglier (eds.), *Laws of nature and human conduct.* Brussels: Task Force of Research Information and Study on Science.

West, B. J., and Salk, J. 1987. Complexity, organizations, and uncertainty. *European Journal of Operational Research* 30: 117–28.

Westley, F., and Vredenburg, H. 1991. Strategic bridging: The collaboration between environmentalists and business in the marketing of green products. Working paper, Faculty of Management, McGill University, Montreal.

Wheatley, M. 1992. *Leadership and the new science: Learning about organization from an orderly universe.* San Francisco: Berret-Koehler Publishers.

Wheatley, M. 1993. Searching for order in an orderly world: A poetic for post-machine-age managers. *Journal of Management Inquiry* 2 (1): 337–42.

Wiener, N. 1948. *Cybernetics: Or control and communication in the animal and the machine.* Cambridge, MA: The MIT Press.

Wiener, N. 1954. *The human use of human beings: Cybernetics and society.* Boston: Houghton Mifflin.

Wiener, N. 1964. *God and Golem, Inc.—A comment on certain points where cybernetics impinges on religion.* Cambridge, MA: The MIT Press.

Williams, J. R. 1992. How sustainable is your competitive advantage? *California Management Review* 34 (3, spring), Special Reprint, University of California, Berkeley, 29–51.

Williamson, O. E. 1975. *Markets and hierarchies: Analysis and antitrust implications.* New York: Free Press.

Williamson, O. E. 1985. *The economic institutions of capitalism: Firms, markets, relational contracting.* New York: Free Press.

Wilson, D. 1980. *The national planning idea in public policy.* Boulder, CO: Westview Press.

Wilson, E. O. 1988. *On human nature.* Cambridge, MA: Harvard University Press.

Wilson, E. O. 1992. *The diversity of life.* Cambridge, MA: Harvard University Press.

Wilson, E. O. 1998. *Consilience: Unity of knowledge.* New York: Alfred A. Knopf.

Winch, P. 1958. *The idea of a social science and its relation to philosophy.* New York: Humanities Press.

Winter, S. G. 1989. Disagreement and reform in economic science: Comments on Simon. *Journal of Business Administration* 18 (1–2): 33–40.

Wolfram, S. (ed.). 1986. *Theory and applications of cellular automata.* Singapore: World Scientific.

Woodcock, A., and Davis, M. 1978. *Catastrophe theory.* New York: Dutton.

Wren, D. A. 1979. *The evolution of management thought.* New York: Wiley.

Index